D1499780

The Resources of Music

Electronic Music for Schools

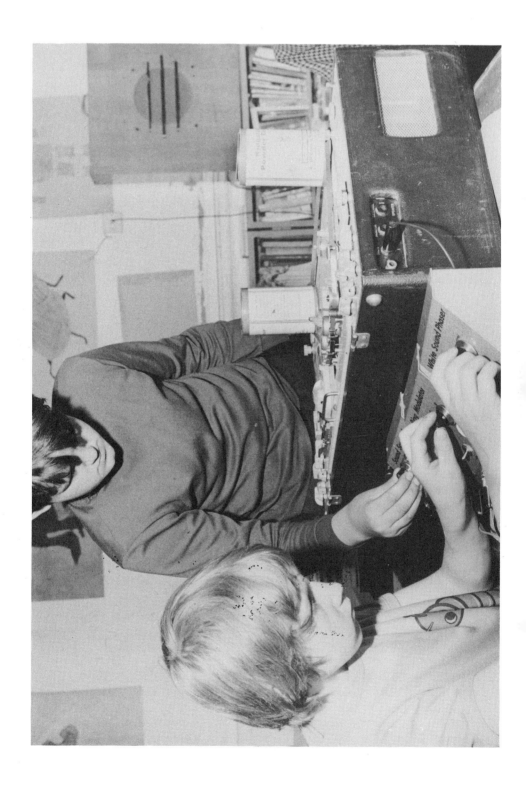

Electronic Music for Schools

Edited by
RICHARD ORTON
Senior Lecturer in Music, University of York

CAMBRIDGE UNIVERSITY PRESS
Cambridge
London   New York   New Rochelle
Melbourne   Sydney

Published by the Press Syndicate of the University of Cambridge
The Pitt Building, Trumpington Street, Cambridge CB2 1RP
32 East 57th Street, New York, NY 10022, USA
296 Beaconsfield Parade, Middle Park, Melbourne 3206, Australia

First published 1981

Printed in Great Britain at the University Press, Cambridge

Library of Congress catalogue card number: 81-3838

British Library cataloguing in publication data
Orton, Richard
   Electronic music for schools.
   (The resources of music)
   1. Electronic music 1. Title II. Series
   789.9   ML1092
   ISBN 0 521 22994 4 hard covers
   ISBN 0 521 28026 5 paperback
   ISBN 0 521 23661 4 cassette

Contents

The contributors   vii

Introduction   *Richard Orton*   1

1 Hardware   *Richard Orton*   3
2 Using the hardware: software, techniques and ideas   *Richard Orton*   26
3 Electronic music in the primary school   *Peter Warham*   45
4 Electronic music in the secondary school: 1   *Phil Ellis*   70
5 Electronic music in the secondary school: 2   *Tom Wanless*   92
6 Simple equipment for electronic music making   *Andrew Bentley*   107
7 What is musicmontage?   *Trevor Wishart*   132
8 Making and performing simple electroacoustic instruments   *Hugh Davies*   152

Appendices I Glossary   175
    II Course outline   179
    III Select bibliography   181
    IV Select discography   184
    V Manufacturers and suppliers   188
    VI Electronic music studios in the United Kingdom   190
    VII Societies and courses   191
    VIII Items on the accompanying cassette   192
Index   194

≡RESOURCES OF MUSIC≡

General Editor: John Paynter

Books for the Classroom

Cantors by Mary Berry
Minstrels by Brian Sargent
Minstrels 2 by Brian Sargent
Poverty Knock by Roy Palmer
Something to Play by Geoffrey Brace
Strike the Bell by Roy Palmer
The Painful Plough by Roy Palmer
The Rigs of the Fair by Roy Palmer and Jon Raven
The Valiant Sailor by Roy Palmer
Troubadours by Brian Sargent
Troubadours and Minstrels, record (Brian Sargent)

Books for Teachers

Folk Music in School edited by Robert Leach and Roy Palmer
Jazz by Graham Collier
Jazz: Illustrations, record (Graham Collier)
Jazz: Lecture Concert, record (Graham Collier)
Pop Music in School (New Edition) edited by Graham Vulliamy and Ed Lee
Pop Music in School: Illustrations, cassette (Graham Vulliamy and Ed Lee)
Sound and Silence by John Paynter and Peter Aston
Sound and Silence, record (John Paynter and Peter Aston)
The Resources of Music by Wilfrid Mellers
Vibrations by David Sawyer

The contributors

Richard Orton is a senior lecturer in music at the University of York. He founded York University Electronic Music Studio in 1968 and has directed it ever since. His publications include units on *Natural Sound* and *Electronic Sound* for the Open University's course 'Art and Environment' (1976) and his compositions include many that employ electroacoustic resources: *Sampling Afield* (1969), *Clock Farm* (1973), *Ambience* for solo trombone and tape (1975), *Scatter* for trombone, piano and tape (1977) and *Emergences* for speaking voice, flute, cello, piano and prerecorded tape (1978).

Peter Warham was headmaster at Barlby Bridge Primary School, Selby, Yorkshire for seventeen years until his retirement in 1979, and started using electronics in school music in 1969. Articles include 'Using the tape recorder in the classroom' for *Tape Teacher* and 'Poetry and sound' for *Headland* magazine. In 1977 he was awarded a Silver Jubilee Medal for services to education. At present he is working on a science project for teachers in N. Yorkshire.

Phil Ellis was head of music at Notley High School, Braintree, Essex from 1971-8. The music curriculum there was based to a large extent on creative activities and made significant use of electronic apparatus. The school has been associated with the Schools Council Secondary Music Project since 1973 and some aspects of Phil Ellis's work have been featured in tape-slide programmes and in printed materials produced by the project. He is now lecturer in music at Huddersfield Polytechnic where he directs the electronic music studio.

Tom Wanless is head of music at the Sheldon School, Chippenham, Wiltshire, where the music curriculum successfully combines electronic music activities with other music making. The school has also been associated with the Schools Council Secondary Music Project and he has contributed to courses and conferences dealing in particular with the assessment and evaluation of children's creative work in music.

Andrew Bentley is resident in Finland and works in Finnish Radio Electronic Music Studio which he has largely designed and built up. He has produced a number of programmes on electronic music for schools. His *Four Finnish Tapes* (commissioned by Finnish Radio in 1975) explore what can be done with limited equipment such as might be available at home or in school.

Trevor Wishart is a composer and environmental musician. He has worked extensively in education, with children in school and in specially commissioned environmental-music projects and also with teachers on numerous courses in Britain and overseas. His many tape compositions include *Machine* (1971), *Journey into Space* (1972) and *Red Bird* (1977). He has written two books of musical games (*Sounds Fun* and *Sounds Fun 2*, Universal Edition, 1977). Other writings include *Sun - Creativity and Environment* (Universal Edition, 1974), *Sun 2 - A Creative Philosophy* (Universal Edition, 1977) and, in collaboration with Shepherd, Vulliamy and Virden, *Whose Music? A Sociology of Musical Languages* (Latimer New Dimensions, 1977).

Hugh Davies was assistant to Karlheinz Stockhausen in Cologne from 1964-6. Since 1968 he has been director of the electronic music studio at Goldsmith's College, University of London. His publications include *The Electronic Music Catalog* (MIT Press, 1968).

Acknowledgements

Thanks are due to the following for permission to use copyright material:
Edinburgh University Press for 'Opening the Cage: 14 Variations on 14 Words'
    from *The Second Life* by Edwin Morgan
Her Majesty's Stationery Office for extracts from Newsom, *Half Our Future*
Universal Edition (London) Ltd for the extract from Murray Schafer,
    The Rhinoceros in the Classroom
Tom Bestwick for cover photograph, frontispiece and Plates 2-4
David Whiteley for Plate 1
Phil Ellis for Plates 5-8
Philip Palmer for Plate 9
Michael Dunn for Plates 10-13

Introduction

RICHARD ORTON

As a means of activity, of discovery of the sound-world about us, of its potential for human expression, the sonic art of electronic music is young. It has little weight of tradition to enshroud us in unquestioned and unquestionable canons of thought and behaviour, to draw its students into possibly inappropriate modes of feeling. Of course, to many there may be dangers of superficiality because of its novelty. Luckily for the children in our schools this question hardly arises - novelty applies to almost every activity which is undertaken. Today the tape recorder can be a powerful means of reflecting and organising our experiences, in documentary, narrative or musical forms. Electronics provides communication among people, and among peoples, on a scale not contemplated in earlier decades. Although its impact has been felt, electronics is not significantly used by the majority of educators in music and the arts. Here and there are pioneers working in schools to direct young sensibilities towards these means of expression; they have found the use of electronics wholly justifiable in its capacity to involve children in their own education, to lead them into unsuspected territories and provide significant and stimulating creative experience.

This book has drawn together some of these pioneers of electronic music in schools, to point the way and to encourage those teachers who have not yet 'taken the plunge'. It has taken the view that although great sums of money can be spent on electronic hardware for making music, this is by no means a guarantee of artistic success or of communicative ability on the part of its users. Indeed, discovering what can be achieved with minimal equipment is a powerful stimulus for invention. As far as equipment is concerned, the authors of this book share a belief that a start can be made with one tape recorder, one microphone and one reel of tape. Beyond this starting point, each additional item of equipment will appear a bonus.

My own chapters serve to outline the equipment and techniques that have evolved for electronic music. The second chapter begins to place the techniques within the school context. Peter Warham, in the third chapter, gives a sketch of how he came to use electronic music in the primary school. Phil Ellis and Tom Wanless then each give their own positive views of electronic music in their secondary schools, and indicate that the CSE Mode III examination provides an opportunity to place the approach firmly within the curriculum.

[1]

The remaining chapters are a little more specialised. Andrew Bentley provides a stimulating plethora of ideas for using simple, cheap and readily available equipment in imaginative ways, and supplies a number of designs for simple circuits for those teachers who wish to introduce elementary electronics construction into the course. Trevor Wishart discusses the principle of music-montage which he has evolved, especially in his tape composition *Red Bird*, and gives an insight into the potential of electronic music beyond the classroom. Hugh Davies brings his experience as an instrument maker to the final chapter. He introduces some projects for constructing and performing electroacoustic instruments, and suggests that in time this activity will supersede that of tape manipulation in electronic music.

A *Course outline* suggests a series of graded activities conceived primarily for a secondary-school curriculum, but which should help teachers plan any course which intermittently adopts electronic music for different year-groups. The series of further appendices will be of assistance to teachers or pupils who wish to further their study of electronic music.

While the text itself is designed to be self-contained, an accompanying cassette has been prepared which illustrates many chapters of the book. Undoubtedly the excerpts of material created by schools pupils will be of especial interest. Appendix VIII gives a list of the recorded items, while the actual cassette may be obtained from Cambridge University Press.

1 Hardware

RICHARD ORTON

The term 'hardware' as used in this chapter indicates the equipment used in making electronic music. We may conveniently divide it into two categories: generators and processors. A generator *initiates* an electrical signal, which becomes audible by interposing a loudspeaker, while a processor *modifies* an existing signal in what should be an audibly recognisable way. Imagine the simplest audio reproduction system: a microphone connected to an amplifier and loudspeaker. Here the microphone will be regarded as the generator, the source of the electrical signals, while the amplifier is the processor. The microphone, of course, derives its pattern of signals from the sound waves in its vicinity – perhaps those of a human voice – while amplification is among the simplest of all modifications. In this direct sound-reproduction chain, the accultured listener will often assume that the sound he hears from the loudspeaker is 'the same' as the sound of the voice that is picked up by the microphone – indeed, it is the aim of the equipment manufacturers to perpetrate this illusion. But the practitioner of electronic music will recognise that each item of equipment between the generator and the loudspeaker is a significant, active contributor to what is eventually heard. In designing a system for electronic music he will be looking for the widest possible range of sound generators coupled to powerful yet flexible means of modification. In such systems the hardware chain can be quite long.

Among the generators may be considered the microphones, oscillators, noise generators, electrical musical instruments such as the electric piano, electric organ and electric guitar and, in a special class as 'recycling generators', the tape recorders, disc players and radio receivers. The processors developed for sound modification include amplifiers, envelope shapers, filters, ring modulators, reverberation devices, mixers, frequency shifters and, again, tape recorders. The appearance of the tape recorder as both a generator and a processor indicates something of its importance for electronic music so we shall start with an examination of its functions.

The tape recorder

Electromagnetic tape is the storage medium for sounds most commonly used in electronic music. It consists of a bonding of tiny magnetic particles on a thin plastic base. In a tape recorder, the tape moves past an array of heads, each with a narrow

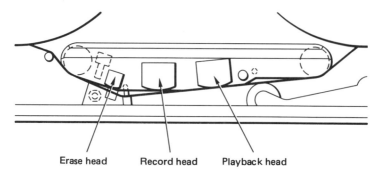

Erase head   Record head   Playback head

Fig. 1.1 Tape recorder heads

vertical gap at its centre, designed to convert a localised magnetic field into an electrical signal, or vice versa. The three heads in a typical tape recorder are shown in Fig.1.1.

The erase and record heads function only when the tape recorder is in the record mode. The erase head scrambles the magnetic particles on the tape with a very high (supersonic) frequency signal, while the record head imposes a new magnetic pattern on the moving tape, the analogue of the electrical signal appearing at the recording input of the tape recorder. The playback head, the last in the line, produces a voltage varying with the magnetic pattern which it reads off the tape.

What is the best type of tape recorder to use for electronic music? Without going into the expensive professional bracket with tape $\frac{1}{2}$ in, 1 in or even 2 in wide, the so-called 'semi-professional' $\frac{1}{2}$-track stereo reel-to-reel tape recorder is recommended, preferably one with three available speeds, $3\frac{3}{4}$, $7\frac{1}{2}$ and 15 inches per second, abbreviated i.p.s. (9.5, 19 and 38 cm/s), although many domestic-quality machines adopt a lower range of speeds: $1\frac{7}{8}$, $3\frac{3}{4}$ and $7\frac{1}{2}$ i.p.s. These machines record two parallel tracks on $\frac{1}{4}$ in tape, each track using approximately half of the width of the tape. In stereo the two tracks are recorded simultaneously, but they may be recorded independently too, and later played back together. The possibility of placing heterogeneous sounds together has proven to be one of the main features of electronic music, and one might consider a four-channel tape recorder, with four parallel tracks available, to be worthwhile. However the trade-off here is quality: the narrower the track, the poorer the frequency response, generally speaking, and a better purchase would be two $\frac{1}{2}$-track stereo machines. Additional useful features one should bear in mind when purchasing a machine are: an easily accessible head assembly (for ease of editing); variable speed controls; and a sound-upon-sound facility, or 'ping-ponging' – the ability to transfer a recording from one track to another while adding a further recording on the second track. This last feature is, however, less important if a sound mixer will be available.

The tape recorder manufacturer should recommend a range of brand tapes to use. It is wise to follow the recommendations, since the frequency and amplitude of the bias signal at the erase head will be optimal for these tapes. Of those recommended, standard thickness low-noise tapes will be the best to adopt. 'Long-play' tape may be used, but it would be unwise to use the very thin 'double-play' or 'triple-play' tapes. If there is a choice, adopt a matt-backed tape rather than a shiny-backed one: it is easier to mark for editing. Once a type and brand have been chosen, it is best to stick to them for all future use, unless a demonstrably better tape for your machine comes along.

Recording

Whatever the source of the sounds to be recorded, whether microphone, electrical instrument, synthesiser or radio receiver, the aim of the recording process should be to gain the maximum undistorted signal from the magnetic patterns induced on the tape. For this purpose a meter is usually provided for each recording track. The meter may be of the VU (Volume Unit) type, in which the needle responds virtually simultaneously to changing amplitude levels – in many musical circumstances the rapidity of movement can be confusing to the eye; or it may be of the PPM (Peak Programme Meter) type, where the needle rises very quickly with a rise in signal, but its fall is somewhat delayed – the effect here is a slower moving needle, easier to read. The meter will indicate a point at which the optimum *signal-to-noise ratio* is reached. Above the point, often shaded in red, there is a danger of distortion. (It should be borne in mind, however, that many tape recorder manufacturers are conservative about this and many sounds can safely be recorded with the needle slightly in the red.) This optimum point may be marked as 0 dBm, the line reference level. The portion of the meter above it will have a range of only three or four positive decibels, while the portion below will have a range of twenty or thirty negative decibels. The decibel is a logarithmic unit of ratio between power levels (or, by extension, sound intensities) and their positive or negative labelling just a matter of convenience. In making a recording of varying sound intensities, the peaks of the loudest sounds should just tip the needle into the red, while the lower level sounds will not necessarily deflect the meter needle at all. In recording sounds for use in electronic music it is wise to ascertain first the range of intensity variation over the duration of the chosen sound.

In order to ensure that constantly optimum levels are maintained from recording to recording, it is customary to record a 10-second test tone of a 1 kHz oscillator at line level. This is particularly useful when making a copy of the tape (see section on copying in the following chapter).

Tape recorder maintenance

There are two important jobs in maintaining a tape recorder for continuously good performance – head cleaning and head demagnetising. While these should be done regularly, preferably each time the machine is used, they are relatively simple and can be taught to responsible children. The equipment needed is a pack of cotton buds, which can be purchased from any chemist, a bottle or tin of an appropriate non-corrosive head-cleaning fluid – check the manufacturer's recommendations – and a device supplied by some tape recorder manufacturers and known variously as a demagnetiser, degausser or defluxer.

To clean the tape recorder heads, remove the shield, if there is one, exposing the heads. Put a little cleaning fluid on to a cotton bud, and carefully wipe the surfaces of the heads. If a lot of brown oxide is deposited on the cotton bud, repeat the operation with a fresh bud. The cleaning fluid should evaporate very quickly so there will be no danger of leaving the heads moist.

To demagnetise the tape recorder heads, ensure first that the tape recorder is switched *off.* Now, from a distance of half a metre or so away from the heads, press the operating switch or button of the demagnetiser. Maintain in the *on* position as you approach the heads. Slowly move the tip of the demagnetiser past each head once or twice – you should be able to feel a slight buzzing vibration. Do *not* actually touch the heads with the demagnetiser – this is not necessary, and it could cause damage. Slowly remove the demagnetiser away from the machine a distance of half a metre before switching it off. The reason for the slow approach and retreat is that a sudden change in magnetic field around the tape heads could leave a magnetic residue which you have been at pains to eliminate in the interests of better recording.

One further word of warning: since there is a powerful magnetic field around a demagnetiser in operation, remove vulnerable watches and especially electromagnetic tapes from the vicinity.

Speed change and variable speed

Electronic music could be said to have evolved from the possibilities which stem from the apparent dislocation of sound in both space and time. The microphone and loudspeaker permitted the dislocation of sound in space, while storage media such as the tape recorder permitted its displacement in time, and the infinite rep-etition of recognisably identical sound events. Where the time-patterns of sound are encoded in space, as in the alignment of magnetic particles on electromagnetic tape, they can be decoded at a different rate, presenting an entirely changed appear-ance to our relatively time-stable sensorium. This is precisely what happens when a sound recorded at, say, $7\frac{1}{2}$ i.p.s. is played back at $3\frac{3}{4}$ i.p.s., or at 15 i.p.s. If played back at the slower speed, the frequency components of the original sound will all be an octave lower, and the sound will have twice the duration of the original. Similarly, if played back at the higher speed, the frequency components will sound an octave higher, and the duration will be halved. There will also appear to be timbral changes in the sounds, a portion of which is due to the change in equalisation in the circuitry of the tape recorder or amplifier.

These octave relationships in the pitches of the sounds are a function of the 2:1 speed changes of the tape recorder playback. By recording and playing back at speeds even further apart, greater transpositions can be obtained.

Some tape recorders may possess a variable speed facility, or it may be possible to adapt your tape recorder so that it will run at variable speeds. A simple, less controllable method is to pull the tape through by hand. In these cases intermediate transpositions of the sounds can be achieved. These may be stable, may continually accelerate or decelerate, or may be somewhat randomly varied up and down. It is difficult to achieve a precise variable transposition since there is usually a lag in the response of the machine. Add to these the possibilities of *recording* with the use of the variable speed control, and one has already a powerful range of transformation techniques.

Further techniques using the tape recorder will be mentioned in later chapters, so we will turn now to some of the other items of hardware for electronic music.

The microphone

Although the title of this section is in the singular, there are many types of microphone. Indeed, in a sense, every microphone is individual, with its own special characteristics of sensitivity, response and directionality (i.e. the response it gives to sounds coming to it from a particular direction). A *matched pair* is two microphones selected by the manufacturers to be as nearly identical as possible for the purpose of stereo recording.

Many microphones, those known as dynamic, ribbon, or the cheaper crystal or carbon microphones, require no power source, but can simply be connected to the appropriate input of the tape recorder. Others, the capacitance microphones, do require an external voltage, usually applied from a special transformer pack connected to the mains supply, but sometimes operated from a battery pack. If you can obtain a number of different types of microphone, it will be of value to try recording the same sound with them and assessing the results. Some will be found to be more sensitive, some to have a better frequency response than others – an imbalance is especially noticeable in the higher frequency areas. Since there is no 'universal' microphone apt for every circumstance, it is wise to know the performing characteristics of the microphones you are using in order to ascertain the most appropriate for a particular occasion. Even the lowest fidelity carbon microphone may be used to effect.

It is important, too, to know the *directionality* of the microphones you are using. Many are *omnidirectional*, i.e. they respond equally to sounds from any direction. Some are *bidirectional*, responding equally to sounds in front and behind, others *unidirectional*, having a strong response in one direction. The *cardioid* is a form often met, having a sensitivity response in a three-dimensional heart shape, being least sensitive behind the microphone.

All of the microphones mentioned, however sturdy in appearance, have fragile parts. They, and the cables between them and the tape recorder or mixer to which they are connected, should be treated with care. The capacitance and ribbon microphones are extremely sensitive to air movement. If used outside or close to someone's breath, they should be provided with a *windshield*, a relatively cheap accessory. During a recording a microphone should be undisturbed by any vibration other than the sound waves it is designed to transmit, so a microphone stand should be used wherever possible. If handling the microphone and cable is unavoidable, use a hand grip, minimise movement during the actual recording and prepare yourself for the editing-out of unwanted rubbing or grating noises later.

Special-purpose microphones

First and foremost here, because of their usefulness for electronic music, are *contact microphones*. These are microphones designed to transmit vibrations not from the air, but from the surfaces of vibrating objects, and require, therefore, direct contact with the vibrating surface. The microphone can be clipped or lightly taped to the surface of any object, which is then excited percussively or by friction. In most cases this will result in sounds not otherwise audible – instant revelation! With care, because of its sensitivity and fragility, the microphone itself can be moved across different surfaces, rough or smooth, and a range of sounds obtained which are dependent for their quality on the texture of the surfaces and the speed of movement across them. Differently textured sheets of paper, fabric, glass, wood, metal and stone could be tried to start with.

Throat microphones are sometimes to be found, perhaps from ex-army or ex-navy stock. These are strapped round the throat, and pick up vocal sounds and guttural noises. They can be used also on other parts of the body.

Miniature microphones, apart from their obvious use as inconspicuous bugging devices, can be very useful in close scanning of large vibrating objects, such as a tam-tam. Since such objects tend to have a complex network of nodes and antinodes of different frequencies, a miniature microphone placed close to a particular point selects only the vibrations radiated from a small area, and assists differentiation from the total vibrating mass. A special type here is the *probe microphone*, placed at the end of a wand, for investigating local sounds in machinery.

Rifle microphones are ultradirectional, aligned closely with the source of the sound, usually some considerable distance away. A device to assist the concentration of distant sounds is the *parabolic reflector*, where the microphone is placed at the focus of the reflected sounds.

The *hydrophone* is a specially sealed microphone for use in recording sounds under water.

Editing kit

To the tape recorder and microphone a few small accessories comprising an *editing kit* need to be added before experiments in electronic music can begin seriously. These are the *editing block*, a one-sided *blade*, a reel of *splicing tape* and some *leader tape*.

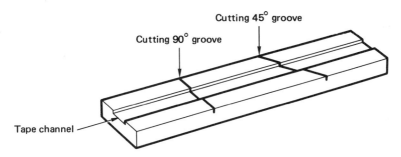

Fig. 1.2 An editing block

The editing block (Fig.1.2) has a channel for holding the tape, and two cutting grooves, one at 90°, one at 45°. The blade should be demagnetised before use. The splicing tape should be slightly less wide than the audio tape – $\frac{7}{32}$ in wide for $\frac{1}{4}$ in tape. The editing procedure is as follows:

(i) Find the editing point on the audio tape by a combination of normal playback and handwinding past the live head (the latter will be facilitated by a pause control or an edit button if your machine has one). Experience will soon inform you of the transformation of sounds due to the very slow movement of the tape across the playback head.

(ii) Mark the point lightly on the back of the tape nearest to the centre gap of the playback head. For matt-backed tape, a soft lead pencil may be used; for a shiny plastic surface a grease pencil will be necessary.

(iii) Lay the tape along the holding channel of the editing block with the pencil mark on the cutting groove; cut along the groove firmly with the blade. Which cutting groove? For most purposes the 45° cut is preferable – the join is stronger. But the 90° splice will give a sharp, 'hard edge' attack and is sometimes used for this reason.

(iv) Discard the unwanted piece of tape, and repeat the cutting operation for the leader tape or recorded tape you have chosen. There should now be two lengths of tape with parallel cuts in the editing block channel.

(v) Abut the two ends of tape, lay about 2 cm of splicing tape across the join, and rub down with the fingernail to remove air pockets and ensure a firm splice.

Some unusual editing techniques will be discussed in the following chapter.

With the equipment so far described a considerable number of techniques in electronic music are available. Much of what the French pioneer Pierre Schaeffer termed *musique concrète* is an assemblage of recorded sounds, edited and transformed. However, we turn now to electronic generators.

The oscillator

Oscillators used in electronic music produce one or more periodic *wave-forms* of variable frequency and amplitude. What we hear when an oscillator is connected to

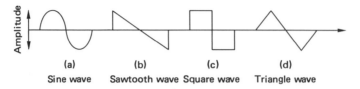

Fig. 1.3 Wave-forms

an amplifier and loudspeaker is a constant pitch (depending upon the *frequency*), of a certain loudness (depending upon the *amplitude*) and having a certain *timbre* (depending upon the wave-form). Wave-forms can be displayed on an oscilloscope; while the number of possible wave-forms is infinite, the simplest and the most common to be seen as outputs from an oscillator are shown in Fig.1.3.

Each wave-form shown here represents a voltage beginning at its zero point, rising positively and remaining positive for some time before crossing back through the zero point, then going negative before rising to the zero point again. The whole is termed a *cycle*, and the number of cycles repeated in each second (1 cycle per second, abbreviated c.p.s = 1 hertz, abbreviated Hz) gives the numerical value of the frequency. On the oscillator will appear a manual control (usually a knob) for the frequency probably covering the entire audio range, from roughly 20 Hz to 20,000 Hz (20 kHz). There will be another control for the amplitude of the oscillator, and there will be one or more signal outputs corresponding to one or more of the available wave-forms.

Since it is important to understand the difference between the amplitude and the frequency of an oscillator signal, Fig.1.4 shows a time-graph of a square wave first increasing in amplitude (i.e. getting louder) and secondly increasing in frequency (i.e. getting higher in pitch).

While this is shown with a square wave the same principle applies to all repeated wave-forms.

The wave-form relates to the timbre of the sound, its sound quality. The sine wave contains no harmonic partials and is heard as the simplest, smoothest kind of

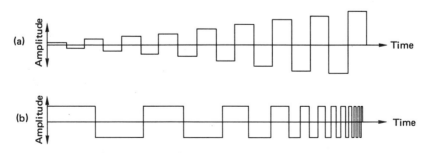

Fig. 1.4 (a) Square wave increasing in amplitude
(b) Square wave increasing in frequency

electronic sound and is used greatly as a test signal on television and radio. The saw-tooth wave possesses all of the harmonic partials in relatively decreasing amplitudes higher up the harmonic series – where n is the number of the partial, counting the fundamental as 1, $\frac{1}{n}$ gives the relative amplitude. It has a characteristically bright, piercing quality. The square wave possesses all the odd-numbered harmonics with the same amplitude ratios as for the sawtooth wave. For example, the ninth harmonic will have $\frac{1}{9}$ the amplitude of the fundamental. The sound of the square-wave oscil-lator is somewhat akin to the sound of a clarinet, having a rather hollow sound particu-larly at lower pitches. The triangle wave possesses all the odd-numbered harmonics in amplitudes decreasing in the proportion $\frac{1}{n^2}$. For example, the seventh harmonic will have $\frac{1}{49}$ the amplitude of the fundamental. It has a timbre brighter than the sine tone, but less strident than the square wave.

Voltage control

Since the 1960s the *voltage-controlled oscillator* (VCO) has become common. The principle of voltage control permits any variable parameter of a device to be operated by means of an applied variable voltage. It is, therefore, a type of automation. A VCO, while usually retaining a manual control for frequency (an 'offset' control voltage), will accept control voltages from a second (and third, or further) oscillator. The connections between the oscillators are made via a patch-cord, or through a central patch-panel, or perhaps with sliding connectors; whatever the system, the principle is the same: the output of one oscillator varies in frequency according to the amplitude and frequency characteristics of the other. As an example, we might imagine a sine-wave oscillator 1 set manually at 1000 Hz. This is controlled by a square-wave oscillator 2 which has a sub-audio low frequency of, say, 2 Hz. Now, twice a second, we hear the square-wave pattern of the low-frequency oscillator causing a deflection of, say, 250 Hz imposed upon the continuous sine-tone output of the first oscillator – first a frequency of 1250 Hz followed by a second tone of 750 Hz in constant alternation. The *amplitude* of the controlling oscillator deter-mines the frequency variation of the sine-wave oscillator; the *frequency* of the con-trolling oscillator determines the rate of pattern repetition. For this reason very low frequency oscillators can be employed to create slow-moving patterns which, in combination, repeat exactly only after a long period of time. Since every wave-form describes a succession of rises and falls in voltage, any wave-form can be used to voltage-control another oscillator. The square-wave oscillator, however, is particu-larly useful for pitch control, since it produces a steady alternation of stable pitches; the triangle wave, of course, would produce constant upward and downward glissandi.

The white-noise generator

A white-noise generator produces a sound somewhat like escaping steam. The colour term comes from an analogy with light. Just as a mixture of all visible frequencies produces white light, so a mixture of all audible frequencies at random amplitudes produces white noise. The colour analogy is sometimes extended to 'pink' and 'blue' noise too. Pink noise is weighted towards the lower end of the audible spectrum through equal amplitude distribution in each octave, producing a sound like a thunderous waterfall. Blue noise is weighted towards the top of the spectrum, and sounds very hissy.

There are often no controls on a white-noise generator, just an output. Otherwise there may appear an amplitude control, and a filter for high or low weighting of the white noise.

We turn now to some processors designed specifically for electronic music.

The voltage-controlled amplifier

A voltage-controlled amplifier (VCA) is one whose degree of amplification, or *gain*, is controlled by an external voltage. It can thus be programmed from an external source to vary in amplitude any signal appearing at its input. Just as a VCO may be controlled in frequency by a varying voltage from a second oscillator, a VCA's output is controlled in amplification. The wave-form of the controlling oscillator will thus appear as a rise and fall in volume of the signal input.

The envelope shaper

The *envelope* of a sound is its total dynamic form – its onset, rise in amplitude, sustaining and manner of decay. An envelope shaper provides a simplified dynamic form with which to shape any sound appearing at its input. It can thus be thought of as a special kind of VCA. Fig.1.5 shows two dynamic contours delivered by envelope shapers. In Fig.1.5(a) the total duration of the sound is divided into three

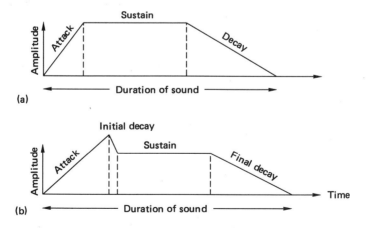

Fig. 1.5 Envelope shaper contours

portions: an attack period, a sustain and a decay period. This is the simplest form of envelope. Each of these three periods can be varied in duration. Typically, the attack period can be varied from 0 (i.e an instantaneous attack) to 1 second, the sustain from 0 to 10 seconds, and the decay period from 0 to 10 seconds or more. In this way a large number of different envelopes can be selected. In Fig.1.5(b) a four-segment envelope is shown, with an initial decay period before the sustain level is reached.

On both types of envelope shaper, in addition to the variable controls for each of the time-segments, three other controls are usual. The first of these is a trigger to set the cycle in motion, probably in the form of a push-button or switch. Secondly, a control for the duration of the *off* time is provided, i.e. the time before the cycle is automatically restarted. There should, of course, be a location for the device to be always *off*, unless overridden by a manual or electronic trigger. The final control will be an overall signal level.

On some envelope shapers, in addition to the signal inputs and outputs, a control voltage output is provided. In this case, the contour of the envelope can be made available to control other devices, for example a VCO, where the contour will describe the rise and fall in pitch of the oscillator, rather than its rise and fall in amplitude.

The filter

A filter will inhibit or increase a selected portion or portions of the frequency spectrum and can be described as *passing* or *rejecting* certain frequency areas. A *low-pass* filter will pass frequencies below a specified cut-off frequency, while a *high-pass* filter will pass frequencies above its cut-off frequency (Fig.1.6).

In Fig.1.6 the shaded areas represent the frequency areas *passed* by the filters. There is always a more-or-less steep slope beyond the cut-off point of the filters: the filters with the steepest slopes, close to the cut-off frequency, are the most valued. Filters used in electronic music usually have a continuously variable cut-off point, though occasionally a filter with a series of fixed-frequency points is found.

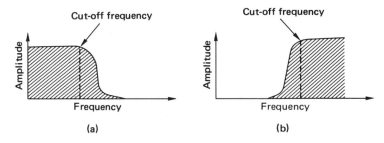

Fig. 1.6 (a) Low-pass filter
(b) High-pass filter

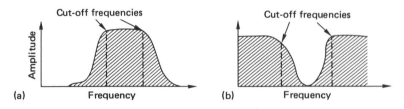

Fig. 1.7 (a) Band-pass filter (b) Band-reject filter

The high-pass and low-pass filters can be combined to obtain *band-pass* and *band-reject* filters. If they are combined in series, then a band-pass filter is formed, rejecting the outer frequencies. If they are combined in parallel, then a band-reject filter is formed, the inverse of the band-pass filter (Fig.1.7). One will often find the two modes available in a dual filter, where band-pass or band-reject modes may be selected by a switch.

A *voltage-controlled filter* (VCF) is one whose cut-off frequency can be controlled by a variable voltage from an external source, such as an oscillator or an envelope shaper. In such low-pass filters, a separate control for the 'Q' or resonance may turn the filter into a band-pass type with a relatively sharp slope around a variable centre frequency. In this case a further tightening of the resonance control may set the instrument into oscillation, and it then becomes a sine-wave oscillator, but can no longer be used to filter sounds. In some filter designs, the resonance control as well as the frequency can be voltage-controlled.

Another type of filter is the *fixed filter bank*. The audio signal is fed into a series of fixed-frequency filters, set at intervals perhaps an octave or half-octave apart. The amplitudes of each of the filters can be controlled separately and a wide range of filtered spectra becomes available. The so-called 'graphic equaliser' to be found in professional sound studios is a type of fixed filter bank, usually with filters set one-third of an octave apart, i.e. about twenty-seven to cover the entire audio spectrum!

The final type of filter to be discussed here is the *comb-filter*. A comb-filter is one in which each frequency in the harmonic series of a fundamental frequency is enhanced or resonated. These resonated frequencies might be termed 'nodes'. At the same time, the frequency areas between the nodes are inhibited. If the frequency of the filter remains static, then a certain hollowness of sound will result, as if the sound is being heard through a long tube. If the frequency is varied, then characteristic 'phase-shifting' effects beloved of much progressive rock music is heard. A comb-filter results from the output of a phase-shifter being mixed with its input signal.

The ring modulator

A ring modulator has no controls, except, perhaps, an output level control; but it does have two signal inputs and will deliver a transformed sound dependent on their characteristics. The output will consist of the frequencies of the inputs both added together and subtracted the one from the other. Let us take the simplest case of a single sine-tone frequency at each of the ring modulator's inputs: say, of 500 Hz and of 750 Hz. The output will then consist of the frequencies 1250 Hz and of 250 Hz (500+750 and 750–500). If more frequencies are present at the inputs, then the resulting sound-mixture will be relatively more complex. In general, the ring modulator tends to complexify sounds, as opposed to the filter, which subtracts from what is given to it.

Ring modulators can be used to effect with oscillator signal inputs in order to produce a wide range of note mixtures or fused timbres. Where one of the inputs is varied in frequency, the ring modulator will produce a characteristic and easily recognisable result in its parallel and contrary motion glissandi.

The synthesiser

A synthesiser is a convenient package of voltage-controlled devices for use in electronic music. Many of the smaller synthesisers that have appeared in recent years have been designed specifically for ease of use in live performance and incorporate a touch-sensitive keyboard. Others, however, are intended mainly for use in tape composition.

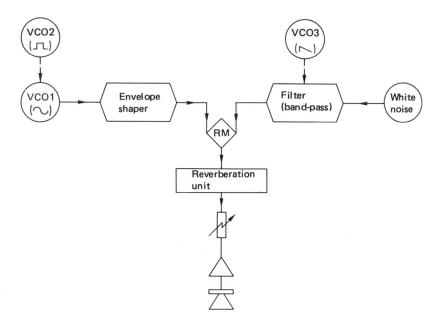

Fig. 1.8 A possible synthesiser configuration

A small synthesiser will typically comprise three voltage-controlled oscillators, a white-noise generator, one or two voltage-controlled amplifiers, a filter/oscillator, a ring modulator, an envelope shaper, and a spring reverberation unit. There will be a means of connecting the modules together, by patch-cords, pin-matrix board, or sliding switches. Such a synthesiser will provide many ways of interconnecting these modules together. Fig.1.8 gives an example of just one possibility.

In Fig.1.8 a low-frequency square wave from oscillator (VCO) 2 is varying the frequency of sine-wave oscillator 1. These alternating pitches are fed into an envelope shaper which imposes a dynamic form on them. This then appears at one of the inputs of a ring modulator (RM). A noise generator is fed into a filter (VCF) with its centre frequency controlled by a ramp wave-form from a third oscillator, and the filter output is given to the second input of the ring modulator. The ring modulator output will vary automatically with that of the envelope shaper, and this is further modified by added reverberation before it appears at the final amplifier and loud-speaker stage.

A synthesiser will certainly have means of communicating with the outside world in the form of signal inputs ('low level' for microphones, 'high level' for tape re-corders, other synthesisers etc.) and signal outputs (connections to amplifiers and loudspeakers, mixer etc.). In addition they should have inputs for control signals, i.e. voltage-varying signals from other devices, of which probably the most important are the *keyboard* and the *sequencer*.

Keyboards

Keyboards are designed to operate with a particular type of synthesiser. Their form is usually that of a conventional piano keyboard restricted to two, three or four octaves. If the keys are of the touch-sensitive, capacitance type they will not move as a piano key does, but will respond nevertheless to the touch of a finger. Keyboard designers have been ingenious in their attempts to increase the variety of control available from a simple act of pressing a key. Keys have been designed which respond not only to their location on the keyboard, but to the pressure of the finger on the key, to the velocity of the key when depressed, to the area of finger in contact with the key, and even to vertical or lateral movement of the finger on the key.

Whatever the type of keyboard, the key responds by sending one or more control voltages to the synthesiser which has previously been connected to give the required range of sounds. The voltages are usually applied to frequency, but amplitude and other parameters may be controlled instead or simultaneously. There will be an 'offset voltage' which, if applied to pitch, will raise or lower the entire register of pitches; and there will be a 'range' control which, if applied to pitch, will determine the interval between adjacent keys. The intervals obtainable can often vary from the smallest micro-intervals to intervals of perhaps a major third. Thus many equal temperaments other than the duodecimal, twelve per octave, are possible.

There may be other, more sophisticated features of the keyboard. The important thing to realise is that it is not a fixed device in any conventional sense, but is simply an additional means of providing a variable control voltage to any synthesiser module with a control input.

The sequencer

A sequencer is a device which delivers a preselected sequence of control voltages to another device. The voltages may be individually set, by a series of control-knobs, or they may be programmed from a keyboard. If they are set by hand, there will also be a means of setting the relative duration for each particular voltage in the sequence; if they are programmed from a keyboard, then the sequencer will memorise the performance time. In either case, there will be a control to change the 'clock-rate' when the sequence is running – that is, the rate of delivery of the control voltages can be speeded up or slowed down. The range of control here is usually very wide – a sequence may be delivered slowly, over a matter of minutes, or it may be delivered faster than the threshold of pitch, 20 Hz, in which case a steady complex sound will be created with the wave-form corresponding to the shape of the preset voltages. The normal use of the sequencer will be well within these extremes. A sequencer output is usually given to an oscillator, providing a variable frequency each of which may be shaped by an envelope shaper. A trigger output from the sequencer is provided to initiate the envelope shaper. However, the series of voltages from the sequencer can also be used to control a filter, amplifier or indeed any device with a voltage-controlled input.

Reverberation devices

There are a number of ways of adding reverberation to a sound during the recording or even after the sound has been recorded. The simplest and cheapest method, used in many synthesisers, is the spring reverberation unit. A transducer converts the audio signal into a mechanical vibration which bounces back and forth along a coiled spring or system of springs before being converted back again into an electrical signal and into the audio line. This kind of unit tends to have a rather thin, 'tinny' sound, though there are very good units of the type. There is likely to be an output-level control and a facility to mix proportions of direct and reverberated sound.

A second type uses a metal plate with transducers. The quality can be high, the unit very expensive. They are often found permanently connected to the output of a *mixer* (see below). With such units the transducers may be moved closer or further away from each other, providing a control for the 'reverberation time' of perhaps 1 to 7 seconds.

Another type, also expensive at present but likely to become cheaper, is the digital reverberation unit. The quality of these systems can be high and they are worth keeping a look-out for.

A technique for adding reverberation to which everyone with a three-head tape recorder can have access is 'head reverberation'. Here the sound is recorded on tape from the record head, is immediately picked up at the playback head and mixed with the sound input back at the record head. This may be achieved with a mixer; or there may be a special internal connection on your tape recorder for the purpose – many machines have the facility built in. The signal output level of the tape recorder will control the amount of mixed-in reverberation. In using this technique, it should be understood that what is really occurring is a series of echo-impulses, the time-interval of which is dependent both on the distance between the record and play-back heads and the speed of the tape. At the slower speeds the echo-impulses will be relatively slow and very obvious (which may, of course, be a useful feature); at 15 i.p.s., because the impulses are very close together, the reverberation is much more natural in sound.

The most direct way to add reverberation to a recorded sound is to play it through a loudspeaker in a reverberant room and record the result. There are, how-ever, many snags to this, the main one being to find a suitably reverberant space which is not subject to noise interference from elsewhere. But if such a space is available, and it can be easily 'wired up' for use as an echo-chamber, then it is likely to give the most natural-sounding results. For stereo reverberation, two microphones can be used picking up different echo paths from a single loudspeaker. The micro-phones should be directed *away* from the loudspeaker, since it is the sound reflec-tion from the walls, floor and ceiling that is wanted.

The mixer – getting it all together

The mixer is the place where all of the more complex signal-routeing and level-balancing operations take place. A mixer is not strictly necessary for many of the simpler techniques in electronic music, but will greatly facilitate the collecting and mixing of sounds from a wide range of heterogeneous sources. The mixer is at the heart of an electronic music studio. Mixers are often described in terms of their ratio of inputs to outputs. Thus a 'ten-into-four' mixer will have ten input channels and four output channels. The implication here is that any level of signal from one or any combination of the ten input channels may be directed to any one or any combination of the four output channels. There are, of course, mixers both larger and smaller than the example I have given. A most useful size for school use would be a 'six-into-two' mixer, delivering a two-channel stereo output from six independent input channels.

An input channel on a mixer needs to be able to accept both very low-level signals from microphones and also comparatively high-level signals from other audio equipment. There may be separate input connectors for these, on each channel, a preamplifier stage being added to the low-level input to bring it up to a higher signal or 'line' level. Alternatively there may be a preset gain control to amplify the low-level signals. Microphone signals may require amplification of 70, 80 or more decibels, while tape recorder signals should not need more than 20 or 30 decibels. The controls to be expected on a mixer input channel are: a preset gain control, an output group selector switch, a 'panoramic' selector for positioning the sound between a pair of outputs, and a linear potentiometer or 'fader'. There may well be also equalisation filters (high frequency, mid-range and bass) and a facility to send the signal to an external echo or reverberation device.

Mixers with two, four or more outputs will have a means of grouping the channels on to each available output. The output channels are often called, for this reason, 'groups' or 'group outputs' and they will, like the input channels, have a fader to govern the output level.

A signal-level meter is usually provided for each group output, the meters operating in essentially the way already described for the tape recorder, though they are usually larger and clearer to see. For any given signal from whatever source, it is therefore relatively simple to determine the optimum level by setting the input channel presets, and moving up the faders on the input channel and the group output selected. Some mixers have a master-fader in addition to the group faders, but this is usual only on mixers with four or more output channels. In setting the signal output level, use the meters rather than relying entirely on the ear for the listening, or 'monitor' level may be independent from the meter reading.

Connections from other devices to the mixer are best made from a *jack-field*, either of standard Post Office size or one of the miniature types. This certainly applies when the equipment is relatively permanent in its location. A jack-field is a network of jack sockets soldered to the outputs of all items of equipment one may wish to interconnect. The operational connection is then made by jack leads between the appropriate sockets. While soldering such a jack-field may be time-consuming, it is well worth considering for serious work in electronic music. It ensures that the equipment is manhandled as little as possible while in operation, and minimises the most common cause of equipment failure, that of cable or connector breakdown.

A plan of a small studio, put together for school purposes, might well look something like the one shown in Fig.1.9. It looks idealistic, but we intend to *be* idealistic for a while. The points to note are:

(1) The central operating position is located mid-way from the two loudspeakers, which are wall-mounted at head height. This position gives direct access to the mixer, jack-field, tape recorders and working surfaces, and is very close to the synthesiser and keyboard.

(2) Two tape recorders are horizontally mounted in the working surface, which is at a comfortable height of 85 cm. A third tape recorder is trolley-mounted and can be moved about the school. Another battery-operated tape recorder for recording outside the school is not shown.

(3) A microphone is available in the room, but cables can also be run to adjacent rooms for recording large groups.

(4) All cable trunking from the equipment to the jack-field runs *under* the working surface, behind a fascia. Below are cupboards and drawers.

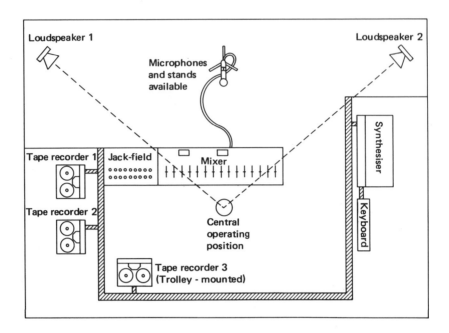

Fig. 1.9 A small studio plan (not to scale)

(5) There are plenty of power sockets around the wall, capable of supplying up to 30 amp of power, though this much will rarely be needed. All equipment is appropriately fused. A master-switch turns on and off the total power supply.

(6) The room is quiet, ideally sound-proofed, and there is good, noiseless lighting and ventilation.

Additional hardware

Extra items of equipment to come into one's hands for making electronic music are likely to have arrived from one of two sources: special purchases to extend the resources, or equipment normally belonging somewhere else (e.g. in the music room, or brought from home by a pupil). Consider that everything capable of generating a sound or of modifying a sound acoustically or electronically is potentially valuable in an electronic music studio.

In this section are items not normally considered a basic requirement for a studio but which will nevertheless prove to be valuable in many circumstances.

Electric piano and electric organ

The synthesiser keyboards are usually monophonic. A true polyphonic or chordal instrument can therefore save a lot of time in recording. The sounds from the instruments may be modified by any of the available processes.

Stylophones, short-wave radios, toy instruments

There is a great variety of sound-making devices, whether designed as 'serious' instruments or manufactured only for entertainment. The children should be encouraged to examine everything from the point of view of its sound-potential. The rule is to be prepared for anything. Some electrical devices may possess an output for amplification or recording, in which case, with the appropriate lead, they may be connected directly to the tape recorder or to the mixer. Others will have to be recorded acoustically.

Cassette recorders

Several pupils may have access to cassette tape recorders from home. These can be used by the pupils to collect sounds initially, to be transferred to reel-to-reel tape later if the quality is good enough (encourage the critical ear; if it is not good enough, try to rerecord the sound with better equipment). Bear in mind that projects can be developed which make use of multiple cassette recorders – see next chapter.

More sophisticated voltage-control devices

(i) *Envelope follower*. An envelope follower converts the amplitude of an audio signal at its input into a proportional control voltage which appears at its output and may then be delivered to any voltage-controlled device (e.g. a VCO, VCA or VCF). The audio signal used may be from any source as long as its amplitude is varying in the way desired. A frequently used source is recorded speech, the amplitude modulations of which may then be used to modify the dynamics of another sound, perhaps a musical instrument. However, the audio signal input may equally be a direct signal from a microphone.

The American composer Morton Subotnick has developed an interesting system employing what he calls 'ghost tapes' which contain a number of tracks of pre-recorded oscillator tones in varying amplitudes. These are given to a number of envelope followers which in turn deliver the control voltages for the equipment used in a live electronic performance or in a 'real-time' composition.

(ii) *Pitch-to-voltage converter* (also known as a *frequency follower*). This is a device which seeks the fundamental frequency present in an audio signal and converts it into a proportional voltage, which may then be presented to any voltage-controlled equipment. A variable sensitivity to certain areas of the frequency spectrum may be one of its features. The device can thus be used to derive a control voltage from the *pitch* of an acoustic instrument (as opposed to the *amplitude* with the envelope follower) by playing into a microphone connected to the device's input. With complex signals containing many frequencies there may appear to be a somewhat erratic response. This is because the device is continuously tracking the strongest fundamental it can find, and in complex signals this may change from moment to moment.

(iii) *Sample-and-hold.* A sample-and-hold device will sample a varying voltage source on receiving a trigger instruction from its variable timing-pulse unit, and will maintain that voltage at its output until it receives the next trigger pulse. It can sample any compatible voltage-varying device, but it is commonly used to sample a white-noise generator, when its output will provide a series of random voltages. A *random voltage source* is precisely this.

Sometimes a series (typically four) of parallel sample-and-hold outputs are provided from a single unit, thus allowing a number of independent control voltages to be derived from a single control source. A polyphony of independent voices can be obtained where the control voltages are given to a series of oscillators.

(iv) *Linear controller.* A linear controller normally provides a single control-voltage at its output. The device consists of a metallic ribbon stretched across a plate. When the finger presses the ribbon down and creates a contact with the plate, a voltage depending on the point of contact is given by the device. If its output is controlling a VCO (its usual application) then the finger can create a continuous melody by moving from position to position. Very smooth *glissandi* are possible with this device. It is thus a useful complement to the *keyboard control*, which normally provides only discrete voltages. A *trigger* output is often supplied in addition to the control-voltage output; this may be used to initiate an envelope shaper to which the signal output is given.

Location devices

Location devices will disperse portions of an audio signal into two or more output channels to 'place' the sound at a desired location. By continuously controlling the device the sound can be apparently moved from one position to another. In stereo a sound can be placed at any point between the two loudspeakers. In Fig.1.10(a) sound A appears centrally; this is produced by equal amounts of the signal being

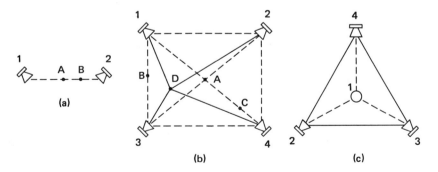

Fig. 1.10 (a) *Linear locations*
          (b) *Two-dimensional locations*
          (c) *Three-dimensional locations*

sent to the loudspeaker amplifiers. Sound B, on the other hand, is closer to the right-hand loudspeaker, and appears there because more of the signal is sent to loudspeaker 2's amplifier.

In Fig.1.10(b) a conventional quadraphonic loudspeaker system is shown. Sound A is heard in a central location because the signal is equally balanced in all four loudspeakers. Sound B has its signal divided equally between loudspeaker amplifiers 1 and 3; sound C's signal is divided unequally between loudspeaker amplifiers 1 and 4, with more amplification in 4. All of the locations between the loudspeakers, represented in the diagram by sound D, are available with different proportions of the signal being sent to the loudspeaker amplifiers.

In Fig.1.10(c) an unconventional quadraphonic placement of loudspeakers, with three loudspeakers in a triangular arrangement at floor level, and a fourth suspended above at the apex of a tetrahedron, permits positioning of sounds in three dimensions.

Location devices to be operated manually are often supplied with a mixer as part of the signal-routeing facilities. The stereo version known as a panoramic potentio-meter (usually shortened to 'panpot') I have already briefly referred to. Since these are usually in the form of a rotary control they are more useful for 'placing' a sound than for creating continuous movement. Though this can, perhaps, be achieved with nimble fingers.

A very useful quadraphonic control is the 'joystick' type, which can be used to locate or to move sounds very easily. The stick can be moved back and forth, and from side to side. With a conventional quadraphonic arrangement of loudspeakers the movement of the stick should map the movement of the sound.

Some voltage-controlled location devices are now available. A single applied voltage is necessary for a stereo model, or a dual control voltage for quadraphonic systems. Perhaps the main advantage these systems have over the manual ones is that very rapid spatial fluctuations are possible, creating complex phasing and other effects rarely heard acoustically.

Frequency shifter

A frequency shifter is somewhat akin to a ring modulator. It will 'shift' the frequencies of any signal input by a variable number of hertz either up or down, by selection. Whereas the ear perceives 'geometrically' in the sense that there are twice the number of hertz in each higher octave, the frequency shifter alters frequency relationships arithmetically and therefore alters the perceived harmonic relationship of frequency combinations in the original signal. Let us take a simple illustration. Suppose the original audio signal contains two frequencies, 500 Hz and 1000 Hz. They are in a frequency proportion of 2:1, and will therefore sound an octave apart. If we now shift them upwards by 25 Hz, the frequencies are now 525 Hz and 1025 Hz, an interval slightly less than an octave. Similarly, if we shift the signal by an equal amount downwards, we have 475 Hz and 975 Hz, an interval slightly larger than an octave. So we can say that in general a frequency shifter tends to transform the harmonic relationships and the timbre of sounds. Sensitively used, it can be a most useful device.

Vibrator-transducer

A vibrator-transducer is, in effect, a miniature loudspeaker except that, in place of the loudspeaker cone moving in and out to create the displacement of air which we perceive as sound, there is instead a moving spigot (Fig.1.11). The normal use of such a device is in the scientific laboratory, where it is used for vibration testing, and it is also widely used in educational institutions to demonstrate patterns of vibration in objects (there may be one in your school's science block). When connected to an oscillator and amplifier the spigot will vibrate at the frequency of the oscillator, but since the contact of the spigot with the air is minimal compared to that of a loudspeaker cone, the sound is virtually inaudible. However – and here is what makes the vibrator such a potentially powerful device for electronic music – the spigot can be brought into contact with any object, turning it into an acoustic radiator.

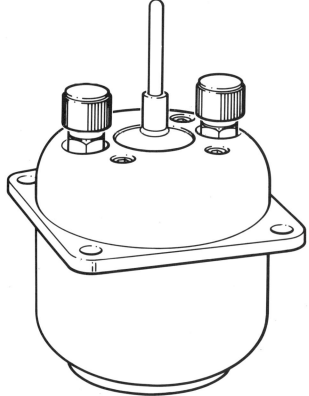

Fig. 1.11 An electroacoustic transducer

Any physical object has a potential for radiating sound. It may be a good radiator for certain frequencies, and a poor one for others. Every object will tend to promote some frequencies and inhibit others, in accordance with its capacities for internal resonance. An object brought into contact with the spigot of a vibrator–transducer can be turned, in effect, into a loudspeaker. However, the difference is that a loud-speaker is designed to radiate all frequencies equally – a 'level response' is highly virtuous in a loudspeaker – whereas all other objects used as loudspeakers in this way will produce a highly 'coloured' response because they are acting as natural filters.

The use of vibrator–transducers for electronic music is very underdeveloped, and yet they can provide a wider range of sounds than most synthesisers at a fraction of the cost. They also suggest some unusual ways of presenting musical performances. Some of these potentialities will be discussed in the following chapter.

Plate 1   The electronic music studio at York University

2 Using the hardware: software techniques and ideas

RICHARD ORTON

This chapter describes some ways of using the hardware discussed in the previous chapter. While this cannot be an exhaustive treatment, it will cover most of the established techniques and will suggest further avenues to explore. This seems appropriate for a medium in which the discovery of new sounds and ways of putting sounds together is a vital impetus. I make no apology for presenting some of the ideas simply as 'fun' - in the right circumstances, many of these projects can be set up as game environments. I feel that exploratory activity within an accepted framework can often release the most creative potential for discovery. This does leave open to the teacher, however, the question of when to 'step in' and bring a sense of form to the process. A successful project in electronic music will have a balance of the two aspects, exploration and formalisation. The latter exists in order to present or perform the results not primarily for the benefit of the audience, but rather for self-assessment. The essential element of play, through which we also learn, is one of the most powerful ways of humanising technology. The point is that the play should be ultimately open-ended, should be capable of extension and development.

The question of the way in which this kind of activity is structured in a classroom is still very much an open one. The best solution would often seem to be that of relatively small groups of children working together on set assignments, and that is what has been assumed for much of the activity suggested here. A teacher's instinct as to what personalities will form a strong interactive group is important and must be relied upon. The group arrangement does have an added advantage in that each group will have a critical audience in the other groups. There are, of course, alternatives. Certainly there is a case for the more enthusiastic children working in pairs - out of school hours if necessary and if it can be arranged easily. And many of the projects, especially those involving dramatic performance, can be tackled by a whole class.

Extending the ears

I remember as a child being intrigued by kaleidoscopes, periscopes and by a device called a 'seebackroscope' which by an ingenious arrangement of mirrors allowed one to see behind one's head. Many children are fascinated by being able to extend the visual sense in such ways. It is possible with relatively accessible equipment to extend the ears in a somewhat similar way. A microphone, preferably low-impedance with a long cable, a tape recorder or other suitable amplifier and a pair of earphones are required. They are connected so that the earphones are picking up the sounds through the microphone directly (i.e. with no recording taking place). Several possibilities now present themselves. If the tape recorder is portable, a single person can carry the microphone to explore a variety of sound environments while wearing the earphones. This should give a sense of the difference between the way the microphone 'hears' and the way human beings hear. When a child tries this, it may be amusing and instructive to ask him or her to pretend to *be* a tape recorder, and to 'replay' the sounds 'recorded'. Such listening exercises are always useful in training attention to sounds, especially when they can be introduced imaginatively.

With a group of children and a long cable it can be interesting to place the microphone some distance away from the child with the earphones and to get the other children to create a special sound environment around the microphone with whatever sound objects are to hand. Guessing games, contests and listening exercises as well as more structured musical performances may be developed from this simple beginning.

Here is a suggestion for an 'artificial sound environment' game.

Blind Man's Microphone

Each child carries an implement with which to create an identifiable sound – his sound-signature. One child, with a microphone and earphones, is blindfolded. One of the sounds is played for him outside the room, so that he can recognise it later. Then he is led into the room where all the children are making their sounds. They should be encouraged by the teacher to vary the density of the sounds, as in a 'musical' performance; this, no doubt, will occur naturally after a time, but at first everyone will be eager to create as dense a sound-texture as possible! There should be a rule that no one can move when the microphone is pointing to him (he may, however, stop making his sound for up to ten seconds or so). In these conditions the task of the microphonist is to find the sound he was given to identify. The game then proceeds as in *Blind Man's Buff* without the violence!

Making recordings

I have given an outline of the recording process in the previous chapter, and other contributors to this book will discuss particular techniques for recording. However, a few words should be given on the importance of isolating the sounds from those ambient sounds in the environment. Schools are not the most silent of places and it would be wise to discover the quietest location in the school in which to make the recordings. Even within a room, there may be a corner that is quieter than elsewhere. Screens of absorbent material, even improvised ones made from a wall of coats, should improve the quality of a recording.

Where it is important that the sound quality of an object is recorded clearly, several factors should be considered. One has been referred to: its acoustic isolation from other sounds. Another is the advisability of restricting the reverberation as much as possible. Reverberation can always be *added* to a sound; it can rarely be successfully removed. So do not record in a reverberant room unless it is precisely this quality that is wanted. Another factor is the positioning of the microphone; a small object should be placed near to the microphone, a larger object farther away, depending on the area of the object presenting a vibrating surface to the air. Beware of recording too closely, for it may well be found that the mechanical or incidental sounds dominate the characteristic sound, a mistake easily made in recording bells, pianos and even voices!

The manner in which the object is vibrated should be considered, and experimented with before the recording is made. When an object is struck percussively the material of the striking implement can be important for the sound quality. It is worth collecting a variety of wooden, metal, rubber or other beaters for the purpose. The point of impact should be tested too: one place may produce only a dull thud, where a few inches away a bright, ringing sound will be produced. Hollow objects can be blown across, to exite the enclosed column of air; some objects can be bowed, with a violin or other stringed-instrument bow, or with a home-made bow of wood and string. Some objects will respond well to coarser friction from sandpaper, hacksaw blade or serrated knife. And so on...

Here are some suggestions for recording objects:

(i)   Get each child in the group to bring along a single unusual sound that he or she has selected. Set the ball rolling by demonstrating some yourself, e.g.:
    rolling a ball-bearing around a saucepan
    blowing across a bottle top
    blowing the edge of a leaf
    twanging the wires of an egg-slicer, while gripping with the other hand to change the tension
    stroking a metal spatula along the inside edge of a deep coffee pot (a sound I used in my tape work *For the Time Being*)

(ii)   Create a 'toy symphony' by recording toys of all descriptions.

(iii) Explore all the sound qualities of a single material, e.g. paper:

    tearing (newspaper)
    crinkling (cellophane)
    shaking (metal foil)
    stroking etc. etc.

(iv)   Create 'scales' of similar sounds by recording similar objects of different sizes, e.g. china vessels:

| egg cups | mugs |
| drinking cups | bowls |

After the main processes of recording have been experienced and understood by the group, the children may be introduced to *acoustic processing*. The principle involved here is that between the source of the sound and the microphone is interposed an object that will modify the sound in some definite way. The clearest example of this is the *tube filter*. A sound heard or recorded through a tube will be changed by a resonance according to the dimensions of the tube. Certain frequencies will be enhanced, while others will be inhibited. Both the length and the diameter of the tube have a bearing on the effect, and to a lesser degree the material of which the tube is made. Here it will be wise to collect tubes of various sizes in advance of the experiment. Longer tubes may perhaps be obtained from carpet suppliers or builders' merchants.

The principle of acoustic processing can be applied by other means. An example is muffling or muting a sound by enclosing its source with a cloth or by placing it inside a container such as a suitcase. Another is recording a vibrating object and modifying the sound with the resonances of the vocal cavity – precisely what happens with a *jew's harp* (or *jaw's harp*).

Recording with a *contact microphone* has been mentioned in the previous chapter. After an initial exploration of what it has to offer, someone with an inventive turn of mind may care to design a 'sound tray' containing a variety of objects which vibrate and resonate in contact with the tray. The contact microphone, of course, will be permanently secured to a suitable position on the tray. Or again, a contact microphone might be attached to a 'bagatelle' table, or even better, a specially constructed board with pins at different heights to give more interesting acoustic results.

I should mention briefly electromagnetic transducers, the principle of which is followed by the electric guitar. Any vibrating ferrous objects, steel rods or hacksaw blades for example, can be detected by the magnet, converted into electrical impulses and amplified. One can find such a transducer in an old telephone earpiece, and its use is shown in Fig. 2.1. Further applications both of the electromagnetic transducer and the contact microphone are given in Hugh Davies' chapter on the construction of electroacoustic instruments.

With a portable tape recorder many possibilities having to do with recording aspects of the sound environment present themselves. There will doubtless be many locations in the immediate vicinity of the school with characteristic, if not unique, sound qualities. Here are some suggestions:

bus station	church
railway station	street
library	pond
coffee shop	wood
department store	

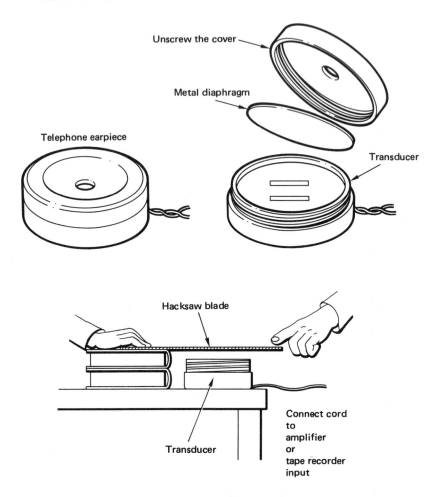

Fig. 2.1 The use of a transducer taken from an old telephone earpiece

Recordings can be made while stationary, or moving from one location to another. Here are some suitable assignments to set for the recordists:

(i)   Seek out the most characteristic sound in each location.

(ii)   Seek out the most unusual sound in each location.

(iii)   Record while moving from an outdoor location to indoors and vice versa. (This has been included to draw the attention to the effect of sound reflection in an enclosed space.)

(iv)   Allow a pupil to make a recording of a ten-minute walk from the school or another identified location. Back in class, play the recording and get the class to try and plot the route taken, using the aural cues on the tape.

A large-scale map of the area may aid this, if one is available. Depending on the choice of routes, it may be advisable to ensure that some readily identifiable sound cues are included on the original recording.

Storing tapes: a sound library

Over a period of time it is likely that many different recordings will be made. If these recordings are to have their full value, it is important that they be easy of access. The experience of many tape composers has shown that a large number of small (4 in or 5 in) spools is most useful during the course of constructing a piece. Sounds of a similar nature can be grouped together on a single spool and labelled.

However, in addition to such a collection of sounds for work in progress, a more permanent sound collection should be considered – the best recordings, the most characteristic sounds and so on. Here the 'cataloguing' becomes, if anything, more important. Recordings of broadly similar categories may be assembled on larger (7 in or 10½ in) spools with a catalogue reference label on both the spool and its box. The more effort put into the catalogue the more useful it will be. The information, whether on label, catalogue-book or card index, should include the following:

title (and number if required)
duration
recording speed
format (mono or stereo)
date recorded
name of recordist
place of recording
leader colour coding (if adopted – see below)

Tapes should be stored vertically, boxed and preferably in a metal cabinet at a constant room temperature. The phenomenon known as 'print-through', which is a faint pre-echo of the louder sounds on the tape, will be minimised with standard thickness tape and by storing the tapes 'tail-out', i.e. the tapes are removed from the *right-hand* spool of the tape recorder, and when they are played again they are run through to the left-hand spool first.

The self-assembled sound library may be supplemented if desired by sound-effects records, of which there are now many. Most record shops have a 'miscellaneous' section where these are to be found.

Leader tape and its uses

Leader tape is a non-recording tape of plastic or paper which is used to 'lead-in' to electromagnetic tape. When passing a live playback head it sends no signal to the amplifier and is audibly distinguishable from a quiescent electromagnetic tape which still accounts for a low-level noise usually known as 'tape hiss'. Leader tape is available in various colours. The most common variety is a clear plastic tape which has been coated on one side with an opaque coloured paint. It should be used with the painted side 'out', i.e. away from the heads, for a number of reasons; the smooth side is presented to the heads causing less wear and the paint on the leader tape is less likely to be rubbed off, and the matt paint presents an ideal surface for writing with soft pencil or felt-tipped pen.

It is a good idea to adopt a standardised colour-coding system for leader tape that all the equipment users know about. It is common to use white before a test signal, green before the sound recording in question, red at the end of a spool and any other colours at intermediate positions along the way. Coloured leader tapes allow rapid access to a coded desired sound.

When editing a number of small lengths of somewhat similar recordings together, it may be helpful to splice-in only a few inches of leader tape between the sounds. Leader for identification purposes should, however, be a few spool-winds thick, so that it can be seen from the edge of the tape when fully wound. The leader at the beginning and end of the tape should be even longer to protect the recording tape from possible mishap.

There is a useful type of white leader tape overprinted with a design at every fifteen inches, and a secondary mark at the mid-points between these. This kind of tape is especially helpful for timed intervals between sections of a piece, where it is easy to calculate the duration by counting the number of such marks while editing, taking into account the tape playback speed, whether 7½ or 15 i.p.s.

Rhythmic templates and tape loops

Lengths of leader tape interspersed with recording tape produce alternations of sound and silence. A construction such as this may be called a 'rhythmic template' since any material that is recorded over it will be broken up into sounding and non-sounding durations. There is an infinite variety of such templates; any desired rhythmic pattern may be produced by converting the durations into calculations of length. Very slow patterns will have long sections of tape and leader, very rapid patterns will alternate them in lengths fractions of an inch long. The disadvantage of these templates is that they take a long time to assemble, but they can be recorded over many times with different types of material. The durations can be made relatively longer or shorter by changing the tape speed – a variable speed facility makes all the 'in between' durations available. And a rhythmic 'retrograde' can be created instantly by turning the tape around.

It may be objected that such stark rhythms imposed upon the recorded material destroys any inherent rhythm contained there. So it may; but one is thereby urged to discover material with which the technique becomes appropriate. It can be very effective where the recorded material is relatively unchanging, or where a strong pulse in a slightly different 'tempo' from the template rhythm is present (this is so regardless of whether the rhythm is regular or irrational). In the latter case the effect of the superimposed rhythms being slightly 'out of phase' with each other creates great tension.

Such a rhythmic template consisting of alternating leader and recording tape may be made into a 'loop' by splicing the end to the beginning and arranging a suitable cyclic path for the loop to go round and round the tape head. In this case the template can be recorded on and immediately transferred to a second tape recorder so that although the template is continually erasing and recording new material a continuous recording is made on the second machine. Whatever the continuous programme material, a periodic rhythm of the duration cycle of the entire tape loop is superimposed, modfied by any changes of tape speed that are adopted during the process.

The use of tape loops is one of the earliest techniques of *musique concrète*. It is much easier to create *ostinati* in which the constant repetition is desirable than it is to create a continuous sound by means of a loop. In most microphone recordings, and even in relatively stable electronic sounds, it is extremely difficult to get the beginning and end of the loop to match exactly so that there is no audible 'bump'. This is much easier, however, in very rapidly changing and complex textures. Take care to listen not only to the sounds you wish to match, but also to the reverberation and ambience matching – all are important to create the illusion of continuity.

Tape loops can be a few inches long, or they may extend to fifty feet or more. The important consideration is that some back tension is created so that the loop is always pressed against the replay head of the tape recorder. (In normal operation the back tension is supplied from the left-hand spool spindle.) The back tension can be supplied for a loop by means of any smooth nonferrous object heavy enough not to be pulled along by the drive motor. For longer loops some ingenuity may be needed to create a successful path around a number of guide-posts. For very long loops it would be wise to employ one or more additional machines as 'slaves' to help the tape along its path.

With tape loops it is worth remembering that the same piece of tape is used over and over again and the rate of wear is therefore much more rapid than with normal usage of tape. Be prepared, therefore, that the quality of the recording will deteriorate noticeably after playing the loop for a long time. If a loop is being used as part of a larger work, to be mixed in with other sounds, its use should be limited until the master-mix is made.

A technique that may occasionally have a use is to create a 'Möbius Strip' loop by giving the tape a half-twist before joining the ends together. Every other revolution the tape will present its back to the heads. The sound should still be present, but very faintly, and the channels will be inverted, on a stereo tape. With this technique, the thinner the tape the louder will be the 'shadow' signal so it may be an occasion to use long-play tape.

Further tape techniques

Editing a sound out of a continuity of sounds may seem a daunting task to the uninitiated, but it is a skill relatively easily acquired and one which is in constant use in the making of a tape composition. It is helpful to set certain exercises in which the act of editing is performed over and over again, and yet constantly demands judgement as to the success of the operation. An example used by teaching studios all over the world is to request the removal of all of the consonants from a sentence of recorded speech. The end product should be two spliced passages, one containing a spluttering of consonants, the other a gliding of vowels. For beginners at editing, it should be recommended that the sentence recorded for the exercise should be spoken very slowly!

A related exercise, more revealing in some ways, is to cut off the attacks from recorded instrumental tones. If a number of these are spliced together, it will be found that the recognition of the instrumental timbres becomes much harder. Much of the information we use to classify instrumental sounds appears at the onset of the sound – the perceptual 'pigeon-holing' occurs in the first milliseconds of audition.

Much of the tape editing performed during the construction of an electronic composition is concerned with the definition of the beginning and the end of the selected sound, cutting the tape at the appropriate points and joining this length of tape to another similarly prepared. The reasons for the choice of sounds thus connected is, of course, primarily a compositional consideration, and determined ultimately only by the composer. But we must recognise that there are many possible reasons for joining two sounds, many of them not necessarily regarded as traditionally 'musical'. While the main reason for the connection may be concerned with pitch or rhythm, it is equally or even more likely to be made for reasons of timbral connection or articulation, or even to create a 'narrative' continuity in some extra-musical context. Many sounds possess both a powerful stimulus for mental imagery and the qualities of definable pitch, timbre, duration and so on which we concede to be primarily 'musical'. Many of the best compositions of tape music have succeeded precisely because the sounds have been used in a dual context. Their iconic qualities and also their musical qualities have both been taken into account in the composition.

It can surely have been no accident that, at the beginnings of electronic music composition, there was a major movement towards incorporating chance in the compositional process. After all, where a new field of exploration presents itself, a random sampling of all possibilities is the most likely to throw up new aesthetic confrontations. Serendipity, accepting the chance results of unforeseen circumstances, remains an important feature of much tape composition.

Editing lengths of recorded tape without reference to a sound's beginning or end seems to have been a discovery of John Cage's collaborative *Project for Magnetic Tape* of 1951. The juxtaposition of sounds chosen from different recorded environments guarantees variety of sonority; random splicing with statistically short lengths of tape guarantees rapidity of articulation – with such guarantees one may wonder upon the significance of the highly structured chance element in a work such as Cage's *Williams Mix*, or the tape realisation of his *Fontana Mix*. But the technique of rapidly spliced, fragmented sounds will produce a powerful effect not really obtainable in any other way, though a fast sweep across the frequencies of a short-wave radio band in the evening hours perhaps approaches it.

Some of the sounds to be heard in the Cage works mentioned are produced by playing a recording backwards. There are two main ways of achieving this. On a stereo ½-track tape recorder, the spools can simply be interchanged. What had been recorded on the upper track and was therefore heard on the left loudspeaker is now heard backwards from the right loudspeaker. The inverse applies to what was originally recorded on the lower track.

The other method is to rethread the tape around the capstan so that it will be pulled backwards. This is easy to achieve only if your tape recorder guides are open at the top. Fig. 2.2(a) shows a normally threaded tape recorder; Fig. 2.2(b) shows the method of threading for backwards playback. In contrast to the first method, this one has the advantage that the tracks are not inverted.

The aspect that is most changed by playing a sound backwards is its dynamic envelope. It will be noticed that many steady sounds appear remarkably similar

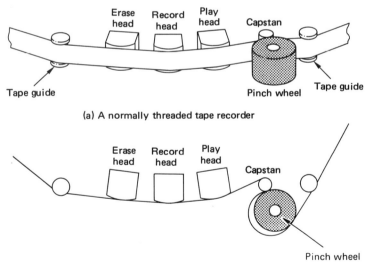

(a) A normally threaded tape recorder

(b) Threading for playing tape backwards

Fig. 2.2

for much of their duration whether played backwards or forwards – it is the attack and decay that most easily 'give the game away'. Recorded percussive sounds, on the other hand, are changed a great deal by being played backwards, since the timbrally complex 'ictus' at the head of the original sound now appears as a sudden climax after a slow crescendo. The 'unnaturalness' of this is sometimes compensated for by reverberation, or by abutting a forwards version of the same or a related sound to it:

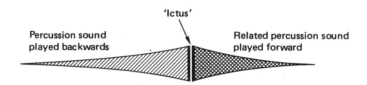

Fig. 2.3

Copying

Copying tapes, whether of complete works or of isolated sounds, is a fundamental technique of electronic music, and it must be done with care so that there is a minimum of distortion or signal loss. The principle is to ensure that the record and playback characteristics of the machines are as nearly identical as possible.

Setting the replay characteristics

To set the replay characteristics of the machines, a prerecorded tape of a sine tone at 1 kHz at a constant line level of 0 dBm should be used. The tape may be a specially purchased test tape; these are expensive, however, and it may be necessary to substitute one you have made yourself. To do this, you will have to rely on the manufacturer's initial setting-up of the machine – so use your most recently purchased tape recorder. Set a sine-wave oscillator to the frequency of 1 kHz – this corresponds to a slightly sharp B, an octave and a seventh above middle C. The exact frequency is not crucial, but the *amplitude* of the signal is. Adjust the record inputs of the tape recorder so that the signal is reading exactly 0 dB on the meter, and then record the whole of a 5 in tape with this signal on both channels.

Before making your tape copy, place the test tape in turn on the machines you are to use, set to the playback mode, and adjust the output level for each channel so that you are reading line level on your reference meter (whether on tape recorder or mixer).

Setting the record characteristics

The copy may be made direct from machine to machine if you have no mixer. A spool of blank tape should be placed on the record machine, your test tape on the replay machine. The outputs of the playback machine should be connected to the inputs of the recording machine. Play the test tape and record this on the second tape recorder, adjusting the record-level inputs to read line level for each channel. Now record at least ten seconds of the signal at the correct level (i.e. after the adjustments have been completed); this can then be used as your 'test tone' before the copy.

To check that the signal has been recorded at the correct level, you may play back this new test signal on the first tape recorder, when it should read line level also on this machine.

Making the copy

Provided all the adjustments have been made correctly, it should now be a simple matter to copy the tape of the sounds desired. Once the setting-up of the machines has been correctly made, the copies will be as accurate as the tolerance of the tape recorders will permit. It is most unwise to tamper with the playback or record levels while making a copy, since it will then no longer *be* an exact copy, and all of the adjustments will need to be made again before further copies of sounds can be attempted.

The procedure for making a copy via a sound mixer is virtually identical to that already described, except that the mixer channels should be left open and not adjusted during the setting-up, and that all tape recorder levels will be referred to the mixer meters rather than to the tape recorder meters.

Multiplying a single sound

From a single sound complex textures can be created. There are a number of ways of doing this. Here are two:

1 (i)   Make a loop of the sound to be treated.
    (ii)   Record the loop many times by copying on to a continuous spool of tape on one track of a second tape recorder.
    (iii)   Repeat (ii) on to the other track of the tape.
    (iv)   Mix both channels together on to another spool of tape, track 1
    (v)   Record the loop again on to the second channel of this tape.
    (vi)   Repeat (iv) and (v) until the desired density of texture is achieved.
2 (i)   Copy the sound to be treated many times on the second tape recorder, slightly varying the speed of playback each time to get variants of the sound.
    (ii)   Splice the sounds together to create a long loop.
    (iii)   Record the loop several times until the desired density of texture is achieved.

Reich's 'phasing' technique

An extension of the first 'multiplication' technique mentioned above is that adopted by the American composer Steve Reich in a number of works dating from the middle 1960s. Here a loop is recorded many times on to one track of a stereo tape recorder. Then the same loop is recorded also on to the second track of the tape, taking care to ensure that the two tracks begin in synchronisation, i.e. what should be heard is a *mono* signal, with the sound image appearing mid-way between the speakers. (Actually this is extraordinarily difficult to achieve immediately, but there is a way of making it appear simple which I will describe in a moment.) Then, while the second track is being recorded, the thumb is placed lightly on the left-hand spool of the playback machine, just enough to slow down the tape fractionally. What should now be heard from the second tape recorder is the sound image slowly separating into two distinct signals, one gradually overtaking the other. Reich called this a 'phasing' technique, and during the course of a single composition would repeat or vary this process a number of times. Later, of course, he went on to extend the phasing principle to live performance.

It should now be clear how to get the two tracks into exact synchronisation. If it turns out that the synchronisation is not exact, then the thumb pressure can be increased a little so that the phasing process is speeded up until the two parts come to an exact unison. Then the pressure can be relaxed to create the desired rate of change. When all has been recorded, edit the tape to where the loops were in exact unison, and it will appear to be a gradual transformation away from a given unitary sound image.

The clearest expression of this technique appears in Steve Reich's *Come Out* of 1965, where the tape loop used is a fragment of speech ('come out to show them'). In this work the process is used several times in succession so that by the end of the piece there are many sound layers within a relatively undifferentiated sound mass.

I should point out that a related technique can be developed by using a variable speed control on the tape recorder instead of thumb pressure to slow down one of the tapes. This is effectively used by Stockhausen at 12′ 27″ of the second region of *Hymnen,* where the dominant chord of *Deutschland* is made to split into contrary-motion glissandi until the harmonies once again conjoin an octave apart at a distance of a diminished fifth from the starting point.

Threading the tape through a number of machines

Where two or more tape recorders are placed on the same level, it is possible to thread the tape through from the left-hand spool of the first machine to the right-hand spool of the last in the line. Even where only two tape recorders are involved, a useful technique can be developed from the tape's passing more than one set of heads.

The principle is that a sound recorded, say, on track 1 of the first machine can be picked up by the playback head of the later machine, sent back to be recorded on track 2 of the first machine, picked up at the playback head of the second machine, and mixed in again with the subsequent sounds recorded on the first track of the first machine, ready to go around once again. In this way quite a long chain of canons can be initiated. The number of times the sound is repeated can be controlled by the replay volume from the second tape recorder; normally this would be set so that the sound repetitions are gradually decreasing in dynamic. This prevents the build-up in noise level otherwise to be expected from using this kind of technique.

It will be noticed that the process is very similar to that described earlier as 'head reverberation' except that since the playback head belongs to another tape recorder the 'echo' is much delayed, the interval depending upon the distances between the tape recorders. With a chain of tape recorders at different distances apart quite complex patterns of echo can be created.

Mixing

The great advantage of having a mixer is that a number of different tracks of sounds can be assembled and later put together by simultaneous playback while recording a 'master tape' from the mixer's output. The technical 'plan' of the piece can be worked out in advance as a number of different layers of successive sounds to be mixed together at a later date. When all of the desired material has been recorded on a number of tapes, different ways of presenting and mixing the material can be tried out before a final version is accepted. The levels of one layer can be adjusted in relation to the others during a mix, the overall dynamic level can be controlled, and the placement of sounds in a stereo or quadraphonic layout can be changed. Very often, too, a degree of reverberation may be added to one or more of the sound layers.

Creating a final mix can be rather like directing a performance in which the instruments are the sounds that have been precomposed. The decision as to how a sound is heard in relation to other sounds is made at this moment.

It may happen, however, that there is simply too much to be done at once, that so many changes need to be made during the 'performance' that it is physically impossible to control them. The answer then is to make a series of *sub-mixes*. For example, from an original eight layers, two sub-mixes, each reducing four layers to two, may be made. Finally, the two stereo tapes will be mixed down to the stereo master.

Electronic instruments

With the wide range of electronic apparatus now available, whether in the form of a synthesiser or as separate modules, probably the most important aspect to be considered is that of assimilation. Children are capable of assimilating a great deal, but if they are presented with a wide field it is likely that the surface of the topic is covered quickly, leaving little interest in developing any aspect to any depth. Better, therefore, to introduce each item of equipment separately, allowing its potentialities to be discovered before moving on.

The *oscillator* must be the most appropriate starting point. A simple project is to 'take an oscillator for a walk', i.e. to prepare a performance or a recording of an oscillator being controlled only in frequency and dynamic. With a variable-frequency oscillator patched, as in Fig. 2.4, to a potentiometer, amplifier and loudspeaker (or alternatively, to a tape recorder if it is to be recorded) there is already enough material for demonstration of musical control.

Fig. 2.4

Each child in the group should be encouraged to get the *feel* of the controls, and then to make an improvisation or recorded performance of perhaps a minute's duration. It should be pointed out that:

(i)   the oscillator covers the entire frequency range, so a particular piece may use the entire range or only a portion of it

(ii)   the frequencies can be changed rapidly (i.e. virtually instantaneously) or very slowly, with all the possibilities in between

(iii) the potentiometer can be used in conjunction with the oscillator's movement to give an interestingly varied dynamic shape.

Normally one would expect a child to control both the frequency and the signal level simultaneously, but a sequenced arrangement, with one child controlling the frequency and another the volume, could be tried. If a mere chance interaction is to be avoided, there will need to be some discussion of the shape of the 'piece', and perhaps even some kind of notation developed for it. A useful investment for such performed scores is a clearly visible stop-clock, preferably silent in operation, which can be used to time the sections of a piece; in this way the feeling for time-span and proportion come to be appreciated.

The next stage might be to introduce any other manual controls for the VCO, such as a linear controller, keyboard or joystick control, if any of these are available. This should certainly precede the introduction of automated control from other oscillators, sequencers or other programmable control sources. When this is introduced, there will need to be a clear explanation of the wave-forms and their applications in voltage control.

The *envelope shaper* is a good instrument to introduce at a relatively early stage, since it can be used to process any available sound. At its first appearance, it would be wise to introduce it as an extension of a system already known, such as that shown in Fig. 2.5, where the shaper is used to articulate an otherwise continuous sound.

The interaction between the amplitude control of the envelope shaper and that of the potentiometer should be made clear, distinguishing it from that shown in Fig. 2.6, for example. In the latter case the envelope shaper can only operate upon whatever level is allowed to come from the oscillator; the hierarchy is inverted.

Fig. 2.5

Fig. 2.6

Fig. 2.7

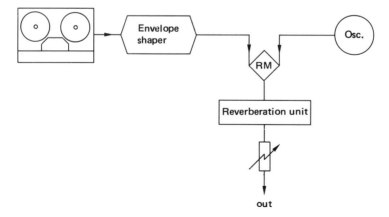

Fig. 2.8

It is quite a good idea to introduce the *filter* shortly after the *white noise generator*, so that some concept of pass-bands and band-widths can be demonstrated. Filters have a wide range of applications, depending upon the type of material they are operating on – so a relatively long time should be spent with this range of instruments. Voice input, recorded sounds and music should be tried, and should be used in conjunction with the classical tape manipulation techniques described earlier in this chapter.

Reverberation can be demonstrated by adding to any chain of events, for example, that shown in Fig. 2.7.

The signal processing techniques we have discussed may be applied to any recorded sound or sounds. Fig. 2.8 shows a patch in which a prerecorded tape signal is being fed into an envelope shaper, which chops up the sounds into lengths of sound and silence, going into a ring modulator of which the other input is a sine-wave oscillator; the output is then reverberated before going to the output channel. Such a processing system is only one of many possibilities for treating previously recorded sounds. Only through experience can the full range of available techniques and combinations of techniques be realised.

Processing sounds with the vibrator-transducer

The vibrator-transducer is able to relay any sound vibration, including prerecorded sounds, into any physical object or material. By recording the process with an air or contact microphone a transformation of the original sound is effected.

Let us take some examples.

(i)   A square-wave oscillator is fed into the vibrator-transducer. A piece of paper is held tautly against the vibrating spigot. The sheet of paper vibrates at the frequency of the oscillator. When held more loosely against it, the paper sheet vibrates more randomly, caused by the looser transference of the energy, and a coarser timbre is heard at a frequency an octave below the frequency of the oscillator.

(ii) A sine-wave oscillator sweeping up and down over a certain frequency range is fed into the vibrator-transducer. A tin can held against the vibrating spigot responds strongly to one frequency in the range, but only weakly to the others. A strong pulsed vibration is heard, accompanied by weaker glissandi.

(iii) A recording of a Mozart symphony is fed into the vibrator-transducer. A taut drumhead is held against the vibrating spigot. The reproduction of the symphony is clearly heard, but modified timbrally by the resonance of the drum. As the spigot is moved across the drumhead, a dramatic timbral change can be heard, and by pressing the drum tighter against the spigot, a momentary rise in pitch caused by the tightening of the skin can be heard. The reverse occurs when the skin is slackened.

Needless to say, these possibilities were chosen almost at random from limitless others. The range of potential sound transformations using this technique is vast.

Setting assignments for children

It is to be hoped that the children's enthusiasm for sonic discovery will be considerable after working for some time with some of the ideas and techniques suggested here. It will be the teacher's responsibility to focus the activities at different stages by setting suitable assignments for a group to tackle. I feel that three points especially must be borne in mind when setting such assignments.

(i)   The techniques to be used in the assignments should have been thoroughly explained and demonstrated wherever possible.

(ii)   The assignments should progress in small stages only from some earlier work.

(iii) They should nevertheless allow some scope for development and initiative on the children's part.

While technical exercises, designed to master a particular technique, are of value, it is important to ensure that an opportunity of using the technique creatively is given. Often only a hint of some imaginative task will be enough to focus creative attention. I have found the following ideas to be helpful in setting the imaginative faculty in operation. Many more, perhaps using these as guidelines, could be developed by the teacher.

(1)   Imagine a journey on an unknown planet, where the plants and other beings emit strange sounds not heard on the earth. Make a sound picture of this journey.

(2)   Illustrate a given poem or other text. I have found the poems of the Scottish poet Edwin Morgan most stimulating for tape treatment. Similarly Emmett Williams' *Anthology of Concrete Poetry* or even Max Brandel's *The MAD Book of Word Power* may suggest a number of possible starting points.

(3)   Illustrate a fantasy-story written by members of the group.

(4)   Investigate all the sounds that can be made with a single source (e.g. a rubber band) and make a piece only from these sounds and transformations of them.

(5)   Create a 'sonic alphabet', i.e. a sound made with an object beginning with the letter 'a' (e.g. munching an apple) and so on throughout the letters of the alphabet.

(6)   Make a seasonal piece with winter sounds, spring sounds, summer sounds or autumn sounds. How best to capture a season only in its characteristic sounds?

Performance techniques

The presentation of work achieved by the electronic music groups should be a constant and natural process, at various times ranging from the casually informal playback to a formal presentation in concert. No doubt the peer group will be interested to hear the results of even the simplest exercises, while more ambitious projects will rightly achieve a wider audience. For these more formal presentations it is important to use the best reproduction equipment available, and of adequate power for the size of the auditorium. The positioning of loudspeakers should be chosen with care, and there should be a constant monitoring of the playback levels during the performance, allowing for subtle but appropriate boosting or attenuation of the sound. In fact, the diffusion of sound in space should be thought of as an art in itself, capable of improvement, and involving initiative and innovation.

Within a school's curriculum there will be many possibilities for performance other than playback of a tape, however, and I should like to draw attention to some of these. The traditional event of the school play can perhaps be enlivened by presenting specially commissioned electronic music for the interludes or intervals; there may also be opportunities for the provision of special sound effects required by the play.

A more ambitious undertaking, involving a group of teachers from the outset, and many more children, would be a tape conceived in dramatic terms and integrated into a totality involving also mime or dance, costume and action, live performance or narrative speech, or any other combination of dramatic arts.

The solo or ensemble concert item, involving composed or improvised musical performance with a prerecorded tape, is another advanced possibility.

A tape and slide presentation is a format that appeals to many children and allows a strong visual element to accompany the sounds on tape. This seems a good medium for involving children of a range of different abilities, particularly where they are able to be really imaginative in the creation of the slides. Illustrations from a wide range of sources can be collaged and photographed from an improvised rostrum camera. There may be a structural link in the way that the visual and aural elements are assembled.

Multiple tape recorders can be assembled for a performance of a gigantic tape loop, even large enough to surround the audience. Sound environments can be created by disguising tape recorders or cassette recorders within an otherwise innocuous space, intermittently sounding their prerecorded message. Questionnaires on the sound environment can be handed to each auditor.

Simultaneously recording on many cassette recorders an improvisation or other performance, and later playing them back in a widely spaced environment can create a fascinating multiple-speaker sonority that increases in interest as the machines get further and further out of step with each other. For a full description of such a system, see 'Harvey Matusow/Naked Software 12-cassette spatial sound system' in Source - Music of the avant garde, No. 10, 1972. Source is published by Composer/Performer Edition, Sacramento, California.

3 Electronic music in the primary school

PETER WARHAM

As a schoolteacher I have devoted a great deal of time to finding ways of awakening children's minds to all the fascinating and wonderful things around us of which our senses can make us aware. Around 1960 I began to feel that the tape recorder had considerable potential for imaginative work of all kinds. I bought my first mains-operated machine for about £20. I found it very useful in school for stimulating dramatic writing and we began to produce 'radio plays'. These were recorded and relayed over the school radio system. The children were soon doing a large part of the recording themselves. I had discovered they could do it as well as I could – except, perhaps, in situations which were fairly complex, such as recording an orchestra and choir, or organ music.

The tape recorder then began to be used for collecting the sounds of wild animals and birds. Because the school was in a small East Yorkshire village it was possible to record many creatures with a mains recorder. The school was surrounded by fields and hedgerows and was only about two hundred yards away from the 'ings', the low-lying grassland by the river, a haven for ducks, waders and other water-loving birds. Then I moved to my next school, on the edge of a small but highly industrialised market town, which was nevertheless within a short distance of the countryside.

It soon became evident that most of us did not use our ears particularly well, and we were often not aware of subtle but quite common sounds going on around us. In some cases we found that we had to *learn* to hear them by persistent listening. Recording on tape made it much easier to become aware of these sounds, whereas listening for them 'live' could be quite hard work. However, once the various sounds had been distinguished, they no longer presented any difficulty and could readily be identified.

Later still, I came across the book *The Psychology of the Use of Audio-Visual Aids in Primary Education* by G. Miliaret. It includes several passages on aural perception which seemed to bear out our observations about hearing sounds. The book made me more convinced than ever that the tape recorder is a valuable tool for developing aural perception and training children to listen. It has tremendous potential as a kind of electronic notebook for collecting sounds, conversation and music. It can be used as an extension of one's self, as is a pen or a paint brush, a potter's wheel or a musical instrument. It can be used, as these tools are, to help us organise our experiences. Many people have discovered this for themselves, but it took me, with the help of the children, many years to appreciate such a simple fact. The road to this discovery was exciting, sometimes hard and disappointing, often great fun, but never boring.

I first used the tape recorder experimentally in the English lesson, because I had been greatly stimulated by an article Charles Parker had written about his work. In 1957 he, along with Ewan MacColl, had been commissioned to prepare a documentary programme for BBC radio on the life and death of John Axon GC. John Axon was a railway engine driver who died at the controls of his engine attempting to prevent a serious accident. Charles Parker recorded some of John Axon's relatives, friends and workmates and found that the language used by them, when talking about personal experiences and situations in which they were closely involved, was very like that found in folk ballads. It had the same simple, dramatic but poetic form.

This led to an entirely new form of radio programme using the words of the people interviewed, with continuity provided by appropriate sounds and music in ballad form as a parallel to the language and feeling of the original statements. It became known as the 'Radio Ballad' and a later programme in the same style called *Singing the Fishing* won the Italia Prize for radio. Some of these programmes are still available on disc and well repay careful listening.

Eventually, by encouraging children to record poems, stories and conversations which contained much personal experience, it began to dawn on me that children also use language in a much more subtle way than I had realised. In the majority of cases the rhythmic pattern of the words matched the ideas they were trying to convey. Because they could listen to themselves, the children became much more interested in what they had written, and they quite often improved their first efforts by critical listening. I was led to the conclusion that the direct but often moving simplicity of their words had similarities with folk music and ballads. This led on to reading ballads and singing or listening to folk songs, and from this work came discussions about the use of words, word rhythms and patterns. Soon the children were encouraged to look at their own work in the way we had examined the ballads and folk songs. They would read some words with special emphasis, or read groups of words with particular rhythmic patterns to suit the needs of the subject matter. What had begun intuitively was now being attempted deliberately, though not always with better results! Nevertheless, the most important point is that the children were exploring the possibilities of language and were thinking about what they discovered.

One result was that several children noticed that simple patterns of words and sounds often suggest a tune. They were sufficiently excited about it to take up the suggestion that perhaps they should try making tunes for the words. The final stage of this exploration was the writing of Christmas carols, both words and music by children none of whom had received any musical training other than that in school. Around these we built a Christmas Service.

Another result of exploring language with the tape recorder was a suggestion that some poems or stories could be enhanced by 'backing' them with appropriate sound effects. This sometimes happened the other way round. On one occasion the famous express steam-engine, *Flying Scotsman*, was brought out of retirement to repeat its legendary non-stop run from London to Edinburgh. The main line passes the end of our school playground and we had prepared to make a stereo recording of the engine's sound as it rushed past. The engine driver saw the whole school waving to him as he went by, so he blew the whistle. One little boy was so excited he rushed into school immediately afterwards and wrote a poem. Later he recorded his poem and we added the recording of the engine and its whistle. Interestingly, the rhythms in the poem matched those of the train. The two recordings enhanced each other, so that the total effect was quite exhilarating and aroused feelings similar to those created by the original experience of hearing the train 'live'. On the cassette you can hear the original recording of the *Flying Scotsman* with the boy's poem, followed by a very early attempt to imitate the effect with electronics (*Cassette example 3.1*). After that, we made similar attempts with poems about the sea, or about the river and the local shipyard, but they were not always as successful. However, there was an eagerness to collect sounds for 'evocative' purposes, and many everyday sounds were now heard in a new way.

We collected sounds on tapes for future use. The children would listen to some of the collected sounds out of interest or in connection with particular assignments. The sounds themselves became the focus of attention and often the starting point for some new work, usually a poem or a story.

While this work was going on, the children had been encouraged to use tape for recording their attempts at making music with percussion instruments, chime bars, the piano or with any other sounds they might like to try. Recording teams had been built up to record stories and music for taping and using as 'lesson' material. Some of this was about composers, the children having written about the musicians' lives and recorded extracts from their music. This meant that everyone had experience in recording and could set up a microphone, fit a tape, adjust the volume, mix two inputs together and do any other straightforward jobs that were necessary.

Fig.3.1 shows a worksheet that I gave the children to enable them to understand the relationship between the length of tape and the duration of a sound at different tape speeds.

Many children, both boys and girls, had raised questions about the technical and scientific aspects of recording. Some attempts were made to answer these questions, but eventually we decided to build a science project around the subject of sound. At the time it was introduced there was considerable interest in recording and a number of children were keen to find out more about it. The enthusiasm was tremendous and the results quite surprising.

One unexpected discovery was that *electronically produced* sounds were a great attraction. I had an old valve-operated audio signal generator, or oscillator,

Tape speed $7\frac{1}{2}$ i.p.s. (19 cm/s)

How much tape would be required to take a sound lasting 1 second? ____ ____

How much tape would be required to take a sound lasting $\frac{1}{2}$ second? ____ ____

How much tape would be required to take a sound lasting 10 seconds? ____ ____

Tape speed $3\frac{3}{4}$ i.p.s. (9.5 cm/s)

How much tape would be required to take a sound lasting 1 second? ____ ____

How much tape would be required to take a sound lasting $\frac{1}{2}$ second? ____ ____

How much tape would be required to take a sound lasting 10 seconds? ____ ____

Tape speed $1\frac{7}{8}$ i.p.s. (4.75 cm/s)

How much tape would be required to take a sound lasting 1 second? ____ ____

How much tape would be required to take a sound lasting $\frac{1}{2}$ second? ____ ____

How much tape would be required to take a sound lasting 10 seconds? ____ ____

15 inches of tape went past the tape head in 2 seconds.
  At what speed was the tape recorder running? _____

$7\frac{1}{2}$ inches of tape went past the tape head in 2 seconds.
  At what speed was the tape recorder running? _____

$3\frac{3}{4}$ inches of tape went past the tape head in 2 seconds.
  At what speed was the tape recorder running? _____

38 cm of tape went past the recording head in 2 seconds.
  At what speed was the tape recorder running? _____

19 cm of tape went past the recording head in 2 seconds.
  At what speed was the tape recorder running? _____

9.5 cm of tape went past the recording head in 2 seconds.
  At what speed was the tape recorder running? _____

Fig. 3.1 Worksheet: Mathematics (tape speeds)

which was designed to produce a series of sounds in steps, from high pitch to low pitch. The sound required could be selected by means of a switch. The children experimented with this and recorded the sounds on tape. Some of these were recorded at 7½ i.p.s. and were later played back at 3¾ i.p.s. by mistake! The children were delighted by the new sounds they heard because they were so *unexpected*. After that they experimented a great deal with material recorded at one speed and played back at another. Not only were electronic sounds dealt with in this way, but sounds of birds and animals, trains and ships. Soon someone suggested mixing together electronic sounds and 'natural' sounds to see what happened. Drums, triangles, cymbals, piano notes, plucked rulers, elastic bands and a host of other sound sources were tried out. In order to create effective sound patterns and sequences the children learnt how to edit tape and splice together the sounds they had selected using our home-made editing machine. It was at this point, when the exploration seemed to have gone as far as it could without further direction, that the idea of making electronic music occurred to me.

'Electronic music' meant making use of any form of sound source, electronic or otherwise, which could be recorded on tape. After all, every time we listen to the

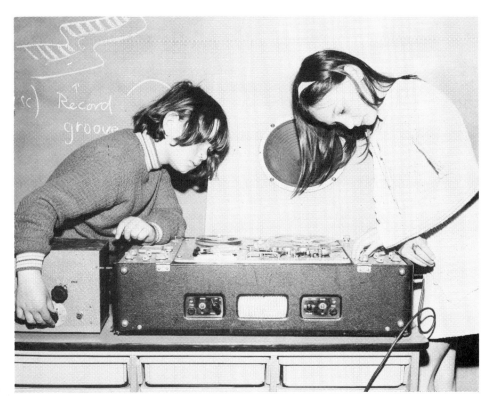

Plate 2   Recording an electric oscillator

radio or to a gramophone record we are listening to sounds produced electronically.

At this time I knew very little electronic music, so I had to begin learning about it and discover something of its possibilities along with the children. It became a genuinely two-way process, where children and teacher share their new experiences with each other and discuss them together. For me, this meant a lot of research, including a considerable amount of reading, experimenting and listening to music. Not only did I learn something about new forms of music, but I found myself listening to more conventional music with greater awareness. The children, too, made exciting discoveries that they shared with me.

I remember one occasion, at the beginning of this work, when the children were finding out what the various pieces of apparatus could do. A boy and a girl were experimenting with the tape recorder and the oscillator. They had discovered how to produce an echo; the rest of the children in the class, who were working on other things, heard the results of their experiments through the loudspeaker. Gradually the class began to listen to the sounds more carefully, and in twos and threes they left what they were doing and stood round the table at which the recordists were working. Soon the whole class was gathered there completely absorbed. I stood with them and after a short time they began to remark on the sounds.

'That's creepy,' John said, about one.

'That one reminds me of when I had gas,' Dawn commented about another.

'That's like angels,' whispered Sandra to me when a gentle, high-pitched sparkling sound came out.

'That's the best yet,' Anthony said emphatically, about a brilliant echo that was produced.

From then on, everyone was eager to experiment. They all wanted to produce 'space' sounds like those they had heard on science fiction films and TV programmes.

It appeared that the instruments which most of them would like to play were those which included electronic gadgetry: the electric guitar, the electric organ. Obviously, such choices reflect the influence of pop music but it also suggests that one way to stimulate and develop an interest in music is to enable children to have access to some simple electronic instruments.

It was not long before someone asked if they could hear some real electronic music. By this they meant electronic music other than that played by pop groups. First I introduced them to a BBC Radiophonic Workshop record consisting of a number of short pieces, mainly music to introduce programmes. Most of these were received with enthusiasm and interest. I then played them some of the music from Walter Carlos' disc, *Clockwork Orange*, consisting of classical pieces arranged for an electronic synthesiser. The pieces included Purcell's *Music for the Funeral of Queen Mary*, the second and fourth movements of Beethoven's Ninth Symphony and Rossini's *William Tell* overture. The effect was completely unexpected. I had never seen children get so excited about music before.

The first time I had heard the Carlos disc I had been thrilled by it myself because of the strong 'dimensional' effects which are possible with electronics. But, of course, this could hardly be called true 'electronic music'. It is conventional music played on an unusual instrument. It serves as a marvellous introduction to the sounds of an electronic synthesiser, but what it also did for these children was to get them talking very enthusiastically about the *pieces* they had heard. It was then an easy matter to introduce the originals, which they listened to very closely.

For some considerable time I did not introduce any of the more *avant-garde* electronic music, for two reasons. Firstly, I didn't think that I had listened to enough of it, or read enough about it, to be in a position to discuss it seriously with the children. Secondly, I believed discovery comes first and I wanted to see what sort of electronic music we could make together. Perhaps our own efforts would give us some insight into what others were trying to do.

Everyday sounds

There are so many sounds going on around us – more than we often realise. An interesting experiment to try with children is to ask them to be quiet and listen: then to list the sounds that they remember. Even when all the sounds are heard, it is surprising how many are not recognised. Another test: play recordings of bird-song and see how many you or the children can recognise.

When some of the children were taken on a camp into Newtondale, north of Pickering in North Yorkshire, one of the foresters took them on a nature walk. He had a marvellous knowledge of birdsong and the children quickly realised that they were almost completely ignorant of these sounds. Some birdsong was re-corded for later discussion and research. Attempts were made to imitate some of the sounds by whistling, or by making noises with the voice. Donna suggested that perhaps some of the sounds could be imitated on the piano, on the recorder or the electric organ.

All of these were tried out and we discussed poems with bird or animal sounds in them, and music in which composers had imitated wild creatures. Donna and Lynn tried the piano and electric organ. Later experiments were carried out with oscillators. The cuckoo was easy, but most of the others were much harder. Part of our discussions centred on notation – how could we write down the sounds so that other people could repeat them? An example of one of our attempts to answer this question is given later in the chapter.

We found recording the commoner animals and birds quite easy – dogs, and cats and farmyard animals – once we had had a word with the farmer to make sure there were no bulls, awkward geese or goats about. Sometimes unexpected sounds were collected. When Geoffrey and some other boys were playing hide-and-seek at camp, they found some wasps building a nest in a pile of old wood they were hiding in. They were very excited and said they would like to record them. Prudence decreed that I should hold the microphone close to the wasps, a few centimetres away, while the boys adjusted the recorder at a distance. No one was stung – the wasps seemed too busy to take any notice of us – and a fascinating recording was made. It was the first time any of us had heard wasps chewing!

This stimulated a general interest in the sounds of insects and we attempted other recordings. Bees, wasps and hover flies were easy to do in the school garden, but other insects were more difficult. We did manage to record some grasshoppers and crickets, both in the field and in captivity. Everyone was most delighted when it was found possible to recognise different species by their sounds.

We collected bog bush crickets from the wild, identified them and recorded them as follows. We put them in an empty fish tank which had a 60W lamp fitted in the cover. The cover also had a hole and a clamp for holding the micro-phone. The crickets were encouraged to sing by the light and warmth of the lamp. When they began to sing, the recorder was switched on. Our crickets were kept in captivity for a few days before being returned to the wild.

If you wish to try out this type of recording, make sure that the lamp is fitted

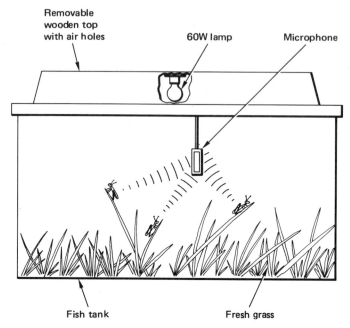

Fig. 3.2 *Recording studio for crickets and grasshoppers*

safely; it need only be switched on a few minutes before recording. With young children the tank should be placed so that they can't play with it but this need not prevent them making recordings or watching the creatures (Fig.3.2).

Montages of wild-life recordings can be very evocative, especially assemblages of insect sounds or of birdsong. A particular kind of day, or time of day, can be suggested by the recording. For example, if the sound of footsteps is heard along-side a dawn chorus, it is someone taking an early morning walk. Put the sound of owls hooting with the recording of footsteps and it becomes someone walking late at night.

Rhythmic sounds grip children's attention and have many possible uses for movement and dancing. Train sounds, traffic and boat sounds and especially the strong rhythm of a pile driver working on the river bank opposite the school have all been used for these purposes. An old pendulum clock provides a good rhythmic sound, particularly if it is recorded and played back at a slower speed. A watch tick recorded and played back at different speeds gives scope for work on sound patterns. Spliced-in with the clock and switched from track to track on a stereo machine, an interesting spatial effect can be obtained.

To record a watch, clock or other small mechanical object such as a toy, it may be an advantage to put it in a box. Place a clean duster or a soft piece of cloth in a suitable cardboard, wooden or plastic box and put the watch or other object in with the microphone. Cover with another cloth and try a recording. It should

Plate 3   Editing on a home-made editing machine

be possible to get a relatively clear recording without serious background noise from such an arrangement (Fig.3.3).

Recording everyday sounds sometimes led to aesthetic discussion. The children had recorded some traffic sounds – motor cars, motor bikes and lorries. Some of the boys like motor bikes and, as they know older boys or have big brothers who own them, there were some arguments about whether the sounds were good or bad: what constituted noise and what was a nice sound. 'It isn't like music,' said one little girl. That led to further discussion. I pointed out that when they brought their transistor radios to school I sometimes said 'Turn off that noise' – and it was often music that was being played. 'Well, you don't like that music' (it was usually 'pop'). I pointed out that this wasn't quite true, as I had some pop records and had played some to them. 'But you listen to classical music most,' said Anthony. 'That may be true,' I replied, 'but you listen to it too don't you?' 'No,' said one little boy, 'violins and that are rubbish.' 'Are they?' I asked. 'You've listened to them at school on records and enjoyed them.' 'Well, it's all right in school, but outside of school there are other things that you want to hear.'

'You say 'pop' is noise in school because you mean you don't want to listen to it then. There's something else to do or to listen to,' suggested Christine.

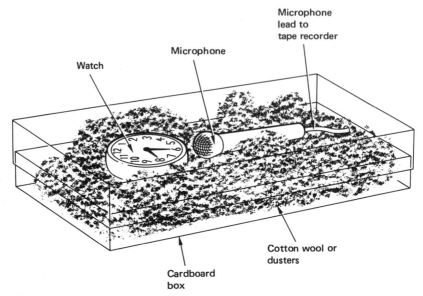

Fig. 3.3 Recording a watch

'That's one reason,' I agreed, 'but I think motor bikes are noisy and unpleasant, but the boys say the sound is great.' 'That's because you don't like them, isn't it?' said Roy. 'You're probably right,' I agreed. 'Loud sounds are noisy,' said Lynn. But it seemed that this wasn't always true, because pop groups play very loudly and that was all right. And quiet sounds weren't always nice – as they were reminded when someone tapped continuously on the desk with a pencil.

This sort of discussion led the children to see that what constitutes noise can be very subjective. It led to a study of 'noise' in the locality, the children making recordings of sounds in the school, in their homes and in the streets, and measuring the noise levels with a decibel meter. It was possible to produce some interesting graphs of local traffic noise.

With some of the vehicle recordings, an attempt was made to show the original sound level in the classroom. We did this by playing the tapes with the decibel meter at about the same distance from the tape recorder as it had been from the original sound source. Then the volume of the tape recorder was set to give the same meter reading as that originally obtained. This gave us a rough idea of the original sound levels and we were able to agree from this experience that what might constitute 'unpleasant' sounds was a combination of loudness, timbre, rhythm and location.

Voice and body music

One of the earliest sources of music must have been the human voice. It is quite possible that musical sounds developed from speech sounds; certainly music has always been very closely connected with poetry.

Over the centuries there have been many changes in the way that words and music have been used together. In some cases it is difficult to differentiate between speech sounds and sounds which are musical. One needs only to listen to a small child saying the alphabet or repeating a multiplication table to appreciate that. One boy did suggest, having worked through a multiplication table by himself, that we ought to make tunes to them so they would be easier to remember. Then he demonstrated how close the table was to singing 'when you said it'.

After many years of recording children's speech and poetry, I believe that the use of sounds and rhythms appropriate to the thoughts and experiences they are talking or writing about is a quite natural occurrence. Linda wrote the little piece below after watching a ship being launched at Selby shipyard. The recording we made of the event can be heard on the cassette (*Cassette example 3.2*). You will notice how she uses sounds to imitate the noises heard in the shipyard, and rhythms that are also to be heard there:

It went with a crash,
It went with a splash,
We all moved back.
The water came rushing, gushing on the bank.
We all screamed as loud as we could.
Luckily the boat didn't get stuck in the mud.
I thought back about the clanging, banging sounds
And the whistle being blown,
But
Now it is quiet, all the fun is over.
We are making our way back to school.

There are many precedents. For example:

The moan of doves in immemorial elms
And murmuring of innumerable bees

These two lines by Alfred, Lord Tennyson suggest a warm summer's day by using words which imitate associated sounds.

There are onomatopoeic words in most languages. I asked the children to list words that seemed to them to imitate sounds. We collected quite a long list (Fig.3.4).

We recorded some of these words, and experimented with them on tape. Speeding up or slowing down the words could alter their 'meaning'. The way in which the words were spoken could also alter their meaning. Even nonsense words and sentences could be given apparent meaning through their manner of delivery. I introduced the children to relevant literature and music: from *Alice in Wonderland* to parts of the Chorus of Frogs in *The Frogs* by Aristophanes, and, on record, children's singing games, the chorus from Berlioz's *Faust* and Berio's *Visage*.

babble	jingle	sighing
bang	lapping	slam
beat	lash	splash
blare	murmur	splutter
blast	patter	swish
booming	pattering	swishing
bubbling	pealing	tick
buzz	ping	ticking
chime	pinging	tinkle
chug	pop	throbbing
clang	popping	thunder
clanking	purr	thundering
clatter	rattle	tramp
clink	rattling	twang
crack	ring	wail
crackling	roar	wailing
creak	roaring	whack
crinkle	rumble	wheezing
dripping	rumbling	whirring
grinding	rustle	zooming
gurgle	rustling	rat-tat-tat
hissing	scratching	tick-tock
hoot	screech	ting-a-ling
howl	shriek	toot
howling	shuffle	honk honk
jangle	shuffling	
jangling	sigh	

Fig. 3.4 Words which imitate sounds

We tried adding tape echo to some of the words, a technique which children seem to find particularly fascinating. We played the recordings of words on tape backwards, and there was some training in listening by getting the children to imitate the word being played backwards and then recording the imitation. When this tape was played backwards, if the imitation was good, the original word could be recognised!

Gradually, a more refined technique was developed for using words to produce 'word music'. One example was a piece called 'Thunder'. The idea was to use the word 'thunder' in such a way that it suggested peals of thunder. Before it was started, the children listened to a recording we had made of a real thunderstorm and, with this in mind, the experimenting and discussion began.

We found a simple 'music sheet' we had devised to be most useful for scoring this performance (Fig.3.5). The final form was arrived at by recording trial performances, listening and trying variations and new ideas until a performance was thought to be satisfactory. The intention in the first part was to give an impression of a single clap of thunder, with the sound echoing away in the familiar rumbling. In the second part, the word was split up into sounds with a group of children allocated to each sound and brought in by a conductor. The 'th...' sounds rep-

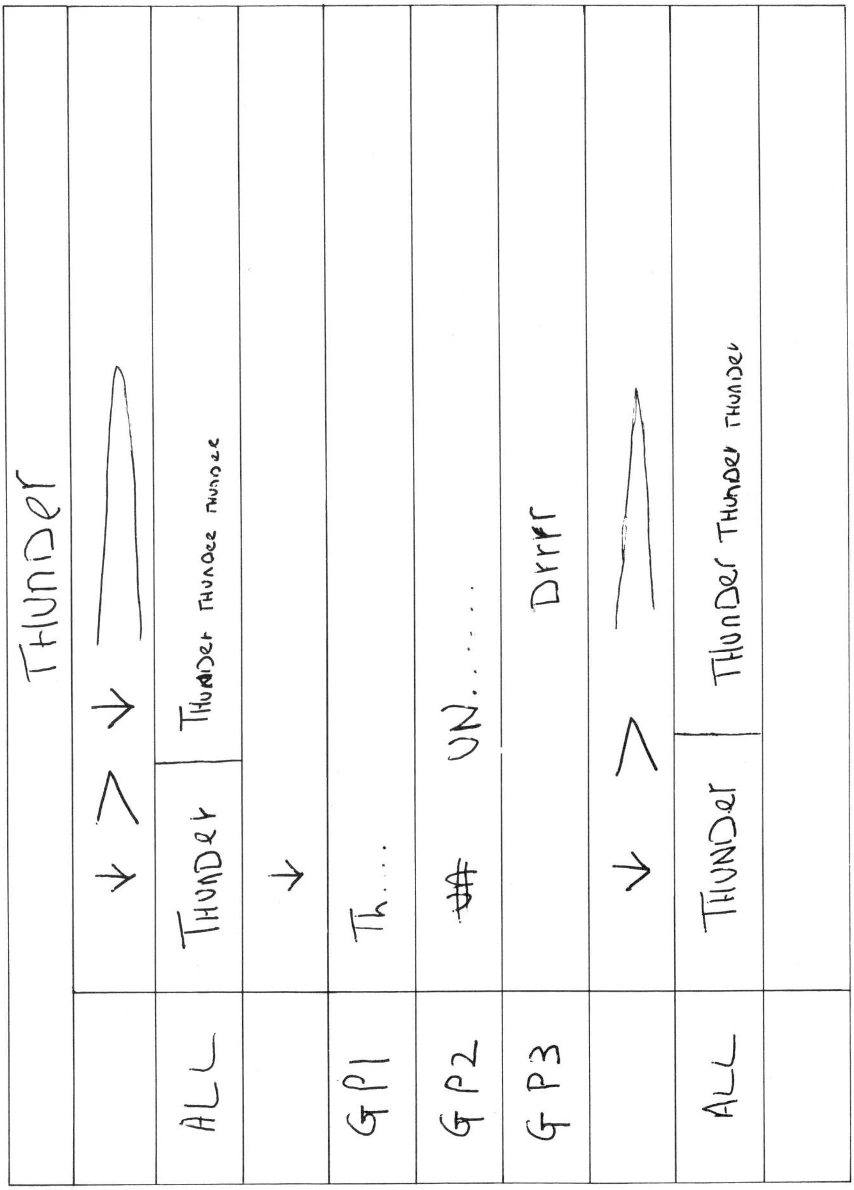

Fig. 3.5 Music sheet for scoring 'Thunder'

resented the rain, the 'un' the initial sound of the thunder and the 'drr' sound the rumbling afterwards. To end the piece we repeated the first part, but allowed the recording engineer to vary the recording if he wished, to give the impression of thunder moving across the sky or to increase or decrease the volume.

'Bonfire Night' was made in a similar way. It suggests, at the beginning, the bonfire burning, and later gives impressions of various kinds of firework sounds: 'b' and 'o' represent the 'bangers', 'ffff' the rockets and catherine wheels, 'igh' and 'nnnnn' the fireworks that scream or hum, while the 'tttt' sounds represent the jumping jacks.

Both these examples of collective sound poems on the title-words can be heard on the cassette (*Cassette examples 3.3 and 3.4*).

We also recorded many sounds made by the body – clicking fingers, clapping hands, stamping feet and slapping thighs all came off well. A close-up microphone gave interesting sounds when hands or fingers were rubbed over various materials like sandpaper or velvet. And we made lots of interesting sound patterns holding the microphone near the feet and then stamping or tapping on various materials like wood, a metal sheet and pebbles.

I have described in a general way how I began work in electronic music with primary school children, and I hope I have shown some of the sometimes unexpected paths we were led to explore. For those who would like to try some of this kind of work, I should now like to suggest some simple recording exercises, and then go on to describe some more elaborate projects.

Recording exercises

The following exercises are ones which I have used on many occasions, both to demonstrate to the children and also to get them to do for themselves. The teacher should try them out in private before attempting them in class. They all acquaint the user with microphone characteristics and recording techniques – the different effects obtained by placing a microphone close to or distant from the source of sound and so on. After beginning with voice sounds, we move on to body sounds and then to sounds from musical instruments, 'noise sounds' and environmental sounds. Each exercise is a suggestion only to point to the wealth of possibilities that exists around us: the teacher and, more importantly, the children will doubtless add variations of their own.

Simple exercises

Exercise 1 teaches us about the qualities of the microphone itself and how its position during the recording can influence the sound quality. Exercises 2 to 7 are really exercises in informal sound composition, which by being connected with the very process of sound discovery will retain a freshness difficult for more sophisticated students to achieve.

Connect a microphone, preferably of the cardioid type (but really any will do), to the input of a tape recorder. If the tape recorder has two or three speeds, some of the exercises should be tried at the different speeds to discover the change in recording quality.

1. (a) The microphone volume control should be set roughly midway and the microphone placed vertically on a stand or desk. Walk around it in a circle at a distance of about half a metre. Say a few words at points around the circle – at 0°, 90°, 180° and 270°. Play back the recording and listen for the differences in quality or sound level at the various positions.

   (b) Place the microphone horizontally and walk round in a circle at the same distance and repeat words at the same places as in exercise 1(a). Play back the recording and, again, listen for any differences in quality or volume – they may be rather greater than in exercise 1(a).

   (c) Repeat exercises 1(a) and (b) with a circle of approximately two metres diameter.

   (d) Say a short piece 20 or 30 cm away from the microphone. (I often suggest to the children that they recite 'Mary had a little lamb' because they all know it and it has a good collection of vowels and consonants.)

   (e) Repeat exercise 1(d) from one metre away.

   (f) Whisper the same words used in the previous exercises at the same distances.

   (g) Breathe gently close to, but across, the microphone. *Do not blow directly into it* as this is not good for the microphone. (If a windshield is handy, put it on, just in case!)

   (h) Click the tongue behind the teeth (i) close to the microphone and (ii) some distance away.

2. *Sound sequence.* Put some of the sounds just experimented with together to last about 20 seconds on tape.

   e.g. Breathe gently then harder.
   Whisper softly then loudly.
   Click tongue close.
   Whisper loudly.
   Click tongue at some distance.
   Whisper loudly then softly.
   Breathe gently.

3. *Voice.* Record different sounds made with the voice.

   e.g. Say and sing sounds like 'oo', 'ah' and 'ee'.
   Put in some consonants.
   Sing at various pitches.
   Sing softly then get louder.
   Sing short, staccato notes.
   Sing in contrast, loud then soft.
   Sing long, sustained notes, loud and soft.

Listen to the recording then make a 40-second tape using some of these sounds.

4. *Fingers.* Record the sounds made by tapping and rubbing fingers on various objects and materials.

   e.g. Tap lightly on desk or table.
   Tap heavily on desk or table.
   Rub hands together.
   Rub fingers over sandpaper and emery cloth.
   Rub fingers along the teeth of a comb.
   Tap on an empty cardboard box.
   Tap on a piece of metal or an old tin.

Make a sequence of 'finger sounds' to last 20 seconds on tape.

5. *Feet.* Place the microphone near the floor or hold it a few centimetres above the floor and record tapping, stamping and shuffling noises made with the feet. (Adjust the volume control to get a satisfactory recording level.)
   Use various materials as in exercise 4: tap, stamp or shuffle on a carpet, tiles, concrete, linoleum, metal sheets, sandpaper etc.
   Children wearing shoes with different types of soles and heels should make sounds in turn.

Make up sound patterns for a 40-second tape recording using various foot movements and materials.

6. *Fingers and mouth.* Tap the side of the cheek gently with the fingers while opening and closing the mouth. Record what happens.
   Work out some rhythms to tap with the fingers with the mouth in different positions.

Make up a 'tune' using fingers and mouth to last 10 seconds on tape.

7. *Tape composition.* Use some of the sounds experimented with in the first six exercises to make up a piece about yourself or about a friend. It should last about 40 seconds. Which sounds will give the best description? Get other children to listen to the tape and guess who it is.

Musical instrument exercises

These exercises suggest recording a variety of musical instruments usually to be found in school. Here what affects the sound quality most is the way the instrument is played; different sounds on each instrument should be sought and then recorded.

1. At about 60 cm from the microphone, record the following groups of instruments, played both loudly and softly and in different ways.

   Percussion
   Drums tapped with (i) sticks (ii) wire brushes
   Castanets
   Wood blocks

   Triangle
   Cymbal struck with (i) hard stick (ii) soft stick (iii) wire brush
   Chime bar struck with (i) wooden-headed stick (ii) rubber-headed stick
       (iii) metal bar

   Wind instruments
   Whistles of various kinds
   Recorder playing single notes
   Trumpet or bugle playing single notes
   Other available blown instruments playing single notes

   Stringed instruments
   Pluck the open strings of several instruments.
   Tap them gently with a chime bar beater.
   Bow them with a violin bow (short and long notes).

   Piano
   Play a few single notes, high/low.
   Play them again with (i) sustain pedal down (ii) soft pedal down.
   Open the piano, put the microphone close to the strings. Pluck and rub the
       strings gently.
   Do the same again with (i) sustain pedal down (ii) soft pedal down.
   Put your head close to the strings, bring the microphone close to the keys and
       sing a note with the sustain pedal down.

Listen carefully to these recordings. Play them through at speeds both slower and faster than the one at which they have been recorded. If it is possible, play the tape backwards. Which are the most interesting sounds?

2. Make a 1-minute tape composition by splicing together a sequence of chosen sounds.

If some of these exercises have been worked through, the children will have been awakened to the immense variety of recorded sounds and will wish to try out some less conventional sound sources.

Sounds from non-musical sources: indoors

Here are some suggestions for sounds which are created from simple objects brought by the children. Most of these sounds are percussive in origin. The recordings made will suggest how the focussing and amplification of quite 'ordinary' sounds can transform them into interesting sound material which can be enjoyed by an audience.

In order to help the children imagine sounds in different contexts, I prepared a simple worksheet (Fig.3.6).

1. Record the following:
   Spinning a coin on a desk
   Plucking elastic bands
   Plucking springs
   Twanging a hacksaw blade
   Clock ticking
   Winding up a clock or clockwork toy
   Clockwork toy running
   Tapping pencil on table
   Tapping on cardboard box (rhythmic)
   Tapping on wooden box (rhythmic)
   Rolling a marble round a saucer
   Shaking marbles in a plastic container
   Shaking a bag of crisps (rhythmic)
   Blowing across bottles of various sizes
   Water tap dripping
   Water tap running
   Pouring rice into a bowl
   Scrabbling fingers about in a bowl of rice or corn
   Squashing a wooden matchbox
   Breaking a match in two
   Rolling a ball-bearing over corrugated cardboard or Perspex
   Crumpling, pulling and tearing paper
   Crumpling and pulling plastic

2. Make a 1-minute tape composition using several of these sounds – 10 seconds of one, 15 seconds of another etc.

Sounds from non-musical sources: outdoors

Take a portable tape recorder into the environment and find what sounds it has to offer. After the recordings have been made, the children should play them back and discover how the sounds of one environment can be imposed on to the sounds of another. Later, some of these recordings may be used as imaginative backgrounds for classroom musical or theatrical activity.

What can we use:	Musical instruments	Non-musical sources	What signs could we use? Invent some.
To play a tune?			
To play a note we can sing?			
To make a sound that lasts a long time?			
To make a loud sound?			
To make a quiet sound?			
To make a sound getting softer?			
To make a sound getting louder?			
To make a hard sound?			
To make a soft sound?			
To make a short sound?			
To make a sliding sound?			

Fig. 3.6 Worksheet: Sounds

1. Record any interesting sounds in the locality.

    e.g. Gate squeaking   ⎫   *These simple sounds could be used*
         Footsteps on path   ⎪   *as a means of stimulating imagin-*
         Knock on the door   ⎬   *ative work: after the door opened,*
         Door opening   ⎭   *what happened next?*

    Bus starting and stopping
    Car starting, revving up, moving away, slowing down and stopping
    Motorcycle or moped
    General traffic noises
    Shop doorbell
    Church clock chiming
    Church bells
    Road drill
    Street cries: newspaper seller, rag and bone men, market stall holders etc.
    Railway station: trains arriving and departing

2. Make a collage of outdoor sounds by combining and contrasting a number of these sounds on tape to last about 1 minute.

Some further suggestions

Water music

Water seems to be a never-ending source of inspiration for artists, poets and painters as well as musicians. We found that the sounds of water can provide a very wide range of textures. The sounds of running water produce their own 'tunes'. Raindrops can give a variety of sound images. The sounds of dripping water, from taps or from wet leaves after a shower of rain, are fascinating to listen to. Imagine the warmth of a summer's day and the 'plop' of a fish in the lake. The sea can stir all kinds of feelings depending on whether it is calm or is being swept by a great storm.

Recorded sounds like these make excellent additions to a collection for *musique concrète*. Listening carefully to such natural sounds may act as an important stimulus to a child's writing a story, a poem or creating music.

We found it quite possible to record sounds under water in an ordinary kitchen sink by using a normal microphone protected from the water. A plastic bag, carefully checked for holes, was placed around the microphone and the bag securely held by elastic bands. Even with the microphone on the sink floor under the water it was found to be watertight. With the microphone in this position the following sounds are especially interesting.

Rubbing the rim of a wine glass. The wine glass stem is submerged and the rim rubbed around with a wet finger until the glass vibrates and produces a sound. A varying pitch can be obtained by the partly filled glass being slowly emptied and re-filled.

Water being poured out of a jug. This is very interesting when played back at a slower speed as the detail of the very high frequencies can be heard more clearly.

Flicking a comb underwater. The comb should be held under the surface of the water and a finger flicked along the teeth of the comb.

Model clockwork boat. The boat is wound up, and the rudder set so that it will go round in a circle. Both the clockwork motor and propeller will be audible on the recording. It sounds, when slowed down, like a real ship, or as someone said 'like a big diesel engine'.

Loch Ness monster. The bottom is cut off a squeezy detergent bottle, the top opened and the bottle placed upright in the water. As it is pushed up and down, a strange breathing sound will be heard. The performance can be recorded both above and below water, and will sound something like a strange monster moving in the water. Slowed down, the recording may sound stranger still.

Feedback

Feedback is the term used for an arrangement which allows part of the signal at the end of the electronic chain to be taken back and reintroduced at some point earlier in the chain. It can often be produced entirely electronically, but it may also be brought about quite simply by allowing air to act as a feedback medium. If a microphone is in close proximity to the loudspeaker which is reproducing the sound fed into the microphone, a wild 'feedback howl' may be produced. The pitch and amplitude of this howl can be controlled by adjusting the positions of the microphone and speaker and the volume control of the amplifier. With careful practice, a position can usually be found where the feedback sound *just* 'keeps going' at a constant level. Care should be taken with this technique, as the equipment could be damaged.

An interesting effect was discovered by one of the boys quite by accident. A plastic map tube had been used for some experimental sound work with the microphone and tape recorder connected up. The boy pointed one end of the tube towards the microphone and the other end towards the speaker some distance away, and a feedback howl was set up. When the tube was turned aside, the sound stopped. The tube always produced a sound of the same pitch. No doubt tubes of different lengths and diameters would have produced different pitches.

Bicycle music

A bicycle is a source of many sounds. One known to all children is the sound that arises when a piece of cardboard is put in the spokes of a wheel and the wheel turned. With a close recording, many of the normally less audible parts of the sound

Plate 4
Playing the Banjophone

can be heard. Other sounds can be obtained by rubbing the spokes with a metal rod or strip.

The gear wheels turning in the freewheel position make an interesting sound pattern. The tyre being pumped up gives a rhythmic pattern, to be superimposed on the other sounds or to use as a constant pulse with conventional musical sounds. The sound of a tyre being let down can be startling.

Ringing the cycle bell in different ways can give a clearly pitched element to the bicycle piece. If recorded while the bicycle is being ridden past the microphone, the unusual change in pitch known as the 'Doppler effect' can add to the interest.

The sound of brakes is a possibility, and tyres running over a wet surface. The children will think of many others and should try different ways of recording them. In order to record many of the sounds it is best to place the bicycle upside down, so that the wheels can be moved freely.

Projects realised by primary school children

'Creepy dance music'

This was made by Linda and Steven for Linda to dance to. The sounds come from an oscillator and feedback from the *Banjophone*, which is the name we give to a home-made instrument. It was constructed out of a metre-length of wood over which was stretched a banjo or guitar string, the sound being transmitted by a piezoelectric pick-up. It was a simple instrument, but one we found very effective and it was used on many occasions (*Cassette example 3.5*).

Donna's tune

The tune was worked out by exploring the piano keys and the electronic organ. Then it was written down on the 'music paper' shown in Fig.3.7, as an aid to memory. By recording the tune and adding other tracks one at a time it was possible for a more satisfying harmonised version to be created. First Donna played the tune on the organ so that it was recorded on track one of the tape. Then she listened to this recording as it was rerecorded on track two, adding at the same time an accompaniment she had worked out and learned. Now both tune and accompaniment sounded as if they had been played together. Ian suggested adding a bass part on the Banjophone later. Various versions of the tune can be heard on the cassette (*Cassette example 3.6*).

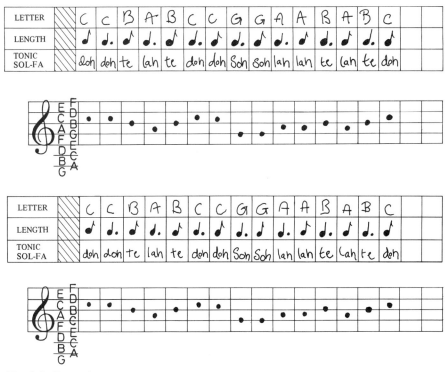

Fig. 3.7 Donna's tune

'The Story of Jesus'

This sound picture of the Nativity was made as a joint effort by all of the children. It really began in November as a Christmas carol, which Helen and Stephanie wrote for our Christmas Service. They wrote the words and then worked out, on the piano, a tune which fitted. These are given in Fig.3.8. The tune is heard at the beginning. To represent Mary and Joseph travelling towards Bethlehem, we hear the sound of the donkey's hooves, made in the conventional way by tapping two halves of a coconut shell together. The sounds of the inn were made in the classroom, with all the children talking to each other about anything that came into their heads. When the classroom door was shut, the children stopped at once, giving the effect of Mary and Joseph being shut outside.

The sadness and despair felt by Mary and Joseph when they were unable to get into the inn was represented by the minor key. Stephanie played the organ, and was obviously not satisfied with the original melody for this moment. Eventually she managed, after examples of 'sad' melodies had been played to her on the piano, to produce a 'sad' version of her tune. This led to a discussion of major and minor keys.

When the travellers arrived at the stable, Steven said that there would be straw in the stable that they would have to walk through, so he and John experimented

Mary rode a donkey,
Joseph walked beside,
Every inn they entered,
They could not stay inside.

Then at last they found an inn,
And the landlord said to them,
'You can stay in my stable,
Here in Bethlehem.'

Mary had a baby,
She called him Jesus Christ,
She rocked him in his cradle,
Every day and night.

Fig. 3.8 'The Story of Jesus'

with paper and a plastic bag and eventually produced the sound in the recording by crumpling the plastic bag.

Then it was suggested there ought to be a baby crying. Helen had a baby sister, so she took the portable tape recorder home for a few days and recorded some of the baby's cries. Kevin had made some recordings of sheep and lambs at the summer camp, so we spliced the sound of a lamb bleating to follow immediately upon the baby crying. The juxtaposition of the two sounds suggested to most of the children not only the shepherds bringing the lamb, but also Jesus as the Lamb of God.

The angels were represented as 'starlike' creatures twinkling and sparkling. These are the metallic clinks, made by some girls shaking pieces of metal on strings. The joyful news for the world is represented by the bells of Selby Abbey, recorded with a portable machine (*Cassette example 3.7*).

4 Electronic music in the secondary school – 1

PHIL ELLIS

The role for electronic music in the secondary school curriculum

The position of music in the secondary school curriculum has been subject to increasing scrutiny during the past few years, partly due to the changing nature of the secondary school itself. The emergence of the comprehensive school has led to a changing classroom situation often calling for new methods of teaching, particularly where mixed-ability classes have been established. The 'traditional' classroom approach to teaching is no longer appropriate, as noted by R. Murray Schafer in his book *The Rhinoceros in the Classroom*, (Toronto, 1975), p.2:

> The old approach: Teacher has information; student has empty head. Teacher's objective: to push information into student's empty head. Observations: at outset teacher is a fathead; at conclusion student is a fathead.

Most present-day pupils will rightly reject such treatment, but it is frequently in music lessons that such an approach to teaching is practised. In the society of the present time, with accelerating change and the prospect of increasing amounts of leisure time resulting from the introduction of microelectronic technology, the education offered must be responsive to change. Pupils of today may not have any job at all in the future; it is certain that they will have a significant proportion of leisure time and the education offered must take this into account. The situation noted by Schafer is unjustifiable: education must encourage a practical, positive, creative, individual response rather than the more passive, receptive, acquiescent attitude engendered by more traditional education practices.

To defend the place of music in the curriculum, one must be able to say that music has a unique contribution to make to the education of *all* pupils – not just the highly gifted few. It is in this unique way of educating that electronics can feature prominently and the use of new technology implies a new ethos and approach. In schools many subjects are already involved in using present-day technology to the full. The computer and calculator have long been accepted as of value in maths, and science subjects are concerned with current techniques and developments, which is reflected in their use of technology.

For a number of years, subjects considered practical, such as arts and crafts, have, as a matter of course, used a variety of modern, sophisticated hardware in order to explore and learn techniques and skills through practical work and also to make a variety of artefacts as part of the learning process. Such personal creativity seems to engender enthusiasm and involvement, particularly where the freedom for personal exploration and development is given.

Music teachers have yet to accept and welcome new technology, and to exploit the *practical* aspect of music in education, where information is not held to be more important than experience, and where the teacher can help, guide, instruct as appropriate, but most important of all, where every individual is allowed to develop in his or her own way and own time. By directing the emphasis towards practical work which encourages individual or group expression, the elitist situation where instrumentalists are involved and the rest – the majority – are not, can be changed. In this style of education, electronics can contribute significantly and effectively.

Exploiting electronic music and instruments in the classroom makes certain demands on a teacher. An involvement in and knowledge of twentieth-century music is essential, and this should be the result of practical involvement. Reverence for the past at the expense of the present is frequently revealed in attitudes towards music in school, and many music teachers know less about contemporary music than their pupils! It is the electric age, and to merit the title or position of teacher we must relate to that. A knowledge of and sensitivity towards the culture of our present time is mandatory. We must be more interested in our pupils as they are than with the transmission of a 'respected body of knowledge' and all its attendant impersonal value-laden implications. A balance between the past and the present can be achieved, but the scales should be heavily weighted in favour of the present. Education must start from the present, from where the pupils are. The medium of music – sound – can be explored in a variety of ways. This can lead to many very valuable musical statements being made, and with all the attendant musical lessons being learnt as part of the process. It may lead to a consideration of music from the past, but need not do so. The change of emphasis in the scheme of education I shall discuss holds the individual, his or her needs and possible development *in the present time* as being of greatest importance.

Perhaps the greatest obstacle to the introduction of electronic hardware into the classroom is that of expense. Music as a curriculum subject has long been low priority with regard to finance. Writing in *Half Our Future*, Newsom noted that

> the (music) teacher has to begin with virtually nothing and build up very slowly through the years, with his equipment supplied by small grudging installments, often of poor quality ... new schools need a foundation grant for equipment in music as for any other major branch of the curriculum.

(Para. 419)

There is little evidence to suggest that this recommendation has been heeded during the past sixteen years, possibly because music is still viewed by many as an academic rather than a practical subject. Even without large sums of money it is possible to build up an extensive and varied electronic capability, albeit over a number of years, quite successfully. A change of heart is needed from music teachers here. A bassoon, for example, costs a great deal of money, is used by one person for a few hours each week for a number of years. A synthesiser costs a great deal of money, is used by many people for several hours every day for a number of years. Possessing a synthesiser may not increase the size of the school orchestra, but in educational terms, by musically involving large numbers of people in practical work, the synthesiser is by far the most productive and beneficial way of spending available resources. Happily, most of the items of electronic equipment which are appropriate for school use can be purchased comparatively cheaply out of departmental capitation and need not necessitate a special grant.

I think that for practical music to be a really effective activity, groups of pupils must have reasonably private areas in which to work. The spaces available for such group work in the school where I worked were wide-spread, ranging from the dining-hall at one end of the building through various empty classrooms – temporarily unused from lesson to lesson – corridors, store rooms, court-yards, etc. to the music room at the other. Other teachers were in the main tolerant of the inevitable noise, and what might at first be distracting for a teacher seemed to have no effect on pupils' concentration, possibly because they knew the cause of the sounds they could hear. Although this meant that a class would be spread around a large area, such small, private work-spaces, free from prying eyes and the unwanted noise from other people were very important.

The electronic equipment which was available for use at my school was in some cases fairly heavy, bulky and relatively fragile. Very few music departments are designed for practical work and mine was no exception. Considerable care needs to be taken when transporting such equipment from the music room to the work area and so I obtained a number of trolleys. Each trolley had two shelves and could easily transport a tape recorder with microphone on the upper shelf, leaving the lower one for other instruments. Other electronic devices – echo or reverberation for example – could be left connected to tape recorders so that time was not wasted in having to connect equipment before work could start. The trolleys could also be securely locked up in a central room at the end of the day, which was an additional advantage.

I view the first three years of musical experience offered to pupils in a secondary school during curriculum time as being largely of the 'primary' kind as identified by Newsom (*Half Our Future*, para. 312):

> To make a pottery bowl involves considerable experience of handling clay: in getting to know empirically how clay behaves when wet or dry, and gradually acquiring the skill of hand and eye in making it obey the potter's will. All this gathering of experience is learning of a primary kind whether the pupil is 10, 20 or 40 years old. But the purposeful employment of this skill to produce a bowl which will serve a special purpose and look right in a particular place – and to be right in one's judgement nine times out of ten: this is secondary education.

The parallels with music are obvious here, and it is only through continuing practical experience that the skills needed to handle electronic and other sound sources can be acquired. Proportion, balance, control, colour, texture and all the other elements of music cannot usefully be taught, they have to be 'felt', and this feeling can only be a result of individual experience. As Newsom goes on to say (para. 312):

> A pupil's secondary education cannot begin until he has enough experience behind him to enable him to make sensible judgements on what he is doing. It does not begin until and unless he makes those judgements.

With these precepts in mind, the following writing reflects the very simple beginnings where basic techniques have to be learnt. At the early stage in particular (the first three years of compulsory curriculum music in the school), electronic instruments and techniques were used in conjunction with standard classroom percussion instruments. The course was continued by some pupils through their fourth, fifth and sixth years and at this later stage, due to smaller numbers of pupils and greater amounts of time, purely electronic music could be produced, although this was not done exclusively. The complexity of the available hardware matches the development through the six years, as equipment was only introduced to individuals or groups as it became appropriate.

Introducing and using basic equipment in the lower school

The way in which new equipment is introduced is very important, and I always attempted to do this in practical ways. In demonstrating a device all pupils could be involved even if only in making sounds which were to be treated by the device, or in question–answer sessions. The style of presentation is vital as the necessary care has to be instilled without being prohibitive or inhibiting. Equipment needs to be approached with respect, but a respect which grows from understanding, never resulting from fear. This I hold to be crucial to all aspects of education even though it might be at variance with the (unstated) ethos of an institution, in which teachers may feel entitled to respect due to the nature of their position rather than the nature of themselves. I found that the respect which grew from understanding as a result of *using* equipment, a respect which grew from within rather than the attempt to impose from outside, led to an absence of vandalism or deliberate damage. Pupils were concerned not to cause damage as this would prevent themselves from working as well as other people. (It is obvious common sense that if somebody – or a whole class – arrives in an inappropriate state of mind, having perhaps had a bad time elsewhere within the school, then time must be given to allow emotions to cool and self-control become possible before equipment is used. Within the education system as it is at present it is often too easy for self-expression to usurp expression, and although self-expression is necessary and therapeutic, it is not always constructive or particularly educational, communication not being a feature of the activity!) When demonstrating a new device I tended to show how it could be used, what effects it could create or how it treated sound, but I always tried to leave considerable room for experimentation and discovery. Areas for exploration were suggested, and it was through the process of discovery and the application of such discoveries in practical ways that involvement and progress became possible. Pupils grew in awareness, and the enthusiasm and general attitude engendered by this approach to practical work was sufficient to ensure full but careful and considered use of very delicate and expensive equipment.

The most widely used piece of equipment, and perhaps the most readily available, is the *tape recorder*. This is basic and essential to work at all levels, from the simplest to the most complex, and as many tape recorders as possible are needed. Three-speed machines are ideal in this context, although they are becoming less easy to find, the advent of cassette recorders having resulted in most cheap reel-to-reel recorders disappearing from the market. However there are some good makes still available from various sources. County supplies or an education authority's central stores may be able to supply such machines but it is well worth looking elsewhere. Not only is it possible to buy equipment commercially and so get good discount, but if repair becomes necessary I always found private firms much more willing and efficient than the 'official' county workshop. (On this subject, second-hand shops and hi-fi dealers often have very good second-hand equipment for sale at very low cost, and it is possible to make valuable contacts with such sources and so build up a substantial amount of equipment at a fraction of the cost of buying only new items.)

Three-speed tape recorders run at $3\frac{3}{4}$, $7\frac{1}{2}$ and 15 i.p.s. (9.5, 19 and 38 cm/s) or $1\frac{7}{8}$, $3\frac{3}{4}$ and $7\frac{1}{2}$ i.p.s. (4.75, 9.5 and 19 cm/s). As pupils most often referred to these speeds as 'slow', 'middle' and 'fast' respectively, that is how I shall refer to them. The most obvious use of such tape recorders, ignoring the straight record/playback capability for the moment, is as a distortion device. The ability, literally at the flick of a switch, to transform ordinary sounds into the extra-ordinary, produces interest, enthusiasm and inspiration, and a desire to work and experiment. For example, if a cymbal were struck once, and this were recorded at the fast speed, when played back it would sound fairly puny (unless your school possesses top quality cymbals!). Playing back the recording at the middle speed instantly changes the effect, and playing the same recording back at the slow speed produces a most impressive sound. An enormous 'tam-tam' sound can thus be created from an apparently inadequate sound source. By varying the output volume on replay, real impact can be achieved, and the tape recorder is most useful in this respect, as one sound can be examined in many different ways any number of times. It is almost the musical equivalent of the scientific microscope.

Recording sounds and slowing them down is perhaps the most evocative and inspiring way of using these tape recorders, and this leads to work in a number of areas which can exploit this effect. Titles such as 'Underwater', 'Caves' or 'Mystery' can be attempted with a fair degree of success at an early stage (with first-year pupils for example). Because the actual sounds are interesting and evocative, no longer 'ordinary', a real and continuing interest can be produced. An example of first-year work which exploits the three-speed tape recorder can be heard on the accompanying tape. This was produced by a first-year group in their third term and was part of a course based on a supernatural theme. Called 'Castle of Horror', the extract comes from the introduction of the piece, all of which was produced by slowing sound down. The eerie effect of this is clear: the effect of the low piano notes is menacing, and by slowing down the organ a most appropriate 'haunted' atmosphere is created. The 'ghostly horse rider' is suggested by castanets, which take on an entirely different character from normal. The complete piece is very evocative and its success lies in the use of a tape recorder (*Cassette example 4.1*).

Speeding up sound (recording at the slow speed and playing back either at middle or fast speed) is more difficult to use successfully in pieces. The effect is frequently hilarious, particularly if voices are used, but in the early years of schooling pupils seem to find such effects more difficult to include in successful work. Slowing sound down or speeding it up will of course alter the time scale of a piece. As most pieces are made by slowing sound down, at first this inevitably leads to work which is far too long, which in turn quickly leads to attempts to plan ahead and take length and balance into account when preparing a piece. This points to what is perhaps the most valuable aspect of using tape recorders in practical work of this nature. By simply recording sound and playing it back unchanged, groups and individuals have the opportunity to listen to the overall effect of their work. Being able to 'stand back' and listen with some objectivity is vital. Real criticism and progress becomes possible when tape recorders are used in this way. Obviously single-speed machines are perfectly adequate for this purpose, and the number of machines available at school can easily be supplemented by the pupils themselves, as large numbers are likely to have portable cassettes with built-in microphones which they can bring in to use at school. The ability to record and then listen to one's own work tends to produce an interest and enthusiasm not possible in any other way, apart from making criticism a real possibility. It is also invaluable in another way. In the school where I worked pupils often extended their expression to include extra-musical forms – art, dance, mime etc. Although it is possible to act or dance and play an instrument, neither can be accomplished perfectly simultaneously. Recording a piece first is obviously more satisfactory and tends to lead the interest on to other things – in other words by using available technology the education became a progression, expression in one medium leading to expression in another. Learning through practical musical activity became a starting point, a catalyst, a stimulus to further work, rather than an end in itself.

One other asset only possible through the use of tape recorders is that of complexity. If a group is able to use a tape recorder from week to week and keep a tape, a piece can gradually be built up, one section being completed and stored, another worked out and similarly recorded, until a piece is completed. In this way, lengthy contrasting pieces can be created. During the first three years of schooling a clear progression became apparent, from simple and short pieces produced by first-year groups through to quite complex, lengthy work in the third year. This naturally led to very advanced work in the upper school. To make this progression possible a large number of tape recorders was gradually acquired. Most were monophonic three-speed machines which could be transported on trolleys as already mentioned, but several cassette players and single-speed reel-to-reel machines were also available. Such hardware does need attention from time to time, and regular cleaning and demagnetising of the heads is very important. This is a simple task, although time-consuming if large numbers of machines have to be dealt with each week. Needless to say various pupils are always happy to take responsibility for such tasks. In order that tape recorders can be fully used, a large number of cassettes and reels of tape need to be available. (3 in spools of tape are quite adequate for lower-school work, larger spools tending to be expensive and longer than most groups require). An efficient booking-out system enables groups to keep a tape for a number of weeks without it becoming 'lost'!

In addition to tape recorders, there is a variety of inexpensive electric/electronic equipment which can be usefully introduced to lower-school pupils. Much of this needs amplification and can be connected directly to a tape recorder for this purpose, although care needs to be taken here that the recorders are not damaged through overloading. Additional hardware calls for numerous *leads* so that connections can be made between different items of equipment. It is well worth investing in a *soldering iron, screened wire* and *jack, DIN* and *phono plugs.* This makes it possible to keep a supply of leads available for use at all times. Making up such leads is not difficult – no doubt the physics department will initiate the ignorant into the mysteries of soldering, and pupil volunteers are quite capable of maintaining a supply of leads.

Very cheap *electric organs* can be purchased from many of the bigger stores (not shops which specialise in electronics or organs). Such very basic organs usually have a three-octave range and a selection of 'buttons' for bass notes and chords. Sound is produced by air being blown through reeds to produce a rather thin, but quite acceptable quality of sound. They are the cheapest way of acquiring sustaining, polyphonic keyboards, and they greatly expand the available soundscape. When used on their own, or with other 'simple' (percussion) instruments they might not sound very impressive, but when used in conjunction with other relatively inexpensive electronic equipment (see below) they can produce very impressive sounds.

For a little over £100, organs of a less basic kind can be purchased. These are electronic organs (sound is generated electronically, not via electric motors substituting for lungs as in the cheaper models discussed above), and usually several different timbres are available. An extra device which is often present is a simple rhythm box which can be used in a variety of ways. Such organs enable *all* pupils to produce interesting sounds and this naturally leads to more varied and expressive work than would otherwise be possible. To stimulate interest is vital, and the demand to use such equipment invariably exceeds the supply – the instruments are often in use all day, every day!

Other cheap items of electronic equipment which can be introduced to lower-school pupils include *echo chamber, reverberation unit, phaser, distortion unit* ('*fuzz box*') and other devices often found in shops specialising in electric guitars etc. Such devices alter or distort sounds which have been electronically or acoustically generated, and this calls for a number of *microphones* to be available for use. Those supplied with tape recorders tend to be rather fragile and somewhat inadequate. I always had a number available as spares, and several were used each year. These, along with considerable amounts of tape, I counted as consumable stock in capitation terms. (With regard to upper-school work it is worth-while buying some good-quality microphones, even though they are expensive.)

The *echo chamber* I found most suitable was the kind which worked on an endless cassette. I did use one which employed a tape loop, but this machine was comparatively heavy and bulky. Because the heads were open it was also much more fragile than the cassette echo chamber, which was compact and easy to carry, with no moving parts being visible. The only thing which is likely to go wrong with the cassette type of echo chamber is for the cassette to break and these can be replaced quite easily. This echo chamber had the additional advantage of actually generating sound as well as providing echo. By feeding tape hiss into the machine a form of 'white noise' could be produced, which can be useful. Echo chambers of this sort can be controlled to produce a number of different speeds of echo of varying degrees of intensity and duration. The varying speed can also be used to produce very effective glissandi. Such a device can transform an ordinary sound into one which is quite impressive. The cheap electric organ described above takes on an entirely different character when fed through an echo chamber. An example on the cassette reveals this clearly. It is the ending of a lengthy piece produced by a group of second-year pupils and its full effect is produced by playing this back with a high volume setting (*Cassette example 4.2*).

A *reverberation unit* will not generate any sound, it will only alter sounds which are fed into it. As it can only do one thing it may seem to be rather limited, but it can be used in a variety of different ways. Its most obvious effect is to create the illusion of space, of being in a large cavern or cathedral. It can also help create a spooky or eerie atmosphere, and it is this aspect which is exploited in the next example on the cassette. Produced by a first-year group working on a supernatural theme, reverberation was used in conjunction with a three-speed tape recorder, and a really evocative atmosphere is created (*Cassette example 4.3*). In more advanced work it can be effective if used sparingly. (In lower-school work, such a device tends, initially, to be over-used, to be used for effect – almost as a novelty. It is important that this stage is worked through, after which its real value as a device can be realised and exploited.) Many reverberation units have several inputs, each with an independent volume control. This makes mixing possible, some models having up to four separate inputs. As the reverberation effect need not be used, the unit can thus be exploited in many different situations as a mixer.

A *phaser, fuzz box* and the many other smaller devices more usually associated with pop music, can be very useful as a variety of sounds can be fed through them. Although tape recorders can be used as amplifiers for these devices as noted above, it is best to try and provide small amplifers for such equipment. Small 'practice' amplifiers used with electric guitars are ideal for this, and are not prohibitively expensive.

One other piece of equipment needs to be mentioned in the context of lower-school work. To broaden the available soundscape and expressive potential, a performance *synthesiser* was made available from the end of the first year. We had a Mini Korg synthesiser, a monophonic keyboard synthesiser which could generate a variety of sounds, but could not be used as a device to treat other sounds. It was simple enough to be used by twelve-year-old pupils as the different sounds were controlled by a series of switches beneath the keyboard. A large variety of sounds could be generated, and the quality of sound was of course very good. Such a synthesiser is rather more expensive than other items so far described, but as it was always in use, and proved to be very reliable, it represented very good value for money, particularly as it was a performance instrument which could be used live as well as in recording. The fourth example on the cassette shows this synthesiser being used as a melody instrument with piano accompaniment. This example is the ending of a piece written by a fourth-year pupil in which the different timbres which could be produced by the synthesiser were exploited melodically (*Cassette example 4.4*).

Using electronics leads to curiosity about sound, and from there to interesting work. Such a development occurred as part of a second-year course based on the theme of water. For this we managed to obtain a large metal tank. (Somebody was replacing their domestic water tank at the time, so we brought the old one into school.) Old baths or washing machines are similarly useful. We had some fairly cheap contact microphones which could be used in all sorts of ways! These were cased in rubber, and we attempted to make them waterproof by coating the joints with rubber solution. They lasted quite well in practice, the two or three which were 'used up' annually being well within tolerable limits of expendable stock.

Most interesting effects resulted when these treated microphones were immersed in the tank of water and sounds made either using the tank itself as the 'instrument', or by playing (mainly metal) instruments in the water. (Different effects could be recorded according to where the microphone was placed, and this led to considerable interest and experimentation.) A proposed development was to attempt to make a loudspeaker waterproof so that water could be used as a medium of distortion – different effects would be produced depending upon the signal fed through the speaker and the position of the microphone. The possibilities for experiment and discovery are endless, and encouraging such exploration results in exciting work – work which shows development and progression over a period of time.

To be able to make beautiful, interesting, unusual sounds from electronic equipment, which all children can, leads to stimulation and captures the imagination and interest. Use of such equipment tends to extend the individual far more than if practical activity is confined to the use of the more usual classroom percussion instruments as the main sound source. In this latter case a limited pallette of sound is available, and it is one which cannot be easily extended after a time. This can become tedious even for pupils who are making rather limited musical statements and can contribute to a lack of involvement, progress and achievement.

All of the equipment mentioned so far can be introduced progressively during the first year at moments when it would be appropriate to subject matter, rather than as just another available sound source which may merely have greater novelty value than other instruments. During the first three years of schooling, the exploitation of such equipment should show a clear development, given a progressive and structured course. Initially, inevitably (as already mentioned), the introduction of such hardware produces an intense interest in sound (what more could any music teacher want?), and instant effect. The novelty value must be accepted, as it is only through using these more obvious effects that pupils can come to terms with such instruments and really use them in musical ways. The preliminary stages of entertainment and novelty have to be explored before this can happen, and seemingly repetitive use of certain sounds can lead to important and essential steps in the process of musical discovery and expression.

Electronic music in the upper school

From this basis, at my school, pupils who chose to continue with music into the upper school could explore electronic music in as much depth as they wished. This was possible as music in the upper school could be pursued on an individual basis – there were fewer people working at any one time – and more time was available in which to work. Electronic music demands time, and in the lower school practical work needs at least one hour per week, preferably as one period rather than as two 30-minute sessions. In the upper school a minimum of two hours per week is necessary if real work and progress is to be possible.

I found two additional items of equipment to be of particular value in the upper school. Both of these are much more complex than any of the electronic equipment described so far, and both demand considerable time and individual work. The first of these is a *studio synthesiser*. The music department acquired a Synthi AKS, a complex instrument which enabled very ambitious work to be realised. I prefer this to other comparable models (a VCS 3 for example), for two main reasons. It is very compact and therefore easy to transport, although it is housed in a relatively fragile case. Unlike other synthesisers it has its own keyboard and sequencer. These two items are very expensive when bought separately, and although the Synthi keyboard is touch sensitive rather than working on conventional lines, it is quite efficient in practice. The sequencer is sufficiently straightforward to allow most people to use it easily, which is not the case with some sequencers.

The second item which I believe to be essential to enable progress to continue in the upper school is a *stereo tape deck with sound-on-sound facility*. One such re-corder is essential, although two would be better as stereo sound-on-sound then be-comes possible. Such a tape deck enables individual work of a complex nature to be attempted, and the spatial aspects of music can also be exploited. Both these items, when used in conjunction with all the other instruments mentioned, can lead the individual towards the creation of ambitious and sometimes highly complex work which need not be confined to purely electronic music. It is important for the in-dividual to be able to work successfully on his own if progress is to be possible in the upper school in a continuing course of practical music. Although both these items are relatively expensive, I believe they are essential, particularly the stereo tape deck.

Upper-school work of this individual nature necessitated an examination. In the school where I worked, the vast majority of subjects could not be continued in curriculum time beyond the third year unless the course led to a public examination. I subsequently formulated a Mode III CSE examination in 'Creative Musical Studies' which catered for as wide a variety of music as possible whilst at the same time encouraging the highest possible standard in terms of individual work. This resulted in a five-year course for those who chose to continue with music beyond their third year of schooling, and much upper-school work can be seen as a development of the first three years' experience, including the use of electronic hardware from the age of eleven. With three years' experience behind them, there is a solid basis of technique and skill upon which quite advanced musical work can be built in the fourth and fifth years, where considerable development resulted because of the in-dividual emphasis. To illustrate the more advanced possibilities for the use of electronics in schools, I have selected five examples of work, produced by five dif-ferent people in the upper school.

Example 1

The first of these examples is a piece called 'Bells' which was produced by Antony over a period of about seven weeks. The idea was to create a piece of music worked entirely on bells, and as source material he used two large cow bells, two strings of goat bells, a length of metal pipe and a set of Chinese wind chimes. He encountered many difficulties in realising this piece, particularly in the first of the three move-ments. Due to the use of microphones and using a lot of sound-on-sound he found tape hiss to be a problem. Although he used the filter on Synthi it was a problem for which he found no satisfactory solution, and this called for very careful record-ing. In addition to the bells mentioned and the filters in Synthi, Antony also used the echo chamber and the phaser during the piece.

The three movements reveal many different techniques. The first section uses bells recorded at different speeds and mixed together. Some glissandi were pro-duced by feeding sounds through the echo chamber and varying the speed of echo. A short extract from this movement can be heard on the tape (*Cassette example 4.5*). The second movement of the piece consists of sounds produced on the length of

Plate 5 Antony recording sounds for his composition 'Bells'

metal pipe mixed with parts of the first section played at various speeds. Parts of the first movement were also fed through Synthi which was patched so as to make various changes to the sound, and much of the result was fed through the phaser. The final movement used the cow bells and goat bells. Only sounds from these were recorded on a long tape loop which was fed through four tape recorders. One of these was in record mode, the other three were merely playing back the recorded sounds. As the signals from these three recorders were fed back onto the loop via the recording machine a very complex texture was created from very simple beginnings. The total effect was recorded on a separate tape and slowed down to make this last movement. From very simple sound sources Antony was able to create three contrasting movements which exploited the sonorities of the bells using various techniques and devices, resulting in a lengthy and satisfying piece of music.

Example 2

In contrast to this piece, the next example is very simple, the whole piece lasting about three minutes. It was made by Tony who had only learnt guitar for a few weeks, although he had considerable experience of using electronic instruments. Part of this piece can be heard on the tape and it shows clearly how one person can gradually build up a piece using the sound-on-sound facility on a stereo tape deck. The first track to be recorded was the guitar chords. The Mini Korg synthesiser was added next, playing a bass line. After this, still using the Mini Korg, the melody lines were added, each one a different quality of sound, and some were fed through the phaser. (Some of these are very faint as the balance was not perfect.) The piece started life from Tony liking the two-chord sequence which forms the basis of the piece. He recorded this and then, over a period of time, discovered the bass part and melodies. As he could play the tape through any number of times and try out ideas until he found what he wanted he was able to take his time and think the piece through. None of this work would have been possible without the hardware, particularly the tape deck (*Cassette example 4.6*).

Example 3

The next example owes little to electronics directly, although the Mini Korg synthesiser is used as a melody instrument. Called 'Long-Shanked Wading Bird', it was written by Jon, a drummer. The way he composed his pieces was to use the stereo tape deck in a similar way to Tony, although he did tend to work the complete piece out in his head first. Jon has some ability on keyboards and electric guitar, and he would play through a piece, usually starting with the keyboard part, record this and then add the other parts using the sound-on-sound facility on the tape deck. Having completed this initial version, a group of players would be brought together and the piece would be worked at by them for live performance. At this stage the other aspect of electronics featured. Quite ambitious recordings of Jon's music were attempted. Using the reverberation unit as one mixer for four microphones and a borrowed mixer for another four, we managed to produce some reasonable stereo recordings. Such work obviously took a long time to set up and this meant that the recording sessions usually took place during the holidays, when

Plate 6   Some of the hardware used in 'Precipitation with Insight'

the building was relatively quiet and equipment could be set up for several hours at a time. The extract from the piece (*Cassette example 4.7*) is taken from the first of four sections, the complete piece lasting several minutes.

Example 4

The fourth example of upper-school work was produced by Jeremy whose work exploited electronically generated sound only. He often made use of all the electronic equipment which was available. Again, the ability to build a piece up gradually, a layer at a time, made his work possible. An extract from the beginning of one of Jeremy's later pieces, produced during his fifth year, can be heard on the cassette. Called 'Precipitation with Insight', it took its starting point from the idea of a distant storm building up. A large number of tracks were recorded for this piece, calling for very careful recording technique and balancing. Even so there is a tendency for the earlier tracks to be very faint. The complete piece lasts for several minutes (*Cassette example 4.8*). Much upper-school work tended to result in pieces lasting anything from eight to fifteen minutes, and occasionally even longer pieces were composed. There does seem to be a connection between the length of work produced and the equipment available. The electronic hardware which was available encouraged lengthy and ambitious work. It is quite an achievement for fifteen- or sixteen-year-old people to be able to produce interesting and successful musical work lasting several minutes. I maintain that the use of electronics makes this possible.

Plate 7   Multitracking with a keyboard synthesiser

Plate 8   Recording from the Synthi

Example 5

The final example of upper-school work exploits extra-musical aspects, and such multimedia forms of expression were a significant feature of much of the work done in the school. We found that when presenting tape music in public performance an audience was much happier if they were given something to look at whilst the music was being played! This was fortunate as many extra-musical elements developed naturally during the composition of many pieces, especially in lower-school work.*

This final example was conceived as a tape piece which would involve dance, theatre and elaborate lighting effects and projection. Its title, 'Albireo', was taken from the name given to a double star of contrasting colours which was the starting point for the composition. The composer, Tim, developed the idea of contrast into this piece, which is in three movements lasting about fifteen minutes. Simultaneous with the composition was the development of the other elements which was necessary for performance.

The first two movements were produced using electronic instruments only, and these movements exploit all the equipment which was available. The third move-

*A more detailed description illustrating the connection which developed between music and other arts can be found in the tape/slide sequence *Music at Notley*, produced by the Schools Council Project: *Music in the Secondary School Curriculum*, and available from the University of York Department of Music, or in videotape format from Drake Video Services, 212 Whitchurch Rd, Cardiff, CF4 3XF.

ment combines electronics with conventional instruments. To produce this movement two stereo decks were needed. The bass line was recorded in one channel and the repetitive whistle in the other. This had to be done with extremely accurate timing. The tape was then played back and rerecorded on the second stereo deck, the other instruments involved – piano, electric guitar and Mini Korg synthesiser – being recorded at the same time. Synchronisation with the prepared tape proved to be a problem, as was mixing all the different lines together so as to achieve a satisfactory balance. A short extract from the second and third movements can be heard on the cassette (*Cassette example 4.9*).

The extra-musical aspects involved complex programming. In the first movement a cloaked figure gradually walked towards a screen on which a series of slides were projected, ending up looking into a magnified view of an eye. During the second movement, the set was flooded in red light and two figures with strange costumes and lurid make-up performed a dance which incorporated two large (cardboard) stars. The final movement was the most complex. Lengths of muslin were hung in front of the screen so that the slides which were projected would form a double image. Two figures dressed in white performed a dance which also involved the cloaked figure from the first movement. (This piece, together with other examples of electronic music, is described in the tape/slide sequence *Music at Notley*.) 'Albireo' reveals considerable skill in using electronic hardware in musical ways. Such skill can only be acquired over a period of time, and the piece is a good example of what can result from practical work extending over a number of years. The final production of the piece, involving the other forms of expression, also revealed how practical education in music can be extending, involving many different disciplines and large numbers of people. It is not an exclusive form of education.

This chapter has very briefly indicated how electronic technology can contribute to the musical education of all pupils during the first years of their secondary schooling and how it can be developed and exploited by older pupils, leading to complex musical work which may additionally involve other areas of expression. The use of this technology is not exclusive, but forms part of the available musical experience, particularly where the individual is allowed autonomy. Much 'education' suffers from divisive thinking – art or skill. Any musical instrument of whatever kind can be made to appear strange, complex, exclusive. The great advantage of electronic instruments is that they can be made readily accessible to *all* pupils and so involve them in the practical processes of music, which can lead to insight, expression, creation, appreciation, exploration, progress... With other areas of the curriculum in mind it could be argued that without a knowledge of, and some practical experience in using, the techniques and technology of the present century the education appropriate to the individual in a secondary school is incomplete. I have tried to illustrate the fact that such work can lead to an interest in music, not in examination terms, or schooling terms, but in musical terms. Education should, in addition to being instructive, help people to want to find out more rather than stay in well-trodden paths; be a beginning not an end of development and discovery.

Music is an expressive art. We have the means to make this a *practical* reality for *all* people at some stage of their schooling. Newsom's 'change of heart' is long overdue.

Conclusion: three projects

In conclusion I will describe three projects which can be attempted by groups of pupils. As many schools do not yet possess significant amounts of electronic equipment I have restricted these projects to the use of tape recorders, as they are basic to all electronic music and are perhaps most readily available. These descriptions should be viewed as ideas, starting points which can be adapted and developed in many different ways, rather than as a set of instructions. Although I will indicate the age range of pupils who worked the ideas, they can easily be used with people of any age.

1. 'Machines'

This task formed part of a first-year course of the same name which was worked during the second term of the year. Because of this the techniques involved are fairly basic, part of the exercise being the opportunity of learning elementary skills in a practical way. A group working this piece would need access to at least one cassette recorder and at least one three-speed reel-to-reel tape recorder. They would also need a cassette and reel of tape for a number of weeks.

Initially the cassette recorder would be used. The first stage is for the group to go round the school recording as many different machine sounds as possible. Obvious places include the metalwork/woodwork rooms, domestic science areas, typing rooms, kitchens etc. The road is also fruitful for collecting various engine sounds. As most cassette recorders have built-in condenser microphones and automatic recording levels, the techniques of recording these sounds can often be limited to merely pointing the microphone in the right direction! This is often a difficult accomplishment for some groups at this level!

Having made a tape of many machine sounds the next stage involves the use of a reel-to-reel tape recorder as well as the cassette player. Using an appropriate lead to connect the cassette to the reel-to-reel all the sounds on the cassette should be transferred on to the reel. (Using a microphone for this operation is most unsatisfactory as the quality of recorded sound becomes very poor.) This recording should be made at the middle speed.

Following this, the group needs to prepare a sheet of paper with three columns headed 'slow', 'middle' and 'fast'. The reel of tape should be replayed. As each different sound occurs its description should be noted in the 'middle' column together with the number of the tape counter so that any sound can be relocated quickly in the future. Having worked through the complete tape in this way it should be rewound and a different speed selected. The tape should then be replayed at the new speed and in the appropriate column a description of the sound written as its effect will now be very different from the original. The exercise is repeated for the third speed. By this stage a large number of widely contrasting patterns of sounds will have been identified. With the written descriptions to refer to, the group then has to choose an interesting, contrasted number of sounds which they feel will make a satisfying piece. These sounds should be written down in their projected order, each description including the source of the sound, the number on the tape where it begins and the speed at which it should be replayed. This will inevitably lead to more of the recorded sounds being rejected than are used, and it is worth encouraging a group to be very selective at this stage as too many sounds can easily result in the task becoming too difficult at the next stage.

Both reel-to-reel and cassette machines are needed for the final stage. This time the output of the reel-to-reel should be connected to the input of the cassette. The chosen sounds can thus be recorded onto the cassette. This will involve many stops and starts as the different sounds have to be found on the reel and the appropriate speed selected. The finished product may seem somewhat crude because of this as many clicks and gaps may be present on the cassette. One way round this is to use two or more machines so that rudimentary mixing can be attempted, one sound being faded out and another faded in so that the stopping of the tape need not be recorded. Similarly a more complex realisation could involve two or more sounds being mixed together on the final tape. There are many possible developments, but the very simple form of this piece using only two tape recorders seemed to be quite complicated enough for groups without previous experience of using such equipment. Only a few groups in any one class would be able to work this piece due in part to the amount of equipment which would be needed. In addition, such work requires extended periods of time, and a group working this piece would need to spend some extra-curricular time in order to complete the piece within a few weeks. If such work takes longer than three or four weeks to complete, it can become discouraging for groups, particularly in the lower school. Although overcoming difficulties and acquiring new skills and techniques forms part of most pieces, it is worth ensuring that a piece does not become too complex, that a group does not become too ambitious in the early stages, as this can easily result in frustration and lack of motivation. One other consideration also affects how many groups can realistically work this piece at any one time: with the best will in the world other teachers can see too much of groups of pupils with a roving commission waving yet another microphone at interesting sounds in their teaching area! As an initial exercise in making music by using tape recorders it worked well, the use of such equipment encouraging involvement, awareness, discrimination, criticism and also demanding skill, perseverance, concentration and cooperation, all of which are valuable in more than purely 'educational' terms.

2. 'Opening the Cage'

The second exercise is more advanced than 'Machines' and was presented to third-year pupils, although certain additional developments also make this suitable for upper-school work. It concentrates on an aspect of tape music which I have not mentioned so far, but one which can be very useful in more advanced work – splicing. Being able to select, order, edit out unwanted sounds and join tape together is very useful. (Such skills would obviously improve a non-edited version of 'Machines' significantly.) As it is a time-consuming activity which requires much patience and manual dexterity I do not introduce work requiring this particular skill until late in the third year, or often not until the upper school. Tape-splicing blocks are needed for this work, and I recommend 'Emitape' blocks as being the best. Although they are more expensive than other makes, they have the advantage of being efficient in use. Some cheaper makes are so difficult to use that the physical problems associated with such equipment can prevent individuals from successfully working this piece. In addition to splicing blocks, it is well worth having a large supply of razor blades, preferably with some form of holder. (Some first-aid plasters could also prove useful!)

The title of this exercise is taken from a poem of the same name by Edwin Morgan. (This appears in *The Second Life*, Edinburgh University Press, 1968.) The title, 'Opening the Cage', partly refers to John Cage whose statement 'I have nothing to say and I am saying it' forms the basis of Morgan's poem. (Cage's statement comes from the lecture 'Composition as Process, III Communication' which is published in the book *Silence*, Calder and Boyars, 1968.) The text of the poem was given to groups attempting this exercise.

Opening the Cage: 14 Variations on 14 Words

I have nothing to say I am saying it and that is poetry

John Cage

I have to say poetry and is that nothing and am I saying it
I am and I have poetry to say and is that nothing saying it
I am nothing and I have poetry to say and that is saying it
I that am saying poetry have nothing and it is I and to say
And I say that I am to have poetry and saying it is nothing
I am poetry and nothing and saying it is to say that I have
To have nothing is poetry and I am saying that and I say it
Poetry is saying I have nothing and I am to say that and it
Saying nothing I am poetry and I have to say that and it is
It is and I am and I have poetry saying say that to nothing
It is saying poetry to nothing and I say I have and am that
Poetry is saying I have it and I am nothing and to say that
And that nothing is poetry I am saying and I have to say it
Saying poetry is nothing and to that I say I am and have it

Edwin Morgan

As can be seen, each line has twelve different words and a total of fourteen words in each line ('and' and 'I' occur twice in each line). Each word can be represented by a different sound, thus twelve reels of tape have to be prepared, each reel representing a different word. The sounds that are recorded can connect with the words they are representing. For example, the 'ss' can be taken from 'saying' and extended; the sighing quality of 'hhh' from 'have'; the sharp ending from 'it'. It is much easier to work the piece if continuous sounds are used rather than patterns which have more than one element. I used this as a way of introducing pupils to some of the sound-generating equipment on Synthi, as many of the qualities of sound present in the text of the poem can be mirrored quite easily using the oscillators, filters, noise generator etc. on this instrument. However, not all groups wished to produce sounds from Synthi, and many other sound sources were exploited.

Having prepared twelve reels of tape (each reel being securely labelled showing which 'word' it represented!), work on assembling the piece can begin. The order in which sounds are put together is determined by the order of the words in each line. The length of each sound can also be related to its word, and should of course remain constant. One way of deciding this is to relate the length of tape to the number of letters in a word: 'poetry', consisting of six letters, could thus result in a six-inch length of tape, and so on, but there are many other ways of arriving at this decision. When the length for each sound has been determined, the fourteen lines of the piece can be assembled by splicing appropriate lengths of tape together in the right order. If a group is working this piece it is probably best for each individual to be responsible for two or three lines. It is essential to label these as they are completed, and then the complete tape can be spliced together.

For some groups this will mark the end of the piece, and will be a considerable achievement for many, particularly if done by a lower-school group. However it is possible to take the piece further. The title mentions '14 Variations on 14 Words' and thus each of the fourteen lines could be treated in a different way to develop this idea and transform the tape into a more interesting piece. Varying amounts of reverberation, echo, phasing etc. are readily available to lower-school pupils, and loudspeakers and microphones can be placed in various acoustics so as to change the characteristics of the original tape sounds. The 'variation' idea also provides an excellent opportunity to introduce some of the 'treatments' that are available on synthesisers. On Synthi this includes filters, reverberation, envelope shaper, ring modulator, and this can lead to considerable variation of the fourteen lines. Further developments could include making two copies of the original spliced tape – splices are liable to break when played often, and resplicing is not always successful. Both tapes could be played back, either synchronised or slightly out of phase, and recorded to make a stereo tape. The two channels could be treated in different ways to provide contrast. A more complex version could exploit the spatial aspects of stereo. There are endless possibilities.

3. 'Environmental Music'

This final project exploits the techniques employed in 'Machines' and 'Opening the Cage' and introduces the consideration of space as an effective and important element of composition. It requires quite a lot of time and perseverance and so is probably best suited to older pupils. I worked this piece through with a group of sixth-form people, some of whom had not had experience of using tape recorders before. We spent three hours each week (a complete morning) over the period of half a term working at this piece, so that about twenty hours were necessary before a performance could be given.

Four groups were formed, each comprising two or three people. Each group was given a cassette recorder and spent a complete morning in the town recording as many different sounds as possible. As this morning happened to fall on market day a considerable variety of vocal inflection and use of language was available for recording! Shops, churches, bus and rail station, banks, pavement conversations, traffic etc. provided the sound sources for this piece. Each group made between thirty and sixty minutes of recording.

The next stage of the piece involved each group transferring the most interesting and usable sounds from their cassette on to a reel of tape, recording this at the middle speed. Each sound could then be examined, replayed at three different speeds, as in 'Machines', and in addition it was possible to play sounds backwards. Each group then had to choose the sounds they thought most effective and splice together a varied tape of a given length. As this tape would be played back at the middle speed, any sounds which needed speed changing had to be rerecorded. (The length of tape required from each group was determined by the performance area – see below.) When the groups had produced their tapes, all four were spliced together to form one lengthy tape. As this contained a large number of splices it was completely rerecorded so that we ended up with one reel of tape of a predetermined length.

The final stage of the composition involved the use of four tape recorders. These were placed in the four corners of a large space (we used the drama studio, and the distance around the edge of this studio determined the total length of the tape). The reel of tape was placed on one of these tape recorders and fed around the studio through the other three tape recorders and back to the first recorder. The two ends were joined together to form a very long tape loop, but with only one splice in it. Each tape recorder had an operator who had to alter the volume control during the piece. This involved a great deal of experiment, as the effect of the piece depended upon how each volume control was used. A length of time was decided upon for the duration of the piece – the time taken for the loop to make two complete circuits for example. Each operator had a watch with a second hand so that a timing score could be followed. This score indicated the output volume – sometimes there would be maximum output, at others silence, and lengthy crescendos/diminuendos were also effective. As there was considerable space between each recorder, echo effects and counterpoint between the machines was possible, the nature of repetition being part of the piece, as sounds heard on one machine could be heard on the next some moments later. In performance we darkened the drama studio. The audience sat in the middle of the studio and the tape loop travelled round the edge, so that real quadrophony was an important and very effective element of the piece. Many different versions are of course possible from the same tape and I feel that this piece is an ideal combination of technical problems and purely musical considerations – having accomplished the difficult task of producing a tape, much time can be spent listening to the different effects which are possible from the endless variety of ways in which it can be played. Such a consideration involves musical judgement, and the finished piece consists of a reel of tape and a performance score. Although there can be disagreement over the most effective way of performing the piece, it is usually possible to arrive at a satisfactory consensus of opinion. The piece is an example of how relatively simple techniques can be exploited to produce a complex final result to which many people will have made a contribution.

5 Electronic music in the secondary school – 2

T O M   W A N L E S S

Creating a syllabus

Sheldon School is a mixed 11–18 comprehensive school and music is a compulsory subject for the first two years, after which it becomes an option. Examination courses are begun in the fourth year, and besides 'O' level we offer a Mode III CSE. It is this latter scheme which includes the electronic element. I devised the course some six years ago when it became obvious that the CSE Mode I examination was not attracting many students. I knew that there were many children who, although not musicians in the sense that they played an instrument or sang in the choir, were interested in the subject. These were the ones I wanted to attract. I felt that the Mode I syllabus did not offer anything like enough practical music making, and whatever I devised had to consider that and also to cater for pupils who could not play instruments but who wanted to take the subject to examination level. My completed syllabus consisted of three written papers, a recording of a practical performance and a project. Paper 1 is basically 'historical'. It concentrates on music of the periods before 1750 and after 1900. These periods were chosen because they contain music which children can perform. Mediaeval dances and songs together with modern pop are relatively straightforward for children to sing and play. Composing using indeterminate and graphic notation can also be attempted. Paper 2 is basically 'electronic' in that it deals with the recording process and all the equipment this entails, together with the wiring up of plugs and sockets. It links up with Paper 1 because so much twentieth-century music relies heavily on the recording studio, e.g. the use of such devices as multitracking, echo and tape manipulation. Paper 3 is a series of simple aural tests based on George Self's *Aural Adventures*. For practical performance I encourage group work because this provides a chamber music approach and involves an element of self discipline. The recording of the performance must be in stereo and can be of published material, an arrangement made by the group of published material, or an original composition. The project can be either a recording or a script on any musical topic. If a recording is made, illustrations must be mixed in; if a script, full details of any musical illustrations must be included. This option has to be given because there is not enough time for every child to make a tape.

The Mode III scheme appears twice in our option grouping and we have had an average of 35–40 pupils taking the subject over the last few years. Each option group studies the subject for 166 minutes a week. This is divided roughly into an hour of historical work and the rest on electronics, aural work and performance. All the recording projects and performances for the examination are done in the dinner hour. Our scheme operates in such a way that a very mixed group will result. Students include potential university candidates who tend to opt for the course as an interest subject and those of moderate or low ability for whom the CSE is the limit of their potential.

My philosophy is that 'music is for everybody'. I will take any child who chooses the subject – provided that group numbers do not become excessive. I would prefer a group of about twenty, although this has risen to twenty-six on one occasion.

Another tenet is that electronic music is anything that involves the use of electronic or recording devices. In other words it can be pure electronic sound produced by a synthesiser, or it can be any sound which is recorded and manipulated. Many musicians differentiate between pure electronics and *musique concrète*, but as far as Sheldon School is concerned no differentiation is made.

The course is planned in what I consider to be a logical sequence. We deal first with the different types of microphone which we have available and the uses to which they are put. Starting with contact microphones we move on to omnidirectional and finally unidirectional types. After this we discuss tape recorders, both cassette and reel-to-reel, their use, advantages, disadvantages, care and maintenance. Coupled with this would be elementary work on the repair of compact cassettes, editing and manipulation of reel-to-reel tapes, together with the use of echo and reverberation. Then would come the use of mixers, multimicrophone recording and specifically designed echo machines. Only after this groundwork do we progress to the use of synthesisers, keyboards and other electronic devices. We do a lot of practical work, the emphasis being not so much on the quality of the music but on the quality of the recording. This is neglected in so many schools. Far too many teachers seem to think that to make a recording all that is necessary is to put a microphone in front of the group – press the appropriate switches and the job is done! They forget that their classes have heard professionally produced records and tapes since they were very small and that children are not content with a second- or third-rate recording.

I would expect the above programme of work to take slightly over three terms to teach, so that by the end of the course certain groups of children would be starting to record their pieces and projects for the actual examination. These pieces can often be used to illustrate techniques which for one reason or another have not been discussed earlier in the course. One such technique which often crops up is the mixing of stereo, or two parallel mono tracks, down to a single mono one, thus enabling other tracks to be added. This often happens because the child realises that the piece as he or she imagined it sounds incomplete, and sooner than start again and multitrack, it is easier to mix down and then use duo- or multitrack techniques.

Space and equipment

The organisation of the course I have outlined presents difficulties. These are principally (a) space and (b) equipment. Because space is at a premium in Sheldon School any available space has to be utilised, however far from the music room. Luckily both the music-room office and stock cupboard have power points and both have been used as recording studios on occasions. I have built up my equipment over a period of years and now have several stereo tape recorders with echo, reverberation and multitracking facilities in addition to a five-channel mixer, a synthesiser and keyboard, an echo machine, stereo amplifier and speakers with enough editing kits for everybody.

The main music room is a converted drama studio and has plenty of electric points so that equipment can easily be positioned wherever it is required. Even so, an extension lead with five or six additional mains points is essential. In an ideal situation I would like to have a large room with work-top surfaces at a convenient height around the walls. These work tops would be divided by partitions so that one group of children could work unhindered by interruptions from the next.

An electronic course can be started with just basic equipment. A bare minimum would be two stereo tape recorders. At least one of these recorders should have facilities for echo, reverberation and multitracking.

I think it important that the teacher organising the course should have freedom of choice over the equipment to be purchased. Far too often when a request is made for a recorder for the music department only a basic model is ordered. Specifications of the various models should be studied. The machine should be stereo, capable of playing at the three standard speeds of $7\frac{1}{2}$ i.p.s., $3\frac{3}{4}$ i.p.s., and $1\frac{7}{8}$ i.p.s. (19, 9.5 and 4.75 cm/s) or 15, $7\frac{1}{2}$ and $3\frac{3}{4}$ i.p.s (38, 19 and 9.5 cm/s). This will enable octave transpositions to be made. It should have three heads (an erase head, a record head and a playback head). This will ensure that echo and reverberation can be added to recordings, will permit on- and off-tape monitoring and will allow recordings to be multitracked. Probably such a machine will only have a preamplifier, therefore a stereo amplifier and speakers will be necessary to complete the item of equipment. However, if a smaller two-headed machine is used alongside the three-headed machine, the tapes made on the larger machine can either be played back directly on the smaller machine, or in dire necessity both machines can be linked with a connecting lead and the smaller machine will then act as the amplifier and speakers. The two-headed machine will have a combined recording and playback head and therefore will not be capable of producing echo, reverberation or off-tape monitoring. The choice of equipment having been made, the teacher should ensure that he or she understands the various techniques which can be applied to tape and what the machine can do.

Techniques: echo and reverberation

There are several ways of adding reverberation to a recording. The crudest is to place the microphones at some distance from the group performing. Disadvantages of this are that you have no control over the reverberation and it is very much a hit or miss affair. It is much better to add the reverberation electronically. To do this you will have to use a three-headed tape machine, and by means of a connecting lead join the replay head to the recording head. This is usually done by plugging one end of the lead into the monitor socket and the other into the input socket and monitoring the sound through headphones from the playback head. Thus any sound reaching the playback head is automatically fed back into the recording head and rerecorded on to the tape. The exact amount of reverberation is governed by (a) the volume of the signal being fed back into the machine and (b) the speed of the tape. To discuss (a) first, if the recording level control is at its lowest setting no signal will be fed back. As the level is gradually raised the reverberation will slowly appear until at a high level the sound degenerates into a very unpleasant feedback, although this can, under certain circumstances, be quite effective. With regard to (b), at $7\frac{1}{2}$ i.p.s. the individual repetitions of the sound are so close together that reverberation is obtained. At $3\frac{3}{4}$ i.p.s. reverberation disappears because the initial sound will have passed the recording head completely before it is fed back in again from the playback head and echo is produced. However at $1\frac{7}{8}$ i.p.s. a more pronounced echo is obtained as there will be a larger gap between the sound and the echo. The amount of reverberation and echo can easily be monitored through the headphones. Without monitoring you are using guesswork and almost certainly only a poor standard of recording will be obtained.

A three-headed machine has the capability of being monitored from both the recording head and the playback head. Usually the monitor switch will be marked 'A' and 'B'. With the setting on 'B' you are listening to the sound as it goes on the tape; with the setting on 'A' you are listening to the sound from the playback head. By moving from 'A' to 'B' while the recording is in progress, you are in a position to compare the sound going on to the tape with the sound after it is on the tape, thus enabling a comparison of the two signals to be made. For echo and reverberation the switch must be in the 'A' position. A good way to introduce your pupils to echo is to ask them to read a passage from a book or newpaper while they listen to the resultant sound with added echo through a headset. It sounds remarkably easy, but it is quite difficult to do as the reader keeps wanting to stop to let the echo 'catch up'. The great danger is that once pupils have heard echo and have realised how effective it can be they will want to use it on every single piece they do. It should be used sparingly. Normally a connecting lead for reverberation and echo is supplied with your machine. It is quite easy to make and Fig. 5.1 shows how such a lead can be wired up for a machine that has DIN inputs and outputs. Use 4-core screened cable.

It is essential that during a recording session the 'recording engineer', besides listening to the piece through his headset, watches the VU meters on the recorder. I always insist that a test of the various microphone and input levels is carried out before a recording is made. The machine should be switched on ready for use but

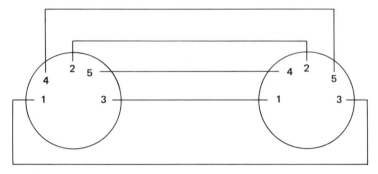

1 Left input
2 Earth
3 Left output
4 Right input
5 Right output

Fig. 5.1 Reversible 5-pin DIN input/output lead

with the 'pause' button in operation so that no recording is made. While the piece is then being played the engineer can watch his VU meters, adjusting them so that at the loudest section of the piece the needles of the meters are just touching the red or 'distortion' section of the scale. If your machine is really sophisticated, besides having two VU meters it will have two small red panel lights which will illuminate as the peak sound is reached, thus making adjustments easier. With the VU meters correctly adjusted the recording can be made.

As my students are assessed on the quality as well as the content of their recordings I pay particular attention to the way their pieces start and finish. Anything that starts and finishes with a click is severely criticised. A common fault is to start playing directly the tape moves, forgetting that any switch on a domestic recorder will put an audible click on the tape. There are two ways of avoiding this. The first is to remove the click by editing the tape when the recording is finished. The second is to mark where the microphone or input levels were during the test recording, turn these levels to zero, start the tape and then reset the levels before indicating that the performance can begin. At the end of the piece always allow time for the natural reverberation to die away before fading out the input signals and switching off. I will not pass any recording unless this has been done, stressing once again that although the quality of the music may not be of the highest standard the recording will be.

Multitracking

Multitracking means the superimposing of several contrasting layers of sound upon each other. In the professional recording studio tape machines exist which can take up to 64 tracks, these finally being mixed down to provide a stereo recording. The 'pop' composer Mike Oldfield excels in this type of work. On his album *Tubular Bells* he performs every single instrumental part. This *tour de force* is quite beyond the resources of any school, but with care, multitracking up to five individual parts is possible on a domestic stereo recorder. The biggest danger is distortion. If the tracks are not carefully balanced you are almost certain to produce an unsatisfactory tape. The thing to remember is that in the studio each track is put on the tape directly under the previous track, so that if you are recording 16 tracks these appear underneath each other. However, the multitracking done on a domestic machine involves switching the signal from track to track as the piece is built up. This method is bound to involve a slight loss of quality, but with care excellent recordings can be made. Five different melodic lines can be multitracked as follows (a diagrammatic representation is shown in Fig. 5.2). Record the first track on track

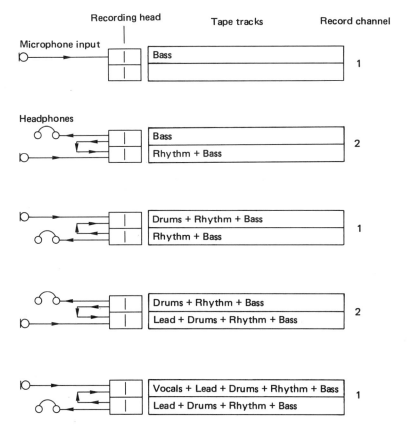

Fig. 5.2 Method of multitracking bass guitar, rhythm guitar, drums, lead guitar and vocals

1 so that your VU meter registers only a 20 per cent input. This first track is usually the bass of the composition or possibly a continuous rythm track. It is useful to give a 'count in' before the first track is recorded because otherwise you do not know exactly where it begins when it comes to superimposing the other tracks. This 'count in' can be edited out when the piece is complete. Having finished track 1, the tape is rewound on to the left-hand spool, track 1 is changed to track 2, the machine is prepared for recording and the multitrack circuit is switched on. During the recording of this second and all subsequent tracks the 20 per cent input level is maintained, the performer monitoring the previously recorded tracks through his headset. The beauty of this system is that, at the end of the second track, the first melodic line is mixed with the second melodic line on track 2 but the original line is still recorded on track 1. This means that if an error is made on the second track only that one has to be rerecorded. At the end of this second track the VU meter should be registering 40 per cent of the total scale. The tape is rewound, tracks are again switched, the multitrack circuit is switched on again and the process is repeated. Both the fourth and fifth tracks are recorded in a similar fashion, and on completion the entire five tracks are on track 1 of your machine. If your input levels were calculated correctly the VU meter should show 100 per cent undistorted volume. The only drawback to this method is that the earlier tracks lose a little of their quality each time they are rerecorded, and for this reason the most important melodic lines should always be recorded last.

Another use for the multitrack switch which can be used on a three-headed recorder where the copying is done via the playback head into the record head is to multitrack a piece against itself without adding a new track. This produces an echo on track 2 of every sound on track 1. The procedure is the same as that outlined above. Assuming that the finished piece is on track 1, rewind the tape, switch to track 2 and engage the multitrack circuit; start the recording process and just monitor the sound. There is no need to worry about percentage levels because you are just copying the first track a fraction later on the other track. The slower the speed you use the longer will be the delay of the second signal. When you rewind, play the tape in stereo and the sounds will appear to travel between your speakers. This effect cannot be obtained from a two-headed machine because both record and playback circuits are combined in one head. One last method of producing a delay is to play your tape on two machines simultaneously. Mount two machines side by side and thread your tape from the left-hand spool of the first machine to the right-hand spool of the second machine. Set both machines to playback and your piece is performed on the first machine before being echoed on the second.

Mixing and editing

Many recordings will need more than two microphones to achieve a satisfactory balance. In order to use multiple microphones a mixer is necessary. We use a five-channel instrument which is capable of receiving a wide variety of inputs. Of the five channels two are left-orientated, two are right-orientated while the fifth is directional. This directional effect is the one which is the most useful. Panning a sound from left to right, or vice versa can sound exciting. Listen to Pink Floyd's *Dark Side of the Moon* and you begin to appreciate exactly what directional sound can do. Another good recording is Steeleye Span's version of 'Gaudete' in which the singers appear to process through a vast cathedral. Operating even a small five-channel mixer demands more skill from the 'engineer' than just making an ordinary two-channel recording. Invariably the first attempt produces a poor result with melodic lines fading in and out at hopelessly inappropriate times. In order to produce a satisfactory recording a working diagram showing exactly what each microphone is doing at any particular moment must be produced. You can simply mark the music, or if the piece is purely electronic then some sort of timed diagram using graph paper can be used. Mixing is a skill which is not arrived at over night.

All recordings need editing. If a tape is not edited then it will probably contain clicks and other extraneous noise. These unwanted sounds can be removed quite easily with the aid of an editing kit. I usually introduce my classes to editing by asking for a volunteer to answer two simple questions, both question and answer being recorded at $7\frac{1}{2}$ i.p.s. This speed is used to facilitate the editing process. One question will have 'Yes' as its answer, the other 'No'.

'Were you at school yesterday?' 'Yes.'

'Did you play truant yesterday?' 'No.'

The answers are then removed from the tape and substituted for each other by editing. The tape is then played to the class and they are asked to note that although the splice can be seen on the tape it cannot be heard. It is really a simple task provided that you remember a few basic rules. The splicing operation should be performed on the tape backing. If you cover up the recorded side with splicing tape then you will either lose the sound altogether or you will get a drastic loss of quality. The blade used to cut the tape must be non-magnetic. If a magnetised blade is used then there is a good chance that you will add a click to the tape. Kits are supplied with blades, and replacements are readily available. Tapes are marked for editing by using a Chinagraph pencil. If you know a tape is going to need editing before completion then it is advisable to use the fastest speed on your recorder to make the initial recording. This will give you plenty of room to make your editing cuts. A slow speed will lead to all sorts of difficulties with tiny lengths of tape which have to be joined together. After editing is completed the master tape should be copied so that all signs of editing disappear. A completed tape should have no aural indications of editing having taken place. Obviously editing needs practice before the process becomes second nature. I always give my classes a length of tape to edit. Give every child about one and a half metres of prerecorded tape. Tell them to cut the tape into a number of assorted lengths and then edit the pieces together again in a different order from the original. Lastly join the two ends together to form a loop. They will soon obtain the skill necessary both to edit and to construct loops. These loops are then inspected for editing quality and played so that the members of the class can listen to their attempts. This is rather a hit or miss affair as the children probably do not know what material the tape contains. It is only an exercise in manipulative skill. Then another useful exercise is to take half a dozen records of a popular group and construct a tape montage of the discs. This demands a lot more skill as the 'editor' has to decide on a particular place to make the cut so that the pieces flow easily and naturally into each other without harmonic or melodic bumps.

Editing can also be used to alter the envelope or characteristic shape of a sound. For example, percussion instruments produce a very sudden attack. If this attack is removed the sound appears quite different. Record a sudden *forte* note on a cymbal and let the sound die away before switching off. Edit out the sudden attack and turn the resultant length of tape into a loop for future use in a composition and you will be quite surprised by the change of sound you have produced. The same type of editing can be done with the decay of a cymbal note. Similar strange effects can be produced by inserting lengths of silence into a sound. If you record another cymbal sound, note how long it takes to die away completely. After the initial, say, five seconds, insert a five-second period of silence before letting the sound resume. This can be done several times because the periods of sound and silence can be measured accurately. One second of silence at $3\frac{3}{4}$ i.p.s. is $3\frac{3}{4}$ inches of tape, so therefore five seconds of silence equals $18\frac{3}{4}$ inches of tape. The only danger is that if you use an insert of blank leader or recording tape the acoustic will change suddenly. This can be overcome if a length of silence is recorded in the same room and then inserted. Alternatively other sounds may be used instead of periods of silence.

Using the synthesiser

Pure electronic sounds are created by synthesisers, and every electronic music course should aim to have access to one. They provide an almost unlimited range of sound. Their usefulness is restricted only by the imagination of the people using them. Yet it is just as difficult to compose electronic music with a synthesiser as it is to compose conventional music using conventional instruments. I am sure that several of my pupils think that by using a synthesiser they can become composers overnight. The truth comes as a rude awakening to many of them. One of the first dangers to avoid is trying to use the synthesiser to imitate conventional instruments. My own feeling is that if you want to imitate a clarinet then you might as well use a clarinet. The same is true of the keyboard. The temptation is to use it as a keyboard without realising that the keys control every device on the synthesiser and even produce exotic scales and arpeggios.

My own method of approach is to give the class 'a guided tour' of the instrument without its keyboard. The pupils know what the word oscillator means but usually do not understand that an electronic circuit can produce a sound. At this point, if there is someone in the class with a smattering of knowledge of electronics I get them to build a small battery-powered oscillator so that an integrated circuit, resistors and capacitors can be seen and heard to produce an audible sound wave. Having explained what an oscillator does, we move to the other devices and treatments on the synthesiser. A filter can remove certain of the frequencies of a note and so change the timbre. One oscillator can be used to control another oscillator. The envelope shaper will give a sound its characteristic attack, on and decay periods. The addition of reverberation removes the dryness of electronic sound, and so on.

Simple sound effects are then demonstrated. If a signal from the noise generator is passed into a barely oscillating filter and the frequency of the filter is controlled by a slow-running triangle wave, then the sound of a gale is produced. This sound can be developed still further by reducing the oscillation from the filter and then passing the signal into the envelope shaper. This produces surf-like patterns, which by careful adjustment of the filter can be regulated for a 'stony' beach, a 'sandy' beach, fine weather or stormy weather.

This type of sound has provided a backing track to several electronic 'pop' pieces and so we naturally move on to demonstrate this. A good example is found on *Zero Time* by Tonto's Expanding Headband. The last track on side two of this disc is called 'Tama' and is a perfect illustration of melodic lines weaving together over an endless landscape of wind and surf. Obviously the next thing to do is to try and imitate this type of piece. The technique is quite easy, just multitracking of melodic lines over the ostinato pattern which is recorded first. It is difficult to produce such an effective piece however. This same disc can be recommended for group listening as it provides several good tracks for the demonstration of elementary techniques. The piece 'Riversong' contains a ring-modulated voice singing in an 'oriental' style over what can only be described as an 'Eastern' background. The track 'Jetsex' demonstrates just how effective panning the sound from speaker to speaker can be. The type of record I avoid is Walter Carlos' *Switched on Bach*. Clever though it is I feel that it presents the synthesiser in the wrong light, imitating orchestral instruments.

The ring modulator and the various inputs I leave until the end. I always feel that the principle behind the ring modulator is difficult for children to understand and even more difficult to use creatively. We start by producing 'Dalek'-type voices and progress, using the envelope shaper, to bell and chiming sounds. One thing I insist on is that every sound the group likes is instantly charted so that it can be recreated whenever it is wanted.

Recording

Making recordings in school is fraught with difficulties. Not only are you creating sounds which are probably annoying other people, but they are creating sounds which are probably annoying you. It is perfectly all right if you are recording elec-

Plate 9   Guitar sounds modified by a synthesiser during recording

tronic sounds, because you are probably taking your sounds directly into the tape machine and are monitoring the results through headsets. The problem is at its worst when you are using microphones. Any unwanted sound is picked up and appears on your tape. It needs great discipline for your group to remain completely silent during a recording – and then to remain silent at the end of the piece until all the microphones are dead. So many pieces end in a sigh of relief, relief that the ordeal is over, the piece has actually been put on tape without mistakes; a sigh of relief is almost called for. Whereas you can control what goes on in the classroom, it is almost impossible to control what goes on outside. To a large extent noise from outside the classroom can be cured, if not altogether eliminated by using unidirectional or cardioid microphones. These only pick up sound from the front, not like omnidirectional microphones from the back and sides. Close miking also helps. Get your musicians, performers etc. as near to the microphone as possible. You might lose the natural reverberation of the room, but reverberation can always be added electronically. If one instrument sounds too loud, then use a mixer and blend the sounds together to obtain a more natural effect. Above all do not be afraid to experiment with microphone placing; you will never have an ideal recording situation.

   It is a good idea to mark the position of the performers on the floor with chalk if you are using microphones. It is easy to get one performer's microphone correctly balanced and set and then find that while the recording engineer gets on with the next performer the first one has moved away. Electronics calls for great discipline.

One part of an electronics course which can easily be neglected is the care of the equipment. Children know that recording apparatus is expensive. It is possible that in a well-equipped school a group could, at any one time, be using microphones, mixers, synthesisers, keyboards and tape recorders with a total value running well into four figures. Most of the maintenance will have to be done by trained engineers using the correct test equipment, but two small jobs can, and should, be performed by the children at regular intervals. The first of these tasks is cleaning the heads of the recording equipment. Over a period of time tape heads become dirty. Tiny deposits from the tape accumulate and gradually build up to form a hard layer of oxide on the heads. The result is that the quality of both recording and playback slowly deteriorates. It is an imperceptible progression and probably you will be unaware that it is happening. Regular cleaning, say once a month, is essential and it is quite a simple task.

The other maintenance job which can be performed by children is to demagnetise the heads. As with the build-up of oxide particles, each head also gradually becomes magnetised and this leads to a loss of efficiency and quality. Ideally the heads should be demagnetised at very regular intervals.

Tape compositions

One of the first exercises I set is the composition of a piece based on a drone. The group is given only the minimum of instructions. The piece must last about two minutes, the drone should be provided by the synthesiser and only percussion instruments should be used. There are two examples of such pieces on the cassette made by two different groups of fourth-year children (*Cassette examples 5.1 and 5.3*). The main differences between the two are in the tape manipulation involved, the nature of the drone and the omission of the triangle from the second piece. A synthesiser is not essential as the drone could be provided by a pair of cellos, clarinets or other instruments. The percussion used included: piano strings, two bowed cymbals, a tambourine, two wood blocks, a triangle, a pair of claves, a guiro, a soprano metallophone and a tambour on which grains of pearl barley were dropped. Two unidirectional microphones and the synthesiser were fed into the mixer and the volume levels were controlled by the engineer. The pieces were recorded at $7\frac{1}{2}$ i.p.s. but this speed was not used for playback. Including the conductor and the engineer, twelve children took part in the first recording and eleven in the second. The children were positioned in a semicircle with the bowed cymbals in the centre just in front of the piano. The wood blocks were placed left and right, the other players had no particular position given them. The conductor was told to indicate by pointing when he wanted an instrument to start and stop. The only other preconceived idea for the piece was that which ever instrument started the piece the same instrument would finish. In the event the guiro was chosen. This was stroked slowly with a triangle beater. The engineer decided that a slow fade would be a suitable way of starting and finishing the piece. Before the actual recording, a run-through was made, the children being warned that they would not be able to hear the drone and that the order of instruments in the rehearsal would almost certainly be different from the order used in the recording. The term aleatory was used and explained. When the correct balance was achieved the recording was made. The drone in the first piece is a bare fifth which was fed into the filter of the synthesiser and the frequency of the filter was changed by treating it with a slow-running triangle wave to produce a slight wah-wah effect. In the second piece a ramp wave was swept by a slow-running triangle wave to produce the harmonic series. On completion the tapes were rewound and played back at various speeds. The first group preferred their piece played at half speed, whilst the second group liked theirs at quarter speed. This manipulation made the first piece last four minutes and the second eight. We realised that eight minutes was a long time for such slender resources, therefore the piece was rerecorded and a time limit of one minute was imposed, which when slowed down became four minutes. The slowing of the tape creates a different timbre on all the instruments, the bowed cymbals become menacing, the stroked and plucked piano strings acquire a quality which it is difficult to describe, the barley grains on the tambour become like distant artillery and the guiro gains a natural reverberation which is completely lacking when played at the normal speed.

After performing these pieces my next step would be to get the group to perform them again with the engineer adding echo to the recording. As the pieces are aleatoric the second performance would differ in many details from the first, although the basic outlines would remain.

In order to show exactly what echo can do I have added echo to both pieces (*Cassette examples 5.2 and 5.4*). This can be done quite easily if you connect two three-headed recorders together. The master tape was placed on one recorder and a second recorder was joined to it using the lead shown in Fig. 5.1. The first recorder was set to playback and the second recorder to record. Another 5-pin input/output lead joined the monitor socket on the second recorder to the stereo microphone input on the same recorder. With headphones connected and the monitor switched to the 'A' position it was then possible to add echo to the copy of the original recording. The amount of echo is set by the position of the microphone input controls. With two microphone controls (left and right) echo can be fed to either channel or both simultaneously. The only difficult part of the exercise was the bowed cymbals. If too much echo was added feedback occurred. It was necessary therefore to watch the VU meters carefully and bring the echo level down whenever the bowed cymbals were played.

The fifth piece was composed by four fourth-year boys and was their first attempt at composition. Their brief was to produce a two-minute piece using electronic sound. Their first problem was how to start – how to attract the attention of the listeners. The opening sequence therefore starts suddenly and only lasts a few seconds. It was created by passing a signal from an oscillator through the envelope shaper and adding reverberation. For ease of control the sound was triggered by the attack button. Directly after this initial sound was finished a 'bass track' was added. This is just a succession of regular beats and runs through the entire composition. These beats consist of a filtered ramp wave with the filter frequency being controlled by a slow-running square wave. The third track was multitracked with the second and uses ring modulation. A ramp wave was ring-modulated with a triangle wave, passed into the envelope shaper and triggered into action by means of the keyboard. The output of bell-like sounds had its pitch changed as keys were played at random. This track was faded in and out to give contrast and unrepetitive, interesting variations. The fourth and final track was another keyboard one. It was not multitracked, just synchronised with the previous material. A sine wave was controlled manually and by a slow running square wave. At the same time a voltage was applied by the keyboard. This track was faded in and out to contrast with the preceding track. The most difficult part of the piece was the ending. In contrast to the sudden opening the group decided that a keyboard glissando of the bell sounds, coupled with a slow fade would provide a fitting conclusion. The piece was composed during eleven lunch-time sessions of about half an hour each (*Cassette example 5.5*).

The sixth piece is an example of what a talented pupil can produce in his own home using his own equipment. This is Chris's first attempt at multitracking a composition of his own, although he has multitracked other pieces on many occasions in the past. The piece is called 'Daydreams' and is in ternary form with a slow middle section. The first track to be laid down was the bass guitar through a microphone on to channel 1. This bass was then transferred through a mixer on to channel 2 using a lead similar to the one shown in Fig. 5.1. At the same time the percussion was also added to channel 2. Headphones of course were used to allow synchronisation. The bass and percussion were then transferred back to channel 1 through the mixer, and the acoustic guitar was added at the same time through the microphone. Finally the bass, the percussion and the acoustic guitar were transferred at a low level back to channel 2 and the electric lead guitar was added to the same channel, first having been passed through an echo unit. The lead guitar was added at a much higher volume level than the transferred parts. Thus the lead is prominent on channel 2 whilst the other parts are prominent on channel 1 (*Cassette example 5.6*).

The final piece was composed by three boys as their entry for CSE. Only one of the boys was a musician in the sense that he could play a few chords on the guitar. They decided that they would have to use their voices as they were unable to use instruments. Their theme was mental illness. They began by listing all the words they could think of on the subject, e.g. 'crazy', 'asylum', 'bedlam' etc., and these were divided between the boys who were performing the piece. The only other sound was an out-of-tune, home-made psaltery. Various attempts were made to perform the piece during normal lessons, but on every occasion the piece broke down into laughter, and they found they were unable to carry on in front of the class or me. Depression set in and the idea of the piece was endlessly discussed and almost abandoned. Finally they came to me to ask for help which, as it was to be an examination piece, I declined to supply, except to suggest they borrow a copy of Berio's *Visage* to listen to. The following day they returned the record telling me that they didn't like it and could not see much point in it. They still wanted to go ahead with their piece so in desperation, after another attempt had broken down, I told them to take the recording equipment to a vacant office and not return until the piece was complete. Half an hour later the composition was finished. As I was not present at the session I was very interested to find out how the piece was finally taped. Various words were stressed in different ways, syllables were accented, echo was used to produce not only echo, but also feedback, the recording speed was changed abruptly and the psaltery was plucked on suitable occasions. I find the piece very satisfying considering the traumas that surrounded its composition. It shows imagination and a grasp of aural awareness on the part of the recording engineer. In spite of the fact that they assured me they did not like *Visage* I find the piece full of Berio's influence. It is a piece for which the bare minimum of equipment was needed. No expensive electronics were involved, just a three-headed stereo tape machine, two microphones and a great deal of imagination (*Cassette example 5.7*).

6 Simple equipment for electronic music making.

ANDREW BENTLEY

The advice and information given in this chapter is intended to serve as a form of 'survival kit' for the first weeks of electronic music making in the classroom. It presumes that only the most modest equipment is available: the classroom hi-fi, an additional tape recorder or two, perhaps augmented by a few cassette recorders brought from home. This chapter does not presume a great deal in the way of previous skills or know-how, and an attempt has been made to go into as much detail as possible about how to apply the techniques suggested, leaving as little as possible to chance. This approach has its dangers, of course, since our aim first and foremost is to make music, or at least to experiment with sound in a musically meaningful way. The technical and rather matter-of-fact slant of this contribution is thus principally intended to provide some ways and means to that goal.

It is also presumed that the reader has no access to a synthesiser. The techniques discussed here go more than a little way to fill the gap, and at the same time cost virtually nothing. What is still better is that they lose none of their value or impact if a synthesiser is available, and can be used to augment and complement its facilities in the same way as such techniques often do in professional studios. Most important of all, they are in many ways explanatory of what is happening inside the synthesiser, which in view of the black-box nature of this instrument can be rather helpful in itself. The primitiveness of simple techniques such as these tends to cheapen their validity – I am not ashamed to admit that I have used each and every one of them at some time in my own compositional work even though I am lucky enough to work in a studio costing many tens of thousands of pounds.

If one's first aim is to make music, the practicalities of classroom electronic music can seem a little tiresome. Certain skills are essential: the ability to record on to a tape recorder successfully, to put together the right leads in order to connect one tape recorder to another for copying and manipulating the material during the transfer process and to edit tapes (described in detail in Chapter 1). Once the art of making connecting leads has been mastered it is only a small step to being able to construct some simple electrical hardware suitable for insertion in the leads between the tape recorders. This is often a matter of using an electrical device where previously an instrument was operated manually. While what I suggest may appear unorthodox, nothing here will cause damage provided the cautions are heeded. It is to be hoped that ingenuity will lead to the discovery of new techniques, and it will soon become evident that lateral thinking and the will to explore new and even wildly strange ideas, when coupled with a thorough understanding of how things work on technical and musical levels, are the two most useful attributes of the electronic music composer-to-be.

As a final word of introduction, it should be said that even though all the material found in this chapter has been tried and tested in the field, problems may arise from time to time which result from the particular characteristics of the equipment available to you. Do not be disheartened if something that you try does not work, either in the technical domain, or the musical. With a technical failure it is simpler to blame your own incompetence first, try again from scratch, and if it does not work the second time blame the equipment. This is the correct course to take, since you lose virtually nothing from failures except time, and usually you gain greatly in knowledge in the process. With failures on a musical level (when you try a particular technique with a certain type of sound material, for example, and nothing spectacular seems to take place) you are experiencing a process of learning the correct matching of materials against techniques which is central to the successful creation of electronic sound compositions. Each case is so specific in this regard that no one would attempt to offer advice designed to cover all eventualities. Each composer builds up a repertoire where techniques are matrixed against musical goals, and he or she should be constantly striving to extend it through varied and preferably reasonably systematic forms of experiment.

Let us turn first of all to the resources nearest at hand. Among those resources most commonly and readily available to us is the tape recorder. It is evident that whatever sounds we are recording with it, we should do so efficiently and effectively. This means, in a technical sense, that we want to record to the highest quality allowed by the equipment. In a musical sense it means not wasting too much time and tape, and not accumulating grossly wasteful and unmanageable quantities of material, because editing then becomes a heavy chore rather than a creative activity, and tape is one of the most difficult media of storage from which to find something when you need it, however many notes you have made about what you have recorded on what piece of tape. Good quality recordings can be obtained by following the practical guidelines outlined here.

Recording materials

Recording is a skill and there are several things one should know in order to do it well.

(1) Use the recording meter, observing that the loudest parts of the sound send the needle just into the red area on the scale.
(2) Use manual rather than automatic, if there is a choice, since the automatic level control tends to make strange changes to the level and the result is usually a continuous *forte* with a lot of 'pumping'.

(3) Record quiet sounds in quiet places.
(4) If you are trying to record sounds from a single object, place the microphone as close to it as possible.

On the other hand rules are made to be broken, and one should explore as many different ideas as possible.

(1) Record with the needle right into the red and against the end-stop: this produces *distortion* which can be used to good effect in the right context.
(2) Try different kinds of microphone if they are available: contact microphones pick up sounds through materials; guitar pick-ups work electromagnetically and respond to vibrations in metal; carbon telephone mouthpieces have the strange advantage of being rather bad quality; old gramophone cartridges are very sensitive to small vibrations and a facility is often provided on tape recorders to accommodate them; normal 'air' microphones are very cheap if you buy the crystal type, enabling you to afford several should you need them.
(3) You can do strange things by 'fooling' the automatic level control when re-recording many sharply attacking sounds in succession.
(4) Neither the microphone nor the sound you are recording need stay still, and if you have the possibility of recording in stereo, you might try to move the sound in the stereo space: moving the microphone also allows you to either mix or sample sounds that are happening simultaneously in the same space.
(5) Some tape recorders offer a built-in facility for mixing microphones, and if yours is not one of this type, if may be worth investing in a cheap little microphone mixer. Record sounds using microphones located at more than one place around the object making the sound, and experiment with mixing them in different ways. Use different types of microphone mixed together. With stereo tape recorders, record with different microphone types on each track. This will allow you to mix them together at a later stage.

Recording successfully in a musical sense demands experimentation and fore-thought. It is not always practical or spontaneous to rehearse what you are to record but it is to be highly recommended where it suits the musical needs of your activity, be it the recording of some water swishing in a pan or several sound events to be recorded as a combination all in one take, where several pairs of hands are involved. When something does not succeed it is better to wipe it out than accumulate rubbish.

Looking for sound materials

Good sounds are to be found in abundance from very simple bits and pieces around us in everyday life. If you have any sense of history or reverence for the early pioneers of electronic music, you may wish to exploit these real live 'concrete' sound sources for their changing qualities which are nearly impossible to replace with synthetic sounds. From a practical point of view two alternatives exist: either the tape recorder can be taken to the sounds, which is necessary if you are recording environmental sounds and for which purpose a cassette recorder is ideally suited, or the sounds must be brought to the tape recorder, which in the noisy classrooom environment can have problems. There is no shortage of sound-making materials, starting with your own voices, but if your minds need jogging this list will help you:

wood	plastic	glass
metal	cardboard	cloth

These materials appear in many forms:

sheets	netting	balls	utensils
springs	blocks	foil	
plates	grating	tubes	

Gather some of these materials around a tape recorder and start experimenting with ways of exciting them into vibration in order to get sound from them. School rulers were made to be twanged, and doing this is not unlike the way a square-wave generator works in a synthesiser. All serrated and ribbed surfaces (combs, washboards, a pile of envelopes) are sources of regular waves and thus musical pitches. If blowing, stroking, beating, bowing, shouting or rubbing with wet fingers does not excite the material into making a suitably interesting sound you may want to turn, disgruntled, towards electronic means to make it for you.

Simple electronic sources

It tends to be difficult to control the pitch of most recorded sounds as precisely as one can control the pitch of musical instruments, though the abstract, indefinable qualities of the former are often highly desirable. An electronic sound source, though it will be far simpler timbrally than many 'concrete' sounds, can offer a more versatile raw material whose pitch can be controlled at the time of recording. For this purpose an electronic organ can be used, or one of the many similar but far cheaper types of instrument now finding their way into toy shops. Besides the evergreen *Stylophone*, one especially interesting example is the *Compute-a-Tune*, which will remember the tunes you have entered into it via its two-octave keyboard, and which also has an output socket for connection to your tape recorder or amplifier.

There is a certain fascination and satisfaction in conjuring sounds out of 'thin air'. An impromptu oscillator can be formed by connecting a microphone to an amplifier (such combinations also exist as toys) or to a tape recorder if it is capable of sending the amplified sound directly to the loudspeaker when the record button is depressed. The feedback caused by doing this can be controlled easily if the microphone is turned to face away from the loudspeaker: among the possibilities offered by this technique is that of rapid fluctuations in volume caused by swinging the microphone around on its cable (but tape the cable to the microphone case to prevent damage to the connections), which can even produce beautiful bird-like twittering. Experiment by putting your mouth around the end of the microphone which allows you to alter the pitch of the feedback according to how wide you open your mouth.

One extremely rich source of often very beautiful electronic sounds is a short-wave radio. If this kind of radio is not available you can try the extremities of the shorter wave bands of a medium-wave receiver, and in either case you should investigate those regions in between stations where atmospheric interference and modulation effects are strongest. These sounds are excellent material when played at lower tape speeds where the rapid high-pitched patterns are extended in duration. For how to obtain *electronic noise* as source material, see later in this chapter (p. 120).

'Musical numbers'

With the aid of two common items of domestic electronic equipment – a pocket calculator and a transistor radio – we are set to explore a rather unusual and fascinating method for producing pitched and other types of electronic sound. The calculator should be placed in very close vicinity to the radio's internal aerial while tuning in to the medium and long wavebands, or alternatively to the tele-scopic metal rod aerial when using FM or short wave. Tune through the bands searching for a very strong steady tone which obliterates all other radio signals. It is likely that you have found the calculator operating-clock frequency, or possibly the frequency which is used to scan its display. This may appear on any or all of the radio's tuning bands. When you have a good signal level, press each of the calculator keys, numbers and functions, and observe their musical effect. Pressing several keys simultaneously in various combinations will produce different sounds, and each type of calculator is unique in this respect so it is a good idea to try all the calculators you can lay your hands on! Not all calculators use the same frequency, and there may be more than one place on the radio dial where sounds will be produced without the steady tone being present. It is just these places, hard to find as they are, which are likely to give the most interesting musical results – glissandi, various types of noise, different musical pitches and 'chord-like' sounds. More sophisticated calculators can give more varied results, but this is not always the case. If a programmable calculator is near at hand, try out programmes which use repeating calculation sequences and loops as these are likely to be the most promising. It is very difficult to offer more detailed advice because of the great variety of calculators on the market.

Once the effects have been discovered, it is very easy to 'notate' them by writing down the relevant keys that you have pressed, allowing you to return to them later. If the radio you are using has a built in cassette recorder, this can be used for recording the sounds directly on to cassette.

Developing recording techniques (one tape recorder)

If you are in command of recording techniques, you may wish to experiment with some methods where the tape recorder's facilities can themselves play a role in the musical results which you are seeking. The tape recorder is not unlike a musical instrument in many ways: it has a facility for varying the pitch (the speed control), loudness (the microphone or line input control or in playback the volume control) and, to a limited extent, the timbre (tone control). With a little ingenuity one can extend the musical characteristics of this very versatile machine even further, even if you have only one tape recorder at your disposal.

Sampling

Your machine may have a pause control designed to stop the tape momentarily by lifting the pinch wheel away from the capstan. Cassette recorders have such a facility which is remote-operable from the microphone switch and which works in exactly the same way in playback mode too. A special lead can be made with a switch wired across the terminals of a 2.5 mm jack plug if you want to control this from a distance. You may use this switching provision to take short recorded samples of sounds occurring over a long and sustained period. This sometimes has a strange by-product (which can either be considered a drawback or something worth experimenting with in its own right) in that a rapid glissando downwards in pitch occurs as the tape gathers speed while recording. When switched in playback mode the glissando is heard to go upwards. A tape recorded in this way, manipulated in the same way during playback, will give glissandi in both directions.

Glissandi and octaves

Manipulation of the speed-change control in either record or playback mode (check with the instruction manual as this is not advisable on some tape recorders) will also produce glissando effects of a longer duration than that offered by the pause control. Using the fixed speeds of the machine, related to one another in octaves in musical terms, is extremely useful: doubling the speed, while raising the pitch of the material an octave, also halves the duration, which means that superb virtuosity is possible if the situation allows you to make the sounds at a lower pitch than you eventually intend them to be heard and you do this at as fast a tempo as you can.

Completely variable pitch

You can also record on to the tape, or play back from it, while hand winding the tape from the reels. Remove the head cover, slip the tape round the back of the capstan (rather than between the pinch wheel and capstan where it usually passes) and keep the tape taut while you hand wind it (Fig. 6.1). Hand winding backwards while you are in record mode will erase parts previously recorded, which if done knowledgeably and with care can result in an interesting telescoping of the musical events as they come into the tape recorder from the microphone or line inputs.

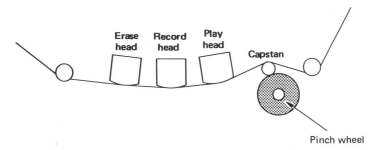

Fig. 6.1 Threading a tape recorder for hand winding

Vibrato

Because the capstan has been ground to be very precisely round, the tape will normally be driven along without any noticeable fluctuations in speed. Wrapping a short piece of sticky tape (masking tape is far preferable to clear adhesive tape in that it does not leave any sticky residue behind when you remove it) around the capstan will therefore provide a splendid vibrato on any material recorded or played back (or both for double the effect). Folding the end of the masking tape over to create a bump will intensify the effect. Vibrato will clearly be far more noticeable on pitched material than on more amorphous sound masses.

Creating textures and masses

Tape recorders are so designed as to erase the tape when something new is being recorded on to it. This happens at the erase head over which the tape passes before it reaches the recording head. If we prevent the tape from touching the erase head, which is a simple matter of bending a small piece of thick cardboard to fit snuggly round the front face of the head, it becomes possible to record a second, third or even fourth layer of sound on to the same stretch of tape, thereby thickening the texture of whatever is being recorded, even to the point of achieving a thick mass of sound when the nature of the material allows it. The last layer to be recorded will always be the loudest when the tape is played back and this is in the nature of things; if you want all the layers to mix equally in level it is necessary to lower the recording level with each successive pass over the same section of tape. Winding back the tape to the beginning is not necessary if all you require is a short piece of material, since the tape can be spliced into a loop (see Chapter 2, p.33), on to which sounds can be recorded continuously with the texture thickened on each full cycle of the loop past the heads.

Acoustic modifications (two or more tape recorders)

While the above mentioned techniques can all be performed using only one open-reel tape recorder, and some of them (sampling, layering, vibrato) even on cassette recorders with a little extra effort, more than one tape recorder enables us to copy from one machine to another via the built-in loudspeaker and microphone. This is not to be recommended for the purpose of making a good copy, but rather for allowing you to make modifications to the sound as it passes from the playback machine's loudspeaker to the microphone plugged into the recording machine.

Reverberation

Reverberation can be added to already recorded sounds by putting the playback tape recorder behind the soundboard of an upright piano and hanging the recording microphone in amongst the strings. Use of the piano's sustain pedal serves to turn the reverberation on and off. Damping upper or lower strings will lend different sound qualities to the reverberation. If you wish to avoid the motor noise from the playback machine finding its way on to the rerecording it is wise to plug an extension speaker into the speaker socket, enabling you to move the tape recorder itself away from the piano. You will in any case need to employ as much level from the loudspeaker as it will reasonably give without distortion, to combat surrounding noises and to stimulate the piano into resonating effectively. If the material is played back and correspondingly recorded at a higher speed than the one at which it was originally recorded, the length of the reverberation will be doubled.

Changing the tone quality

Many ways can be found to colour the sound on its way between the loudspeaker and microphone ranging from use of the acoustics of the room you are in (as Alvin Lucier employed in his composition *I am sitting in a room*, in *Source*, No. 7, 1970) to putting a loudspeaker unit in a bucket, a sock, an empty milk bottle, a guitar or virtually anything that comes to hand. Passing the sound more than once through the object will, of course, serve to intensify the effect which it has on the sound (Lucier went on passing the sound through the room until none of the sound of his voice was left, merely the resonances of the room). Tubes of all sorts and sizes are excellent for this purpose because they are 'tuned', like organ pipes, to a certain frequency. They will resonate at this frequency like a drum (drums can in fact be used too) if they are 'hit' with a short sharp sound from a loudspeaker. Putting one tube inside another like a telescope allows the length of the tube, and thereby the frequency, to be varied while recording is in progress, but this can make undesirable noises. Lateral thinking provides us with an alternative solution if a stereo tape recorder is available, whereby the effective length of the tube can be altered. Record your material on to one track of the tape and play this back through the extension speaker placed at one end of the tube. Record from the microphone, situated at the opposite end of the tube, on to the second track, using the hand-winding method described above (Completely variable pitch p.112). With the tape wound slowly forwards the effective resonance of the tube will turn out to have a higher pitch when the tape is played back; when run more quickly it will appear to be lower in pitch. The fact that this only becomes

apparent when the tape is subsequently played back means that it is rather difficult to estimate what the effect will be. One has to 'listen upside down' and make
a guess!

One is not restricted to passing sounds through the air; fixing a loudspeaker
down on to some object or material in order to pick it up at the other end with a
contact microphone proves to be an interesting alternative. Wood or glass work
satisfactorily for this purpose, and if metal is used a guitar pick-up can be employed in place of the contact microphone. A large metal plate can act as a
reverberation device in this fashion, though an impromptu rig-up such as this will
not be the equal of the professional type of reverberation plate described elsewhere (Chapter 1, p.17).

The mouth tube

A variation on the acoustic methods of filtering just described, and equivalent
to the band-pass filter often found on synthesisers, is the mouth tube. A glance
at the diagram (Fig. 6.2) should explain all. A funnel large enough to cover the
loudspeaker on the tape recorder or cassette recorder is stuck in the end of a piece
of hosepipe about a metre in length. It is then taped down over the loudspeaker
with masking tape to effect a well-sealed join. The end of the tube is placed in

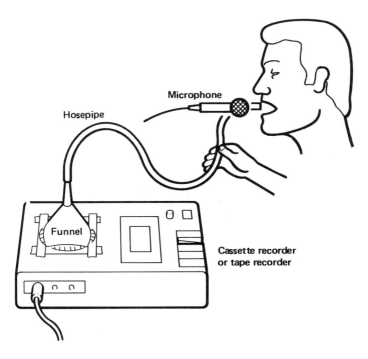

Fig. 6.2 The mouth tube

your mouth with the recording microphone as near to your mouth opening as possible. Opening and closing your mouth around the tube will alter the filtering frequency in the same way as it changed the pitch of the feedback 'oscillator' described earlier (p.111), and in the best of cases the sound material can be made to 'talk'. Tuning your mouth sharply to a resonant frequency can be difficult to do well in the first place but improves rapidly with practice. This is, in a sense, a type of acoustic *vocoder*. All the tone-colouring techniques described here are the acoustic analogy of what is happening in electrical filters, where a 'tuned circuit' is used to replace the tube's role in colouring the sound.

Making leads

The advantages we have seen from using two tape recorders can be exploited far more effectively if we have the possibility of copying from machine to machine using a direct electrical connection. In order to do this it is necessary to buy or make the appropriate leads. The price of ready-made leads and the demands of different situations are usually reasons enough to make it worthwhile learning the gentle art of lead-making.

The tools you will need for making leads are as follows: a pair of side cutters, pliers, some tool with a sharp point (the smallest of a set of watchmaker's screw-drivers or a filed-down paper clip), a soldering iron with a reasonably fine bit, and solder. A vice is very handy to hold the plugs while you are soldering on to them, and a multimeter is a boon for checking that good connections have been made and that there are no shorts from the signal wires to earth, but these are not alto-gether essential.

Audio leads should be made from single-screened cable. Double screened cable may be used for connections between stereo devices, but in most cases two separate leads will prove handier. In order to solder the lead on to the plug, the plug should be dismantled and the lead passed through the plug cover. You will need to pare away the outer covering of the cable, using the side cutters, to ex-pose about 2 cm of the screen braiding underneath. Your sharp point now comes in handy for separating the plaits in the braiding starting from the tip of the cable. Twist the braiding together and tin it with solder, applying the solder and iron sim-ultaneously (this is the golden rule of soldering). A few millimetres should be pared off the plastic covering of the signal wire which has now been exposed from under the braiding. The signal wires are twisted and tinned as before and then soldered on to the appropriate pin on the plug. Information on which pin is which can be gleaned from Fig. 6.3. The screen braiding is soldered on to the earth pin, and the plug reassembled.

If you plan to build your own equipment at some later stage it may be wise to standardise on a certain plug and socket combination where it is possible to do so, e.g. mono jack plugs or the smaller and cheaper alternative the 3.5 mm jack plug. At the tape recorder and amplifier end you are unfortunately stuck with what you are given.

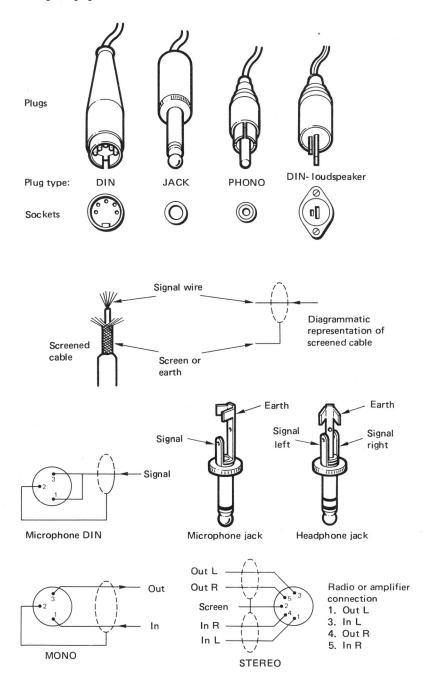

Fig. 6.3 Tape recorder inputs and outputs

Amplifier		*Terminology used*
Inputs	– from record deck	PHONO, PICK-UP, X-TAL MAGNETIC
	– from tape recorder	TAPE, REPLAY, RADIO, AUX, LINE-IN
	– from tuner or radio	TUNER, RADIO, AUX
Outputs	– to tape recorder	TAPE, RECORD, AUX OUTPUT, LINE-OUT
	– to loudspeakers	LS, LOUDSPEAKER, MAIN, REMOTE, 8Ω/4Ω

Tape recorder		
Inputs	– from radio, amplifier or tape recorder	RADIO, AUX, LINE-IN, DIODE
	– from record deck	PHONO, PICK-UP
Outputs	– to amplifier or tape recorder	RADIO, AUX, LINE-OUT, PRE-AMP

Cassette		
Inputs	– from microphone	MIC (microphone remote control – REMOTE)
	– from cassette recorder	MIC (only from EAR when no other choice is available)
	– from radio or amplifier	AUX
Outputs	– to cassette recorder	EAR (only to MIC), AUX
	– to amplifier	AUX

Symbols used

    ◠◡ to or from tape recorder
    ◡ from record deck
    ◌ from radio
    ◖ from microphone
    ◠◖ to headphones
    ◗ to loudspeaker

Fig. 6.4 Connections between equipment

Whether you choose to make leads or buy them, it is still necessary to know which plugs (and, in the case of DIN plugs, which pins on each plug) and which sockets should be connected together to ensure a successful transfer of the signal from device to device. This can be tried out by experiment but the combinations are often many, and not all are equally successful. Those readers who have heard such terms as 'impedance matching' and 'balanced lines' should rest easy because these problems rarely raise their ugly heads when dealing with domestic equipment. It is usually a question of finding combinations of inputs and outputs which suit one another in terms of signal level, or 'sensitivity' as it is usually unhelpfully described in instruction manuals. The table of connection terminology (Fig. 6.4) should be your guide. If your equipment uses sign language on the sockets, the key to the symbols will clarify matters. A bad combination of output and input will be evident if the sound quality deteriorates or if a hum is induced on the inputs. Look for alternatives too if you find that the signal level arriving at the input is too low and that you therefore have to use more than half the level available at the input level control. With suitable leads available for connecting the tape recorders together it becomes possible to try some techniques which work most effectively when the sound material is being played back and copied on to a second tape recorder. Listening on headphones to what is arriving at the second machine's input allows you to monitor what is happening to the sound. The techniques which we applied when recording sounds on to the tape, such as sampling, layering, octave changing and hand winding, are equally applicable here, but in addition to these we may try the following.

Distortion
Distortion, which in electric guitar players' terminology is flatteringly called 'fuzz', can be obtained electronically by overloading the inputs of the tape recorder, which is not generally considered to be good practice. The alternative is overloading the tape itself by recording very heavily into the red on the recording meter. This will not do any damage but is likely to render the tape less usable for recording thereafter. The simpler and purer the sounds recorded (a suitable candidate being the mouth feedback described above), the more effective the distortion for making them timbrally interesting: thicker textures usually sound distasteful when distorted. If the distortion is recorded at a quieter dynamic level in the final musical product, it is likely to sound more as if it was intended as a timbral decoration than a mistake. This is a characteristic of perception rather than an electronic phenomenon. Later in this chapter you will find a very simple electrical circuit for obtaining fuzz and controlling it more effectively. Electric fuzz has the strange characteristic of sounding more pleasant than the gross overmodulation of the tape described above. The 'harmonics' produced by these two methods are related in different ways to the original sound.

Bending the pitch
Once the sound has been recorded on the tape it becomes possible, by holding the tape at two carefully chosen points with the fingers and thumbs and stretching it slightly, to make small downward bends in pitch. This, needless to say, renders the tape completely unusable afterwards but its artistic merit may justify this expense. The stretched sections can be edited out of the tape before it is used again. However, there can be no equivalent way of making the sound bend up.

Tremolo and fluctuating dynamics
There are several ways of creating variations in the dynamics of the recorded

material when it is copied on to a second tape recorder. Taking a blunt and non-metallic instrument, or your finger if it is small enough, and using it to bounce the tape on and off the head as it is playing is a technique which can be performed at various tape speeds. When the material is copied at a lower speed than that at which it was recorded, the fluctuations can be made to occur at a faster rate than your own dexterity would otherwise allow. The variations in dynamic are accompanied by drops in the high frequencies as the tape wavers away from the surface of the head. With tape recorders that are equipped with pressure pads to keep the tape in contact with the head it usually suffices just to waddle this backwards and forwards.

If an electronic organ with built-in Leslie loudspeaker (this is a type of loudspeaker which rotates) happens to be available, it is sometimes possible to plug the output of the tape recorder into its preamplifier (usually a jack or phono socket is provided for this purpose somewhere under the keyboard) and the various speeds of tremolo can then be rerecorded on to the second tape recorder using a microphone placed near the Leslie. The technique for doubling the speed of fluctuation is just as effective in this case also.

It is not out of the question to build your own rotating loudspeakers. The most difficult problem in this regard is getting the signal to the loudspeaker when it is turning round. Wires simply will not do, since they get wrapped in knots after a few revolutions. The solution I came up with was to use a jack plug and socket combination, fixed vertically to act as a kind of bearing on which the loudspeaker could rotate. This will not take the weight of a large loudspeaker, nor will it last indefinitely, but it does work.

Electronic noise

This is a useful source material for creating percussive effects and lends itself admirably to tube filtering and dynamic modifications. No expensive noise generator is actually needed to obtain it, since by plugging in a tape recorder output to another recorder's input and turning up the input level to maximum it is possible to record nothing – nothing, that is, except noise. If this does not give enough noise level, play the tape you have recorded on the first machine and repeat the operation until the level is satisfactory.

Dynamic shapes

This is an extension of the technique described in Chapter 2 under 'Rhythmic templates' (p. 32). A little fancy work with the scissors and the low speeds available on domestic tape recorders work effectively together as a way of changing the dynamics of sounds by cutting the tape at acute angles. If two tape recorders are available we are not restricted to the tiresome process of cutting up each individual sound recorded on the tape, but we may cut empty tape into the dynamic shapes that we want and record the material, where it happens to be fairly continuous stuff, on to the readily cut sections. These shapes, made from bits of tape with leader tape for the silences, can be formed into a loop for convenience (Fig. 6.5).

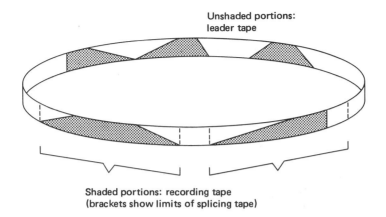

Unshaded portions:
leader tape

Shaded portions: recording tape
(brackets show limits of splicing tape)

Fig. 6.5 A chopping loop for making dynamic shapes

When the sound has been recorded on to the loop it is then replayed and recorded on the first tape recorder, or a third should it be conveniently available, for storage in its new form. The loop can then be re-used for another sound. With tape recorders equipped with three heads, it is possible to 'pass the sound through' the chopping loop on to a third recorder all in one operation. Mono tape recorders work best for this technique. With stereo tape recorders the sound appears to move in space, unless the two outputs are mixed into mono.

Painting the tape
'Painting' is meant here in only a figurative sense. The idea is that by stroking the tape with a demagnetiser, it is feasible to record the 50 Hz mains frequency on to the tape, thus producing tones whose pitches depend on the speed that the demagnetiser is guided along the tape. Some demagnetisers do not produce this effect; instead they erase the tape entirely, which is something which can quite equally be used for causing changes in dynamic if the demagnetiser is not allowed to come into close contact with the tape. With a stereo tape, erasing one side of the tape rather than the other causes the sound to wander. Those demagnetisers which produce tones can also be used to make rather pretty modifications to material which has previously been recorded on the tape, including spectacular sweeping sounds. It is wise to experiment with some unimportant materials at first, and to keep the demagnetiser away from any important tapes while you are working with it, for reasons which should be obvious. This means that one should cut out the parts of the tape to be treated in this way and replace them afterwards.

As a final word on tape recorders it may be worth noting that the reel of tape is not the only method of storing recorded sound material. One entertaining alternative is the Mapophone.

Mapophone

This is the name I have given to a realisation of the idea suggested by the American composer Jon Hassell in his compositions *Map 1* and *Map 2* (*Source*, No. 5, 1969). Strips of empty or prerecorded tape are glued down, with the oxide coating (the side normally touching the heads) uppermost, on to a sheet of cardboard or plastic to form a rectangular area on which the sounds are to be recorded. If you are lucky you will be able to appropriate some 2 or 1 in tape which will make the job of laying down the strips much easier and which will also last much longer in use, owing to there being fewer adjoining edges. A record head, or record/playback head must be obtained, either surplus or from a component firm, and connected to your tape recorder's record/playback head terminals. This should be done with extreme care so as not to dislodge the leads that are already there. It should be connected with a cable that has two signal wires for the connections between the head terminals and a screen which should be attached, as shown in Fig. 6.6(b), either to the central tap on the tape recorder's head or to the machine's chassis. Not doing this will result in hums or the cable acting as a radio aerial. It is wise then to wrap the tape head in insulative material so that only the front face is to be seen, which prevents your hands from touching the cover. This helps to prevent hums. Put the tape recorder in record mode and record the sounds at the input of the tape recorder on to the map surface in any and all directions, keeping the head as upright as you can, using fairly swift and even strokes of the head. Playback is done in a similar manner, with the machine in play mode, with the added freedom to explore different regions and directions of the map using your artistic licence. Tilting the head slightly results in the higher frequencies becoming fainter, and a mellowing of the sound.

A more recent use of unusual tape and tape recorder head mountings was demonstrated by another American, Laurie Anderson, in his *Violin Tape Bow*. This

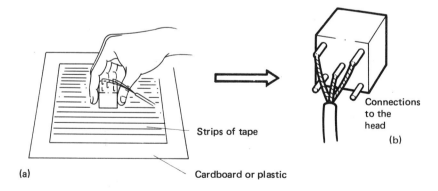

Strips of tape

Connections
to the
head

(b)

(a)   Cardboard or plastic

Fig. 6.6 (a) The Mapophone
(b) Tape recorder head and screened cable

comprises a tape head fixed to a violin, and the hair of the bow replaced by a length of prerecorded tape. As with the *Mapophone*, the prerecorded sounds can be played at any speed, with the possibility of enormous speed changes and rapid changes of direction between forwards and backwards.

The poor man's synthesiser

The tape recorder has so far gone a long way towards providing us with many techniques for the origination and manipulation of sounds which we would normally expect from a synthesiser: sources of oscillation, vibrato, pitch-bending, changing of the tone quality by filtering, creation of dynamic shapes or 'envelopes' and reverberation to give an impression of acoustic space. The tape recorder's only drawback, as can rapidly be deduced from the techniques described above, is that it can rarely do more than one of these things at a time. If build-up of noise from many generations of tape is inclined to be a problem, however, and you really know what it is that you want in advance, it may be worth rationalising your procedures a little to see just how much you can manage to do in one operation.

With the tape recorder thoroughly explored, and some confidence gained from making leads and connecting equipment, the time may be ripe to employ your constructional skills in building small devices which can cut a few corners in an operational sense and at the same time overcome some of the problems of performing techniques with machinery not really designed to do the job. The circuits to be described below are logical extensions of the techniques which are already familiar from working with the tape recorder, and are whittled down to the most minimal versions which will still work with reasonable quality. They are simple enough for the pupils themselves to assemble on terminal blocks. The more adventurous can transfer the units that have been tried and tested for their musical usefulness on to 0.15 Verostrip or Veroboard for permanent use. Verostrip (0.15 in. matrix) is a rather close equivalent to terminal blocks. As they stand, these projects do not demand any soldering skills other than the attaching of leads to the potentiometers to enable them to be screwed into the block. This could be done by the teacher. No tools other than those which were used for lead-making are necessary. You can lay the components out and insert them into the blocks using the diagrams shown in Figs. 6.7 – 6.11 as a guide. Lists of components are given to make ordering or buying easier. With everything connected together properly they should work first time, but the terminal block arrangement does mean that you have to be careful not to let wires touch each other unless they are connected to the same hole. Observe the polarities of such things as diodes and capacitors, and be careful to insert the transistors in the way shown on the diagram. None of the components is terribly vulnerable and should not be suspected first if the device does not work. To connect these units to tape recorders or other equipment you will need three or more cables with bare ends to insert into the terminal block and plugs to suit the equipment at the other end. These too could be provided ready-made by

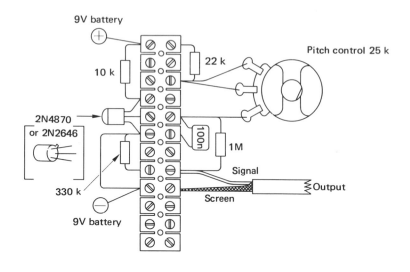

Component list	
10 k	resistor
22 k	resistor
330 k	resistor
1 M	resistor
100 n	capacitor
(= 0.1 μ), polyester radial	
2N4870	transistor or 2N2646
25 k	potentiometer
9 V	battery
	battery connector

resistor colour codes

10 k brown black orange
22 k red red orange
330 k orange orange yellow
1 M brown black green

Fig. 6.7 The oscillator

the teacher. If you suspect that the inputs and outputs of your equipment may not be adequately protected ('decoupled') against DC voltages from the outside world, you should insert a 0.1 μ (100 n) capacitor in the signal lead of each of these cables for safety's sake. This will prove to be a wise precaution in any case.

The oscillator (*Fig. 6.7*)

Though many electrical oscillators work in a way which is analogous to the teacher. If you suspect that the inputs and outputs of your equipment may even simpler. It is a *unijunction relaxation oscillator* built around a unijunction transistor, and its frequency is controlled by a voltage applied to the fifth terminal from the top via a potentiometer. This potentiometer could be replaced by a set of keyboard contacts separated by a chain of resistors or preset potentiometers if the need were felt. This way one would be able to obtain discrete intervals of pitch. The voltage could equally well be derived from some other source.

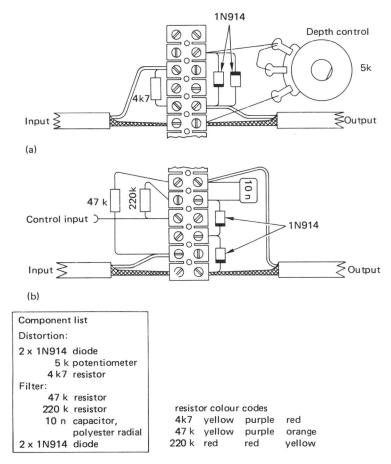

Fig. 6.8 (a) Distortion and fuzz circuit (b) Voltage-controlled filter

The fuzz unit Fig. 6.8(a)
This unit will distort the sound passed through it by symmetrically clipping the tops
and bottoms off the wave-form peaks. It is entirely passive, i.e. it needs no battery
power to work. The potentiometer controls the amount of distortion. It is possible
that signals of too low a level will not be distored by this circuit, but normal tape
recorder outputs should work quite happily.

The voltage-controlled filter Fig. 6.8(b)
This is a passive low-pass filter of the RC (resistor-capacitor) type. It needs to be
supplied with varying voltage at the control input from some source, which might
be a similar arrangement to that used in the oscillator. This control voltage can also
be supplied by the output of the attack–decay generator or the envelope follower,

described below. The higher the voltage (up to 9V) supplied to this terminal, the lower the frequency of cut-off and the more treble is removed from the sound being passed through.

The voltage-controlled attenuator (Fig. 6.9)

This is for controlling the dynamic shapes of sounds and works in conjunction with the attack–decay generator or envelope follower, either of which will provide a voltage to vary the amount of the signal which is allowed through the device. It uses the variable resistance of a P-FET transistor to sap away larger or smaller amounts of level from the signal.

The attack–decay generator (Fig. 6.9)

This is a very simple form of envelope generator, capable of supplying an upward-going ramp of voltage for the attack portion and a descending ramp

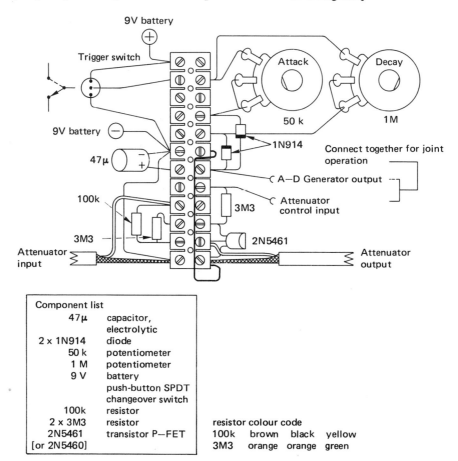

Fig. 6.9 Attack-decay generator and voltage-controlled attenuator

for the decay portion, achieved by charging and discharging the capacitor. The durations of the attack and decay can be altered using the potentiometers: the push-button switch, which should normally be resting with the centre terminal connected to earth (battery negative terminal) should be pressed for as long as the attack portion of the wave form lasts if it is intended that the sound reach full volume.

The envelope follower (Fig. 6.10)

This is a handy device which follows the dynamic shape (envelope) of the input signal and produces a varying voltage which traces it. With its output connected to the control input of the voltage-controlled attenuator, the level of the signal passed through the attenuator will vary in exact correspondence with the dynamic of the sound connected to the follower's input. Thus new material can be synchronised with previously recorded sounds, and rhythmic materials created. The output of

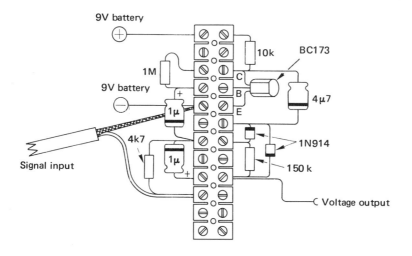

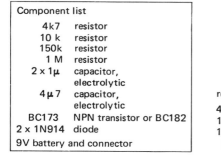

Component list	
4k7	resistor
10 k	resistor
150k	resistor
1 M	resistor
2 x 1μ	capacitor, electrolytic
4μ7	capacitor, electrolytic
BC173	NPN transistor or BC182
2 x 1N914	diode
9V battery and connector	

resistor colour codes

4k7	yellow	purple	red
10 k	brown	black	orange
150k	brown	green	yellow
1 M	brown	black	green

Fig. 6.10 Envelope follower

the follower can also be applied to the voltage-controlled filter's control input, causing the filter to dip in frequency as the input to the follower grows in dynamic; when the signal present at the follower input is mixed with the filter output, the two sounds will appear to alternate. When connecting any of the above devices together, it is essential to use either a common battery or common earth connections, which entails connecting all the battery negative terminals together.

The mixer (Fig. 6.11)

Suitable for use with the signals from the above devices, and of great help in other more general tasks, is the mixer built from passive circuitry shown in Fig. 6.11. Although, in the form described here, it is laid out in the same way as the previous projects on a terminal block, this is a rather ineffective method of constructing it. Its general usefulness will make it worthwhile to transfer the connections on to 0.1 in Verostrip, the holes of which very conveniently match up with the pins on slider-type potentiometers, thus making the job very much easier to accomplish. Suitable sockets might then be mounted on to the strip, or attached to an angle bracket fixed to the strip, enabling the mixer to be plugged in where and when required. Contrary to what is often said about the 'loading effects' of passive

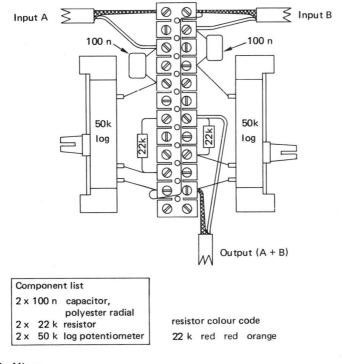

Fig. 6.11 Mixer

mixers, this one works very satisfactorily in the great majority of cases. If an active two-input mixer is preferred, a very simple Josty Kit is available, but the passive mixer works out much cheaper and adds no distortion or noise to the signal !

Ready-made alternatives
Comparable in many ways to the little construction projects just described, but designed and constructed to better specifications and boxed for permanence, are the effects accessories which guitarists often use for processing the sound from their instruments. These are excellent devices for classroom experimentation and, though not cripplingly expensive if bought singly, they can usually be borrowed from some willing person to enable you to try them out for a few days. The *fuzz box* has an effect similar to the circuit described above, with the added advantage that its active circuitry guarantees good distortion in all cases. The *wah-wah pedal*, a foot-operated low-pass filter with a resonating peak approaching that of a band-pass filter, will give a sharper filtering effect than the passive unit described above. Other units include *sustain*, which gradually increases the dynamic on a new sound being inputted in order to compensate for the decay inherent in plucked guitar sounds, and the *octave divider* (hiding under many different pseudonyms such as 'sub-octave generator' or 'blue box') which provides a square-wave signal of a pitch one or two octaves below the input frequency. It is only able to follow fairly pure tones with any accuracy, but responds excellently to voice sounds and makes a fair mess of anything complex in character. The *phaser* causes a sweeping effect to be added to the sound not unlike the variations in a jet engine sound of an aeroplane flying overhead.

Building equipment

Even though the music lesson may not be the time or place to engage in serious electronics construction, some words of advice and encouragement may be welcome to those who would like to try this in their spare time or initiate such a project as part of school science activities. Electronics teaching is becoming a more familiar phenomenon in British schools, due in part to the impetus and excellent literature provided by the Schools Council Science Project, and volunteers for experimenting with electronic music circuits may well be found in your own class or school. Use them: home-made electronics are very cheap and, if constructed from a well-known published design, can be quite the equal of commercially available equipment. Try construction yourself: it is certainly not as frightening a prospect as it seems, but a rather relaxing and satisfying activity. If you are able to solder leads together you are halfway there; any further know-how that is necessary revolves around the components – identifying them, making sure that they are put into the circuit the right way round and assessing which of them may be causing problems if the circuit does not work. Excellent literature is available to cover all these aspects.

Start with a kit; the simpler the better. Kits are child's play to assemble in most cases, and the suppliers often include copious notes to accompany them. Some even offer to put the matter right if you do not succeed in getting the circuit to work under your own steam. There are firms which specialise in kits for electronic music modules (see Appendix V), many of which are taken from articles published from time to time in the popular electronics magazines. Kits have many advantages over homebrew construction: professionally made, printed circuit boards are included, almost guaranteeing the success of the project by itself, since alternatives such as using matrix boards of the Veroboard type are more fiddly and it is relatively easy to make mistakes or leave some connection out. Making your own printed circuit boards is a messy business involving etching acids and home-made boards rarely come out to the same standards as the professional ones supplied in kits, which often have diagrams printed on their upper face to show where the components are to be inserted. All the components are supplied in one package, simplifying ordering immensely, and the total cost rarely works out more expensively than 'shopping around'.

Surprisingly, electronics construction usually involves more metalwork and woodwork than it does electronics, since when the printed circuit board has been furnished with its components, soldered and tested – which may take one hour – the problem still remains of how to house the device you have built, involving the drilling of holes to accommodate potentiometers, switches, plugs and sockets. Not only is this more time-consuming than the electronics assembly but these components and the box will often cost several times the price of the electronics inside. Boxes are one area where great savings can be made if you do-it-yourself in the school metalwork shop. Compatibility of electronic music modules from different sources can sometimes be a problem. This applies less to audio signal levels, though some synthesisers work on so-called 'hot' levels of a few volts' swing, and others on lower levels more closely matching those found in domestic audio equipment. Sadly, information in kits or constructional articles far too rarely give clues to these and other problems, nor to the nature of the required control voltages and their polarity. An oscillator's frequency, for example, might be controlled by a voltage which rises either linearly, 1V per 1000 Hz, which is musically less useful, or exponentially at 1V per octave which is a widely accepted standard among professional manufacturers. This voltage can be rising for an increase in frequency, or falling, and furthermore it may be positive with respect to earth, around earth, or negative going. These systems are not necessarily compatible with one another and the best policy is therefore not to mix circuits from one synthesiser design with those of another if you are in doubt.

Access to further information for the beginner

Whether you are merely experimenting with tape recorders or are adventurous enough to try out the constructional ideas presented here, many questions will be raised which require answering. If access to equipment proves to be a problem, then access to information, tools and know-how can prove often to be a far more serious matter. If ideas or information are what you are lacking, look near to home: there is always an expert near you. The list of university studios in Appendix VI may be of help – you can contact the studio director for advice, arrange a studio visit, or ask for a willing composer to bring a synthesiser to school and discuss what you are doing, even arranging an impromptu concert-demonstration if there is enough interest. A resident technician may be available in some cases to answer your technical queries. Books are plentiful but are often too general to cover specific problems relating to your equipment. Magazines tend conversely to be rather too specialised, demanding specific technical knowledge of the reader. Summer courses can be a rich source of inspiration but are inevitably too short, and regrettably few societies exist to promote these kinds of activities. The answer lies, in the final analysis, in exploiting the best of all these sources, some guidance to which will be found in the appendices to this book.

Musical goals

No quantity of tape recorders, synthesisers or techniques for applying this equipment can ever replace the combined cooperation, endeavour and imagination of a class of thirty pupils. Although the activities described in this chapter are inevitably destined for small-group activity, there are many simpler activities which can be used in the first instance to gain familiarity with the equipment and involve the whole class: some of them, such as collecting sounds from the environment, lead naturally into investigating recording techniques and developing a strong sense of appreciation for sound materials and a responsibility towards their creative application in improvisation and composition. Aural games, in which the tape recorder can take part as a storage medium for sounds, help to sharpen the ear towards different aspects of the living sound. Building instruments, including electroacoustic instruments, helps to gather the threads of how sound is made in a physical sense while providing ideal material for the techniques described in this chapter.

All these resources must be turned into music, and in guiding pupils in the kind of activities described here it is wise to lay extra emphasis on the musical significance of what is being done in order to counterbalance the technical nature of its execution: use musical terminology rather than technical terms where you have a choice; quiz your pupils on what it is they are trying to achieve on a musical level. Draw attention to the way that the sound has been transformed from its original state to its present one, and encourage the use of material from all stages of the transformation process. In this way musical similarities and differences, processes and coincidences, conscious execution and discovery, can all play their part in whatever turns out to be the musical product. In this sense this chapter can only hope to help you in your technical survival: the rest is up to you.

7 What is musicmontage?

TREVOR WISHART

I hope that my contribution as a composer to this book (intended primarily for teachers of music interested in electronic music) will serve to show the potential of electronic music beyond the boundaries of the classroom and will give some insight into the processes of electronic music composition.

The world of sounds

When dealing with recorded sounds, rather than just the sounds of conventional instruments, we are able to choose any sound as material to work with. Thus we might choose recordings of conventional instruments, electronic sounds or sounds from the natural world. Or we might choose segments of available music (such as those which are overheard on short-wave radio during a performance of Stockhausen's *Kurzwellen*) or recordings of events in the real world (as in a news broadcast). Again we might choose sounds which sound *like* events in the real world (e.g. an electronic sound which sounds like footsteps or breathing etc). Radio drama constantly makes use of both real-world sounds (doors opening and closing) and fake 'real' sounds (e.g. electronic sounds suggesting a flying saucer landing or taking off; the voices of Daleks, and so on) to create the right theatrical illusion. Such sounds used in this context are usually called 'sound effects', but they are actually no different from other recorded sounds. In fact, making a radio drama or any recorded 'aural theatre' is very similar to making a piece of tape music. Sounds from various sources (e.g. actors' voices, sounds of doors opening and closing, cars passing etc.) are mixed on tape to complete the effect. The difference between aural theatre and a piece of tape music therefore lies in how we listen.

It may seem obvious to say that in an aural drama we are listening to what the words mean, and to what the 'sound effects' tell us about the context (large room, small room, outdoors etc.) of the action. However it *is* possible to think of making a radio play where the dialogue doesn't mean anything immediately obvious, doesn't 'tell a story'; or where the context cues are very difficult to interpret (e.g. set on an alien spacecraft or a completely imaginary environment). With tape music, on the other hand, we are listening to how the sounds are organised *in themselves*. But if, in our music we use different kinds of reverberation, are we not suggesting different kinds of 'space' similar to large room, small room, outdoors, in radio drama? If we begin to utilise sounds such as pre-existing bits of music, or the sounds of birds and animals, are we not suggesting (perhaps unwittingly) some kind of 'context' in which our music takes place? When we use a text we are often concerned with the meaning of the words and on tape we can suggest the context in which it is sung or spoken. Think, for example, of the voice of the young boy in Stockhausen's *Gesang der Jünglinge* . . . note how the voice becomes 'disembodied' by its use in changing aural perspectives, created by the use of rapidly changing dynamics or reverberation . . . quite unlike a straightforward recording of a song.

Thus, when we begin to examine closely the apparently simple distinction between aural drama and tape music, the boundaries begin to become rather vague and unclearly defined.

In this chapter, therefore, I intend to deal with the strange and exciting area which lies in this 'no-man's-land' between so-called 'abstract' tape music and conventional aural theatre ('radio drama').* I will introduce the ideas of musicmontage and aural landscape and discuss how these may be applied in making tape compositions.

Musicmontage: composing with recognisable sounds

What would happen if we attempted to preserve the original context of our real-world sounds, and avoided modifying them to any great extent (especially in ways which destroyed their recognisability)?

Here I would like to make an analogy with the visual arts. Just as the twentieth-century invention of sound recording has made almost any conceivable sound or combination of sounds available for making music, the development of printing and especially photography has provided a vast store house of texts and images which the visual artist may use directly.

The technique of arranging wholes or parts of unmodified or modified *pre-existing images* in two dimensions is known as collage (e.g. the work of Kurt Schwitters). Doing the same thing with moving images on film or television is known as montage. Such a collage or montage may focus attention on the formal properties of the images used (size, shape, colour etc.) or on their representational aspects, creating a representational 'composition' which comments on the original images used.

Now it is not very difficult to see how we may adopt the same approach in using pre-existing real-world sounds (now called *sound images*). As sounds exist (and change) in time, this approach could be more akin to the techniques of montage in film or television, and I intend to refer to it as *musicmontage*.

Clearly a musicmontage could be representational (or apparently so), or a more 'abstract' arrangement of sound images. More importantly, because sounds and

---

* The reader will benefit by listening to some or all of the following works in conjunction with this chapter: *Visage* by Berio; *Gesang der Jünglinge* by Stockhausen; *Symphonie pour un homme seul* by Schaeffer, *Red Bird* and *Journey into Space* by Trevor Wishart.

music can and do evolve in time, the way we move from one sound image to another, the way they are superimposed, contrasted and so on, is very important, just as it is in what we normally refer to as music. Finally, we are of course free to use so-called 'abstract' sounds as well and to pass at will from the apparently representational to the apparently abstract.

The idea of musical landscape

Imagine that you are sitting in a concert hall listening to a symphony orchestra play Beethoven's Fifth Symphony. Apart from hearing the music, you are also aware of where the sounds are coming from – lots of musicians playing instruments on the concert platform. Now imagine you are sitting at home with a record-player and you put on a disc of Beethoven's Fifth Symphony. In this case the sound is actually coming from loudspeakers, being produced by the vibrations of cardboard cones. However, despite this we would still say that we are listening to an orchestra playing Beethoven's Fifth Symphony. In this case we conceive of the sounds as coming from the orchestra.

This notion of *where we conceive of the sounds originating* we will call the *landscape* of the sounds.

In both the above instances, the landscape of the sounds was fairly clear-cut. In a radio play we might wish to create the illusion of a particular landscape. The use of 'sound effects' such as doors opening and closing, or sounds of a busy street, used as background to a dialogue creates landscape (inside a room, in the street) for the dialogue (which in reality is taking place in a recording studio).

Another example: we often find that electronic music is used as accompaniment to science-fiction dramas, or 'eerie' scenes in television programmes. Why is this? It would seem that, apart from the few who are familiar with synthesisers and electronic sounds, most people find these kind of sounds disorienting and eerie – just what the programme intended. This is precisely because the listener can't conceive of where these sounds might originate or how they might be being produced; the sounds have no identifiable landscape.

We might also consider the difficulties experienced by some people in listening to concerts of tape music in the concert hall. Many people express the feeling that the lack of a visual focus, of anything happening (visually) on stage, is disorientating. It is more likely, however, that their inability to conceive of a landscape for the sounds they are hearing causes their disorientation.

What are the features of a sound image which enable us to identify its landscape? Perhaps the two most significant features are:

(a)   *aural cues* (such as those used in radio drama discussed above)
(b)   the *aural space* in which the sounds appear to occur.

Let us examine these a little more closely.

Aural cues: recognition

The simplest example of aural cueing is the case where a sound is immediately recognised by the listener. In this case the sound is its own 'aural cue': it creates its own context. When recorded sounds are heard separately from one another, many are easily recognisable: spoken voice, traffic, dripping taps etc. However in the context of a tape piece containing many other sounds, especially where the other sounds create an unfamiliar (or 'impossible') context, it can be surprisingly difficult to recognise even the most commonly heard sounds. Of the three examples previously mentioned, normal speaking voices tend to retain their recognisability, but the sound of a dripping tap could be very easily misinterpreted. Even traffic noise could go unrecognised in certain kinds of sound context, e.g. where other continuous drone-like sounds of low frequency moving between the loud-speakers are being used. Therefore, in all but the simplest contexts, we cannot rely on the recognisability of sounds.

Aural cues: context sounds, clarity and ambiguity

The next most obvious type of aural cue is the use of simple 'sound effects', or *context sounds* in radio drama. As mentioned before, these sounds need not be 'true to life' (e.g. real doors, real traffic etc); they need only create an illusion of a context. We will refer to landscapes which appear to be real as *pseudo-real*.

It is important to point out the difference between creating a satisfactory landscape illusion by the use of aural cues, and directly recording real-world landscape. At first sight it might seem logical that the best way to create a convincing landscape of, say, a busy street would be to record your material in a busy street. The problem here is that the ear is a selective listener, whereas the microphone is not. In the street the ear (or rather the brain) will focus on the information which it considers significant, e.g. dialogue and specific aural cues as to context. The microphone will merely record everything, and once this is projected on to a stereo (or, even worse, mono) listening system the apparent clarity of the original will often seem incomprehensibly confused and muddy.

It is this selectivity of the brain which allows us to hear one particular conversation at a noisy party, where many simultaneous conversations are taking place probably against loud music, even though the conversation we are listening to is relatively quiet (the signal-to-noise ratio is very low). It is also these focusing and interpretative abilities of the brain which allow us to use aural cues at all, and to create illusions of reality which are in fact not at all 'realistic' in the normally understood sense.

When deciding upon aural cues, therefore, we should aim to use the minimum number of cues compatible with a convincing landscape illusion. Using many sound cues (or many sounds) together easily creates confusion of the aural image (as you will discover if you try to mix a large number of complex sound materials on to a single stereo tape).

In addition, without the aid of *visual* cues it may not be apparent which of the many sounds we hear we are meant to focus on, and which are background phenomena. The task of clarifying this relationship between foreground and background is similar to the analogous task in a conventional musical composition.

On the other hand this lack of obvious focus may be a feature we wish to exploit. In *Journey into Space* we hear a man driving along in a car (we hear the sounds of the car and of traffic) and we hear him switch on his car radio (knob-click, sounds of tuning in to stations) and the sound of a space-rocket launch on the radio. In a real situation it would be immediately clear which of the two sets of sounds we were hearing came from our immediate reality (the car, the traffic) and which from the radio (the space sound). Not only could we very clearly locate the direction from which each sound came, but we could see the real events (the interior of the car, the gear-changes, the passing traffic) and not see the events heard on the radio.

On the tape however, the relationship between these two threads remains unresolved. Although *initially* it seems clear that the space-rocket sounds are on the radio (the aural cues of switching on, tuning in), as these sounds persist, and eventually become louder than the traffic and car sounds (which finally die away completely), the conceived relationship of the sounds shifts. Are we now located in the space-rocket – or even in the imagination of the car driver? This ambiguity of the landscape is a central feature of *Journey into Space* allowing us to pass from the pseudo-real to the imaginary to the 'abstract', so that the nature of the landscape becomes one of the factors with which we can compose.

Here is a slightly different example: at one stage in the same pseudo-real car journey we hear the sounds of motor-horns amongst traffic noise in the almost narrative context of the man driving off from his home on a journey. At a later stage, at a point where there are no recognisable environmental cues in the music, these horns are used in the context of other 'pure' sounds, i.e. sounds which in themselves do not suggest any particular landscape (not even that of instruments being played, as they are largely produced, live, from unconventional sound sources). Because of the previous context in which the horns appeared, however, the context of 'journey/traffic' adheres to them.

This is enhanced and transformed by two other factors: (a) the use of sustained (slightly wavering) sounds on toy trumpets which sound like the motor-horns elongated in time, transformed in a strange way; (b) the fact that these sounds and others drift about the stereo space, moving, but in a slow and disordered fashion. In this way the landscape 'journey/traffic' has been transferred to what (out of context) would appear to be a 'pure' music sequence, and at the same time has taken on a completely different ambience. This is now a mental or mythical 'journey', having no apparent direction, through a totally unfamiliar landscape.

Aural cues: naming sounds – counterfeit cues

A very particular use of aural cues is the use of words to denote, or name, what something is, where we are etc. This device is commonly used in radio drama but is not so suitable for use in musicmontage unless the use of a text can be justified for some other reason.

As an example, in *Red Bird* we hear the very creaky voice of the Philosopher. This particular voice quality is introduced because it can (and does) transform into the sound of a creaking door (the door being one of the important sound-images in *Red Bird*). At the same time however the speaker is heard turning the pages of a book. This sound, especially when heard against a background of other sounds (here not only the speaker but several whispering voices) and in a strange context, is not easily recognisable. The speaker however says, 'Here in our Book of Knowledge . . .', drawing attention to the sound of the book. Once this denoting has been done, the pages may be used on their own, or in conjunction with any other excerpt from the Philosopher's speech (i.e. not necessarily containing the word 'book') and still be recognised.

Next we hear the book being slammed. This sound is so brief that in the tape context it would be almost impossible to recognise. However, it must not only be recognised but also differentiated from the sound of a door being slammed, as at one point in the piece it gradually transforms into the later sound. This landscape requirement is impossible to meet without the use of the sound of pages being turned *prior* to the sound of the slam, providing a clear context for recognising this later sound . . . and the use of words to denote the book allows us to recognise the former.

At the same time the 'Philosopher' turning the pages of the 'Book of Knowledge' has a clear place in the narrative structure of the myth, which is another way of hearing the *Red Bird* piece. The idea of myth and parallel interpretations is discussed later in this chapter.

A final word on the subject of aural cues. Even though a sound may be used as an aural cue to create a convincing context for another, the cue sound may in fact not be what we heard it to be! In *Red Bird*, for example, a sound which appears to be a metallic hammering (but was originally a 'chorus' of screams) slowly changes into the sound of a clock ticking. The final confirmation that this is a clock is given when a clock alarm goes off. However, this later aural cue is in fact the transformed sound of birds which itself rapidly changes into birdsong!

This last example illustrates how involved (or subtle) control of landscape can be.

Different types of landscape

Having decided to work with landscapes, we must now ask what kinds of sound landscape there are, and how we can go about using them. The most obvious category of landscape is that which we name *pseudo-real*. Thus the disc recording of Beethoven's Fifth Symphony is (or rather, appears to be) realistic (although in practice it may be made from several separate 'takes' – possibly using slightly different musicians or instruments). The illusions created by context sounds in most radio dramas are also *apparently* realistic. Here we can see that the events which take place (people talking into microphones in a recording studio, a door closing – probably recorded somewhere else) are not the same as the events portrayed (people talking naturally in a small room). We would still retain the image of a real landscape just as documentary television drama is effective in being apparently realistic. As we are not, however, constrained by the real world (things which just happen to sound at the same time in the same place), being 'realistic' is not a restriction.

More importantly, perhaps, even the most clear sound images are not so instantly recognisable as are visual images, (making convincing 'reality' in radio plays is much more difficult than in television drama!). There always remains some doubt or ambiguity about the 'reality' of an aural landscape and this is a significant feature when approaching the composition of a musicmontage piece. As our pseudo-real landscape therefore is only apparently real we can easily step outside possible or known realities, e.g. imagine two people talking in a busy street; one of them opens a door, goes through and appears to be underwater. Both landscapes involved here are pseudo-real, but the combination is an impossibility.

As a more interesting example consider a duet for bellowing elephant and singing wren. This event can be 'orchestrated' on tape and both elements would remain realistic; the result is however an impossible landscape. As a visual analogy one can think of surrealist paintings in which incongruous objects are juxtaposed to create an impossible reality. This approach can be extended to create a whole world of imaginary landscapes, in which events recognisable in themselves appear in impossible contexts, behave in unlikely ways or combine with sounds which are not recognisable. We can, for example, observe in reality a fly flying round a room. On tape, however, we can create a room flying around a fly, a voice flying around a room, a voice flying around a fly, and so on.

There are many other kinds of landscape. One particular example is the style of verbal delivery of a disc jockey and its combination with snippets of music, vocal slogans and fade-ups and fade-downs of adjacent pieces of music. This very specific kind of landscape is not real in the sense that it is just the sound of naturally occurring events (it is in fact often collaged from prerecorded tapes, especially in totally automated rock-music radio stations such as are found in California) but it is sufficiently familiar within our culture to be easily recognisable. Similarly, the aural format of news magazines, quiz programmes or even the formal radio presentation of broadcast concerts may be viewed as other special types of landscape associated with the broadcasting media and we can refer to these as *media landscapes*. It is possible to imagine presenting something which conforms entirely to the style and format of a disc-jockey show but where, in fact, all the sound constituents are changed. In this way we use a known landscape with incongruous material, and this is in all ways similar to our previous discussion of the creation of imaginary landscapes from pseudo-real landscapes.

It may also be seen, however, as one particular type of category which we might call *cross-landscapes*. Here in effect the characteristics of one landscape are imposed on another. Thus the typical crescendo, fall in pitch and decrescendo as sounds pass from one speaker to the other (Doppler effect), which one might associate with passing traffic, could be superimposed on the voices of a conversation. In this way the characteristics of two separate landscapes are superimposed (crossed) to create an imaginary landscape which however carries 'resonances' of both of them, and may suggest some meaningful link between them or ideas associated with them.

Another example of cross-landscape is the 'Word Machine' in *Red Bird*. We hear what appears to be a machine (aural cues are the repeating cycle of operations, and also often some quiet superimposed metallic noises, actually a double-speed version of a recording in a sheet-metal factory, which create a factory-like context) but on closer inspection the sound is constructed entirely out of verbal material ('t, t, t, t, t', 'rea', 'i', 'nnn', 'sss'), which are themselves syllables or elements of the phrase 'Listen to Reason', prominently used elsewhere in the piece. In this way a deeper link is suggested between the purely rational use of language (the idea of listening to reason is itself odd!) and a mechanical world or mechanistic world-view.

This idea of *substitution* is apparent in other parts of *Red Bird*. Thus in the opening section, where the prisoner appears to be being thumped, a closer inspection reveals some of the thumping sounds to be words, books and doors – the aural image is not so literal as appears on first hearing.

This type of ambiguity of images can be created however without recourse to such complex sound constructions. Thus the other machine ('Body Machine') in *Red Bird* might be interpreted as a machine or as the sounds of breathing and a heart pumping. How we hear it depends on aural cues and space context. On its first appearance, the previous sounds (of a person running and crying out) are the aural cues for us to hear it as body sounds. As it continues, however, the reverberation gradually increases dramatically (to give the spatial illusion of a large factory) and the aural cue of factory noise (the sounds mentioned previously) together make us reinterpret it as a machine (bellows and pump). In this case we have transformed the landscape (or interpretation) of a sound, without changing the sound itself.

Vocal landscapes

An important family of landscapes is that which uses the human voice. People conversing in a room, or a soloist singing a song are types of 'real' landscape which we might recreate on tape. But with voice on tape we can go far beyond this. Voices can now be 'disembodied' and made to move rapidly through vast spaces, or to leap inexplicably (in terms of our experience of real landscapes) from one reverberant space to another, or to merge into 'abstract' sounds (all can be found in *Gesang der Jünglinge*), or to sustain impossibly long sequences of activity (*Visage*), or to transform into other recognisable sounds (e.g. birdsong, as in *Red Bird*) or to flock together and move off like birds (ditto). The very recognisability of the human voice makes it particularly suited to these 'impossible' transformations because, no matter how unlikely we make the context, we continue to associate the voice with its immediate source (a human being); the conflict of the clearly recognised and known source with the distinctly unnatural context can create powerfully affective sound imagery.

The style of verbal delivery may also vary in so many ways, from the type of voice (man, woman; young, old), to the mode of delivery (whispering, speaking, various modes of singing, shouting), the style and manner of delivery (hesitant, exaggeratedly expressive etc.), the 'channel' of delivery (natural speech, speech through a telephone, speech apparently underwater, broadcast speech) and so on. (This is without discussing accents, languages and meaning.) All these factors contribute towards suggesting a landscape for the voice which may be enhanced or contradicted by other aural cues. Although many of these factors may be, and often are, exploited in musical composition for concert performance they are usually not thought of in landscape terms. This is partly due to the music tradition of listening to sounds *as if* they were essentially abstract. It is also, however, due to the conflicting *visual* landscape of the concert hall.

Consider, for example, a recording of a contemporary piece of vocal writing which uses the voice entirely in various unconventional ways (whispering, shouting, use of words broken up into their constituent syllables and so on) accompanied by a piano. The presence of the piano immediately suggests the landscape of 'concert performance' (though it need not – we could perhaps be listening to a recording of a deranged person in a room with a piano!), a socially formal context in which these unusual vocal sounds are produced. In a sense therefore these new sounds lose some of their dramatic power – the vocalist is doing what is indicated in a score, just like the pianist, as we know from our experience of concerts.

Next imagine a similar piece on tape in which the vocalist is accompanied by a variety of tape-recorded environmental sounds, e.g. the sounds of machinery or birdsong, which themselves may be recorded and/or transformed in numerous ways. Looking at this latter material in a conventional musical way it is clearly possible to organise it in such a manner as to produce an interesting piece of music, just as if we were writing for voice and piano. However, at the same time, the removal of the piano removes the contextualising sound which makes us think 'concert'. We are now free to hear the voice and accompanying sounds as suggesting numerous other contexts. The deviations from normal singing (whispering, shouting etc.) can thus suggest transformations of the total landscape of the sounds, the vocalist may in fact *be* deranged or dreaming or 'speaking in tongues', or a disembodied voice floating in space, and not merely conventionally 'pretending' to be the same – there is no conflicting real context (a singer/speaker actually standing in front of us) to contradict our immediate aural perception. It is this power of tape to transform aural landscape which is of special significance.

Although many musicians have argued that tape-music is generally speaking a second-rate alternative to live musical performance, this is a very one-sided view.

Clearly the lack of the visual/theatrical element and the spontaneous interpretative aspect of live performance cannot be matched by a work on tape. However there are many features of composition on tape which are not available in a live performance and this potential for the radical and convincing transformation of sound landscape is one of the most powerful features of tape composition not available in live concert music.

Understanding the sounds

Having reached a general understanding of how we might use recognisable sounds in musicmontage composition we still have to come to grips with their musical organisation. Most recognisable real-world sounds, outside the specialist field of *conventional musical* sounds, are not only immediately complex (timbrally very rich) but also are complexly articulated in time.

Complex timbre may be explained as follows. We are used to thinking about sound primarily in terms of pitch, duration and volume. In the recognition or differentiation of complex real-world sounds, however, these may be the least significant factors. We might more usefully look at the pitch-bands (or formants) in which the strongest frequencies occur, the noise and grit (random unpitched click-like attacks) content and its 'rustle-time' (the rate of occurrence), the type of glissandi through which constituents (pitched or unpitched) move, the complexity of all of these and so on.

Complex articulation may be explained by considering a birdsong. Such a song cannot be specified by a single note but only by a group of characteristic phrases. Thus the musical object we start from is already quite developed. In addition the internal pitch-structure of such a song (which we can often only hear clearly when it is slowed down abour four times) is not only untempered (lying outside our normal 12-note scale) but contains many notes whose pitch is vague because of rapid portamento, or the use of modulation producing bell-like chords. At the usual speed of birdsong, to the human ear all these details meld together to produce a characteristic perceived gestalt. We need to be able to compose with these gestalts.

Relating to conventional musical sources

The first problem we might consider is how to integrate a complex recognisable real-world sound with more conventional musical sources. From the very beginning I have largely abandoned the use of normal musical instruments, for two reasons. First of all, they are much too inflexible with regard to timbre (and most of them to pitch – most real-world sounds do not conform to tempered scales!). Secondly, either they or the real-world sound appear incongruous – the landscape is contradictory (musical instrument with machine sound – is it a concert in a factory?). Voices on the other hand are almost universally useful. As the voice is used in many other locations outside musical contexts we do not produce such a jarring landscape contradiction by using voices with other real-world sounds. At the same time the voice is uniquely malleable with respect to both timbral modification and pitch inflection. In the most difficult of musicmontage techniques, the 'natural' (see below) transformation of one sound into another, the malleability of the voice is almost indispensable, and most of the successful transformations in *Red Bird* will be found to involve vocal sounds as one of the constituents.

The simplest approach to integrating real-world sounds into a more conventional musical context is to use the real-world sounds live in a performance, which is then recorded. A simple example is the use of car horns in the section of *Journey into Space* mentioned above. Here correspondences and musical relationships are established partly by the choice of complementary sound sources (in this case, toy trumpets) and partly through the intuitive judgements of the performers. This technique may of course be extended to live-performance pieces using either everyday sounds or rerecordings of the latter as elements in live-performance pieces (e.g. the use of dogs barking and other animal noises in *Beach Singularity*).

To achieve a more defined relationship between the real-world sounds and others we select specific audible characteristics of the real-world sounds and attempt to relate musically to these. In a simple improvisatory procedure for the tape piece *Machine*, steam-outlet noise from a power station was collaged with filtered noise from a synthesiser and whispered words with prominent sibilants taken from a list provided by me. Likewise in *Journey into Space*, the syllable rolled 'rr' is caused to pan across the stereo space at the same time as motorbikes are similarly panning (actually driving past the microphones).

My earliest approach to composing with this kind of material (in the tape piece *Machine: an electronically preserved dream*) was more controlled. Here I captured certain complex machine sounds on tape loops and then asked a choir to imitate these sounds (or some aspect of them) as closely as possible and then gradually diverge from them. This process of imitation and divergence, although improvised, was very carefully controlled. The initial imitation was decided upon by a principal conductor who got the choir to imitate him. Control of different parts of the choir could then be divided among up to eight conductors as the process of divergence proceeded.

In all these cases much more material than was required was generated by these procedures and a selection made for use in the tape composition according to how successfully the sound relationships (or the processes of gradual divergence) had been achieved.

The Word Machine in *Red Bird*, mentioned previously, adopts a much more sophisticated approach to this same problem – how to establish a musical link between vocal and real-world sounds. Here edited bits of words are used to construct in sound on tape a gestalt which appears to be a machine. In this way there is no longer any dichotomy between the sound constituents of the words and of the machine – they are one and the same. This approach does however rely on the ability to create the convincing aural illusion 'machine'.

This is not always possible. Hence in *Red Bird* I also attempted to transform a vocal sound ('zzz') convincingly into the sound of a fly. This could be achieved half-convincingly when the two sounds were not juxtaposed. However as the rationale for attempting this construction was to be able to make a continuous transition from the vocal 'zzz' to the fly, this limitation was crucial. Given the equipment at my disposal I was obliged to use a different approach (I in fact recorded a bluebottle and made the necessary transitions from the vocal sound by sudden edited changes through a loud staccato sound).

Montage

We need not, however, attempt to relate our real-world sounds to conventional sound sources. We may consider techniques more appropriate to the real-world sounds themselves. The most immediately obvious approach is that of sound-image montage, where we superimpose (mix) or juxtapose in time (edit) a number of sound images.

In a series of superimposed images (e.g. the 'garden' sequence in *Red Bird*) we need to consider some of the following questions.

(a)   How many sound images may be reasonably superimposed without masking one another, or creating a confused aural image?

(b)   How similar or different do such sound images need to be to produce a clearly defined (or a blended) texture? We must consider not only the pitch areas of each sound image (e.g. avoiding using similar sound-images. in the same pitch area if we're aiming for clarity of each image), its timbral qualities (e.g. its stressed formants etc.), but also its style and complexity of articulation (e.g. a complexly articulated sound is more easily differentiated from a simply articulated sound than from another complexly articulated sound; a glissando articulation from a non-glissando articulation, especially if the sounds are similar in all other respects).

(c)   How can the separation or melding of such images be enhanced? The careful use of stereo, dynamics and reverberation will help to separate sound images clearly (in the *Red Bird* 'garden' montage we can hear sounds in eight separate locations).
Conversely, to blend sounds we may project them in mono.

(d)   What are the important musical characteristics of the montage? We may want a very dense texture becoming less dense, or vice versa; a gradual frequency spread from treble only, to treble with bass; a change in the articulation of the constituents (e.g. becoming more internally varied, becoming less active, becoming narrower in range etc.); a change in the variety of the constituents (e.g. from a texture of constant novelty to one with fixed, recurring constituents) and so on.

(e)   How are we to move from this particular collection of sound images to another? And so on.

'Classical' approaches to the voice

If we now wish to control the sound images themselves we have many techniques available. The treatment of vocal material in tape pieces such as *Gesang der Jünglinge* and *Visage* may be viewed as a point of reference for certain voice techniques in musicmontage. Although these two compositions are usually viewed as being in the tradition of conventional tape music the fact that they employ words or vocal gestures means that they are already using complex and *recognisable* gestalt sounds as material for composition. Landscape considerations therefore come into play, even if only in a subconscious manner.

Given a consistent set of vocal materials, e.g. the sounds of a particular voice, or alternatively a specific text spoken by different voices, the use of certain classical techniques defines a landscape. Within this landscape there are of course interesting and uninteresting, effective and ineffective ways of ordering the material. Whether the landscape or the ideas about musical organisation occurred first in the conception of the piece, the musical problems remain the same. (With *Gesang der Jünglinge* it seems likely that the latter predominated, though some unconscious grasp of a particular aural landscape seems apparent in the very concept of the piece – exploring the continuum between vocal sounds and pure electronic sounds.)

Knots and strings

One very useful advanced technique involves the formation of a dense texture out of the original sound gestalts. Imagine we have a scream lasting half a second. We can copy this at various slightly different speeds, thus changing the pitch of each copy to various slightly different extents. Mixing these together would produce a chord of screams. Instead however we could try putting the pitch-changed screams on short loops of different and unrelated lengths. When these are played back simultaneously we will produce a continuous texture in which the time relationships and vertical combinations of the screams are constantly changing, a 'screaming' texture.

In practice however this simple technique is unsatisfactory. No matter how dense the texture, the regularity of loop repeats is noticeable, and the total effect sounds 'unnatural'. By this I mean to suggest that textures of related sounds occurring in nature, e.g. a flock of herring gulls, are similarly constructed to our 'flock' of screams except that there are no absolutely regular repetitions of the elements. To achieve this natural texturing we must in fact make our loops, make numerous copies from each loop and then edit-in leader tape (or edit-out silent tape) in such a way that the distances between repeats of the same sound are totally irregular. When the thus adjusted tapes are mixed together we produce a 'natural' texture. This is how various such textures in *Red Bird* were made.

Of course it may be that we want a particularly unnatural texturing, but this must be thought out in landscape terms. In a piece like *Red Bird* where the sound world is focused on a semi-naturalistic, if mythical, landscape we wish to avoid at all costs the listener's sudden realisation, 'Ah! that's made with loops'; we only wish to draw the listener's attention to a mechanical procedure when a mechanistic landscape is intended. At one point in *Red Bird* we do hear a bird-like sound which repeats absolutely regularly but here the natural/mechanical ambiguity is intended.

These textures of gestalts (which I call 'knots' if short, and 'strings' if long) may have internal structures of their own, e.g. they may diverge continuously in pitch from a central point, as with the flocking words in *Red Bird*. Whatever their internal structure, provided they do not diverge too widely in pitch (speed) from their source gestalt, they have certain compositional advantages. Such a 'knot' retains the sound characteristics of the original gestalt, but these characteristics are averaged out and blurred by the multiple superimpositions involved: this makes them more malleable to conventional *concrète* techniques. It also makes them very useful in achieving sound-transformations.

Transformation

The ultimate technique, and the most difficult, in making powerful musicmontage composition is that of transforming one recognisable sound 'naturally' into another. In *Red Bird*, words change into birds, books into doors, water into birds and so on.

The technique is analogous to film animation. In cartoon films people's necks may be twisted into impossible shapes, one object changes into another, with apparent ease. Film animation is time-consuming, but not difficult, and the two-dimensional image is almost infinitely pliable. Sounds are, by comparison, intractable. However, transformations in sound also have a different affective quality and this is similar to the difference between music and sequences of silent images. Perhaps it is the fact of transformation of images combined with their powerfully affective quality which links the experience of musicmontage so strongly with that of dreams.

When we say that a transformation is 'natural' we imply that the transformation process does not contradict the landscape of the sounds being transformed, and this is the source of technical difficulty. To explain more clearly what is meant, let us imagine attempting to transform the sound of a scream into that of a bird 'naturally'. It would be very easy to make this transformation without this latter condition, e.g. using standard voltage-control techniques we could modulate both sounds with a complex electronic signal to produce a very dense electronic sound. Then by careful use of the controls we could cross-fade continuously from the scream to this electronic complex and out again to the bird.

However, in doing this we have introduced clearly electronic-source sounds, immediately changing the nature of the sound landscape. In particular it tends to suggest immediately that someone is artificially *making* the transformation by using electronic apparatus. In fact even the smallest trace of sound having an 'electronic sound-source' landscape will destroy the 'natural' illusion. We must create the impression that we merely went out with a microphone into somebody's imagination and made a direct recording of a scream becoming a bird!

In this particular case (the opening sound in *Red Bird*) the transition is made by choosing a birdsong phrase whose opening part is characterised rhythmically (a series of rapid clicks). This is used to modulate the loudness of the scream (itself at half-speed and therefore quite long). The transition then moves from the scream, through the scream cut up into a series of separate attacks, to a series of exactly synchronised clicks (the birdsong itself) to the final two glissando notes of the birdsong (which make it instantly recognisable as birdsong). All this happens extremely quickly. Here no suggestion of sound from an electronic source is allowed to contradict the landscape.

Experience suggests, unfortunately, that there are no general methods for making transformations from one sound gestalt to another. Each transition depends critically on the nature of the two original sounds. In the above example the pitch content and continuity of the scream alongside the unpitched click-like quality and the discontinuous pulsation of the birdsong allowed a simple transition to be made. Our first task in attempting any transition, therefore, is to find two suitably 'matched' sounds. This implies that any score we make before composing a piece must confine itself to general descriptions of sounds, rather than particular descriptions.

Let us examine this more closely. One of the principal discoveries a composer makes when moving to the studio after working with notes on paper is that *sounds themselves* are infinitely richer than he might have suspected. What can be written down in conventional notation is only a tiny fraction of the qualities of a sound, and all these qualities can be used and controlled in the studio. Most composers therefore spend a long time learning about how to control these aspects of sound lying outside conventional notation, and learning to compose them by experience, and without scores. Unless he wishes to ignore this new experience completely, a composer must be very familiar with working with sounds in a studio before he can begin to precompose what he intends to do in a score. Then a new problem arises: not only are there no accepted conventions for notating most aspects of sound (e.g. filtering, reverberation, articulation of formants etc.) but, practically speaking, it is impossible to capture all aspects of a sound in any notation system.

Therefore any precomposed score is necessarily to some degree an outline of events which are to take place in the piece, a *generalised* version of events of which the piece will be the *particular realisation*. With *Red Bird*, which was largely precomposed, most of the transformations which occur were written in a score. But these transformations were specified in a *general* way, e.g. *scream changes into birdsong*, with notes on the musical effect desired. The studio task was then to find and 'match' a particular scream with a particular bird and make the particular realisation of this specification.

In making transformations the voice, as has already been mentioned, is a particularly valuable 'instrument' because of its almost total malleability. Another im-

portant factor can be speed of transformation. Thus the transition *Reasonab(le)
to the sounds of bubbling water* was made quite simply by speaking the sound
Reasonab-(vocal imitation of water), filtering the latter half of the sound to make
it approximate more closely to the frequency band of the second sound, and cross-
fading very rapidly to the sound of bubbling water (actually at half-speed). In these
situations the details of filtering and fading are crucial to achieving a successful
result.

Another extremely useful technique is the use of knots or strings (see above).
The problem with complex gestalts is that they have such *particular* sound
characteristics. If we can somehow average out and blur these characteristics, the
task of finding a matching sound is much simplified.

One of the most successful transformations in *Red Bird* is the syllable 'Lis', of
'Listen', changing into birdsong. The first stage of making this involved saying
'Liss. . .' with an extended 'ss' and gradually introducing (in performance) bird-
like whistling into the 'ss' sound. This was a matter of performance and numerous
attempts were recorded before a satisfactory transition was achieved. Next, a
reasonably closely matching birdsong was chosen and altered in pitch to correspond
with the pitch area of the whistling. Finally a string of *'ss'* to *whistle-tones* was
made superimposing four *different* performances, but mixing these so that they
appear to originate in a single voice's 'Lis . . .'. This was then cross-faded (slowly)
with a string made up of four different stretches of the birdsong superimposed
on one another in such a way that they appeared to lead into a single bird. In this
way a focused 'Li' leads through a defocused area of whistling and birdsong where
the crucial transition is made, back to a focused bird.

An example of musicmontage composition

I propose to finish by looking at one particular complex example of musicmontage:
the machine finale of *Red Bird*. This consists primarily of two machines, the Word
Machine and the Body Machine, both of which have been discussed earlier.

The context set by a recapitulation of the thumping sequence and the slamming
of a door at the start of this section is one of a horrific mechanical prison or torture-
chamber. However, the symbolic nature of the two machines and the non-realistic
sequence of events makes this a symbolic prison, the *Universal Factory*.

The general effect of this sequence is of the oppressive interminability of the
machines which have entrapped the prisoner. However, for the machines merely to
cycle on would not create this effect at all. It would very quickly become boring!
We must create this illusion, surprising though it may seem, by having the machines
constantly pause and change speed. To complicate this picture, each machine has
linked to it a number of 'squeaks' (i.e. the machinery appears to squeak as it turns).
These 'squeaks' are however made out of not immediately recognisable human
screams, and animal and bird noises. From time to time these emerge as recognisable human screams or animals and birds from the sounds of machinery, then re-

merge into the machinery. In addition, the particular 'squeak' constituents of the machines change gradually. Both these facts imply that the volume levels of these constituents are changing in a gradual manner for most of the time.

Let us determine how we will construct this sequence of sounds (ignoring all other factors). The basic machine sounds could be on loops. As the 'squeak' constituents change in volume, however, unless we have a multitrack tape recorder, we cannot put these on the same loop. With normal tape recorders we need to synchronise (in length and starting position) the machine loop with the loops carrying 'squeaks' and mix them, varying the levels of the 'squeaks' as we mix. If we have a large number of 'squeak' constituents we may need more than one such mix. There is no way we can keep these separate loops in synchronisation with each other over a long period of time. However it is best to make such complicated sequences of sounds in short sections, so that we can deal with only a few problems at a time, editing the segments together later. So the long-term synchronisation problem is not crucial.

To change the speed of the machines we cannot merely vary the tape recorder speed as this will change the pitch also, which we don't want. What we have to do is shorten the loop. However we can't edit the loop *anywhere* as at most places it will merely sound edited, destroying the landscape 'machine' (and replacing it by the landscape 'tape loop'). We can therefore list all the possible edit points in the loop, and note how much of the original can be removed. This enables us to shorten the loop (speed up the 'machine') in various ways. Once however we have added the 'squeaks' to our machine there are even fewer places where we can edit convincingly. In practice the 'squeaks' must be added to each *edited* machine loop, which involves making up a new set of 'squeak' loops synchronised with the edited machine loop for every differently edited machine loop.

Considering all these problems we need to break down the construction of the section into as small units as possible. Take, for example, the sequence of pauses in the machines. Apart from varying the timing and length of these (and their sound context, for when the machines stop we hear other sounds, such as the prisoner and the clock) we have three types of pause to consider. The Word Machine may pause while the Body Machine continues (a); the Body Machine may pause while the Word Machine continues (b); or both machines may pause (c):

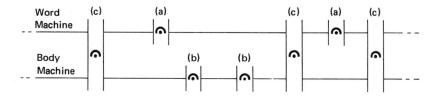

We may imagine the two machines (together with their associated 'squeaks' and interruptions) as two contrapuntal lines in a sound composition. The way we then lay out their pauses, the duration (sound content as well) of these pauses and the machine speed changes becomes a two-part contrapuntal exercise in achieving the particular musical effect we desire.

To complicate matters, every time a machine stops we produce an 'unnatural' effect as we are merely editing a tape; machine sounds don't instantaneously cease when the machine stops. These stops must therefore be masked in some way, and in *Red Bird* various loud attack sounds from the rest of the piece are used for this purpose.

Finally we can decide how to put all this together. When both machines stop at once we can edit across the total sound, putting the masking sound at the beginning of the next bit of tape. When these are later edited together and appropriate reverberation added, the effect of continuity is convincing. Thus we can divide the score into a number of sections running from one two-machine-stop to another. These can be made separately:

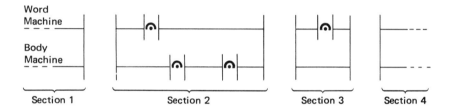

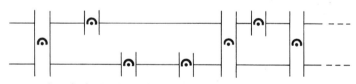

sections 1—4 edited together, with silent pauses between them

Within each of these mixes we may have either machine stopping by itself (and possibly restarting at a different speed). This can only be achieved by mixing-down each machine sequence separately, making the necessary edit insertions in each, and then mixing the two lines together.

First these eight sections are made:

These are then edited together appropriately:

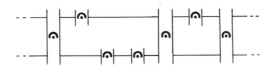

These larger items are then mixed together appropriately:

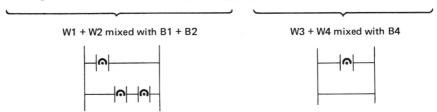

These mixes are then themselves edited together:—

Hence our sequence of operations is strictly defined by the musical structure of the material.

A final and very significant factor has to be borne in mind. If we are making a section of tape involving lots of previous mixing, and this is to be edited (via an interruption) to a similar section of tape which is meant to appear, aurally, as a continuation of the first, the two tapes must match exactly. Therefore a very precise note of the volume levels (and possible filter settings etc.) of all the constituents must be kept through all the previous mixes involved in making the two tapes. Only with this degree of control can we assure a perfectly convincing aural landscape.

From this outline it can be seen that very detailed work on tape requires, apart from anything else, a systematic approach to organising and documenting practical work. However with this detailed approach we can produce striking results. Thus, at one point in this sequence we hear just one of the machines and its many squeaks which up till now we have heard only as squeaks. Suddenly the machine stops and the squeaks continue, still mechanically repeating. For an instant we continue to hear them as squeaks, but as an additional 'squeak' type sound enters we suddenly realise these are all animal and bird noises, the 'garden' image of the piece is suddenly revealed. Almost at the same moment the machine starts up again and all these squeaks, including the new sound, resume their previous role. The *Universal Factory* grinds on. This all happens in a moment and depends partly for its effect on the context created by the remainder of the piece.

Such an effect of instant and surprising landscape transformation can clearly only be achieved through the very careful organisation of materials and detailed working we have described. However, when after endless preliminary editing, mixing, edit-testing, loop-synchronisation, list-making and frustrating mistakes one finally hears what one has been aiming at for weeks, or even months, it can be a magical experience.

A sequence of excerpts from *Red Bird* can be heard on the cassette (*Cassette example 7.1*).

8 Making and performing simple electroacoustic instruments

HUGH DAVIES

Historically almost by accident, the principal development of electronic music so far has been inextricably linked with the storage of sounds on magnetic tape. If the pressure of wartime scientific research in Germany had not hastened the final stages of improvement of magnetic tape and tape recorders in the early 1940s, it is possible that the experimentation in early electronic music and *musique concrète* which was under way in several countries less than ten years later might have led to methods of producing these sounds directly in concert performance.

Breakthrough to commercial viability is not, however, necessarily the final technological leap forward. For example, it is expected that digital tape recorders will be widely available at compatible prices by the mid-1980s, with very considerable improvements in recording quality compared with present standards. Yet it is interesting to note that, until the development of the telephone and the phonograph in consecutive years during the 1870s, audio and optical communications devices were *primarily* digital (such as those that used the Morse code) up to and including the misfunctioning prototype *Harmonic Telegraph* (Bell) and the speeded-up replay of the *Telegraph Repeater* (Edison) that stimulated these two inventors into their breakthroughs which ushered in a century of *analogue* devices.

If we look at the musical precursors of electronic music as we have come to know it, two of the four main areas of experimentation were concerned with recording (manipulated or retrograde gramophone records and hand-drawn or retrograde film soundtracks) and two with live performance (electric musical instruments and mechanical or electromechanical noise machines). The most significant compositions in this period up to 1948 that primarily feature such equipment (apart from the use of electric instruments, such as the ondes Martenot, as one element in works for large conventional forces, by Varèse and Messiaen for example) are a series of *Imaginary Landscapes* composed by John Cage between 1939 and 1942. These three pieces formed one aspect of Cage's current explorations of unusual percussion instruments (including the prepared piano of 1938) and use, among other things, a contact microphone, a gramophone cartridge to amplify a coil of wire, oscillators and oscillator tones recorded on discs which are manipulated by hand; the whole designed to be recorded live in a radio studio, but easily performable live in a concert once such equipment, together with reasonably portable amplifiers and loudspeakers, became generally accessible during the 1950s.

[152]

Without wishing to deny the value of tape in electronic music, I should like to suggest (and have done so for several years) that it is likely that live performance with electronic music apparatus will become the principal method of presentation, with tape reserved for certain more complex operations that cannot be carried out in real time. The relationship has existed throughout musical history in the West, the Middle East and the Far East: nearly all music has been performed live, with a few pieces specially composed for musical clocks, musical automata, mechanical (mainly keyboard) instruments and other antecedents of the musical box (for which Hassler, W. F. Bach, C. P. E. Bach, Handel, Haydn, Mozart, Beethoven, Stravinsky, Hindemith and Stockhausen – among many others – have composed works). The tensions that come into play during performance in front of an audience are an important part of the final musical result, and many performers find it hard to re-create the same feelings artificially for themselves when in a recording studio. Today the composer–performer is once again on the increase, after a decline during the last one and a half centuries, and thus 'live electronic music' is a quite natural development; many composers who were dedicated to working with tape during the 1950s – including such opposite poles as Cage and Stockhausen – became equally involved in live electronic music during the 1960s.

From the several areas of live electronic music, which include the use of devices such as filters and ring modulators to modify the sounds of voices or conventional instruments and performance on synthesisers, I shall limit myself here to electro-acoustic instruments.

The processes of choosing the sound qualities that a composer wants are considerably restricted by the instruments or apparatus available. Often a composer is forced to limit these to the narrow range imposed by the instrumentation that he or she has selected or which has been externally defined by the terms of a commission; on other occasions the composer may hear music in his or her head and will search to find the most suitable instrumentation for it. If the latter is not possible with traditional instruments recourse may have to be made to the electronic music studio. In a small studio the equipment required may be its complete installations; in a very large studio it will be only a small proportion of it. A notable example of the latter is Stockhausen's 35-minute-long *Kontakte,* which only employed thirteen devices (plus five tape recorders), but with great technical ingenuity and expertise, to produce an enormous range of sounds.

Thus the basic way in which a composer works until he or she is as familiar with the possibilities of a particular electronic music studio as with those of an orchestra (a knowledge that is largely assimilated unconsciously in the course of day-to-day experience of music over many years, starting in childhood) is very much trial and error, exploring sounds and sound combinations that he or she likes. Exactly the same process applies to inventing new musical instruments, acoustic as well as electroacoustic. The inventor accumulates experience in assessing the suitability of cetain materials and the unsuitability of others, in knowing which type of microphone will be the most appropriate, and even why one microphone is much better in the instrument in question than one which is apparently very similar. I have sometimes found that a microphone or sound object that I have bought in the hope that it will be particularly effective initially turns out not to be so, but at a later date proves to be ideal for something else; thus the instrument that has the most extensive range of sound possibilities of all those that I have made was built in a single day as a result of 'giving another chance' to a type of microphone that I had bought as second-best because the shop in question was out of stock of the type I was really looking for.

All this is rationalisation after the event. My own development has been briefly as follows. After limited experience both of small tape studios and of live trans-formation of instrumental sounds, I started to assemble my own private studio with limited funds, and expanded my very small range of sound materials by amplifying everyday items (such as combs, small springs, broken light bulbs etc.) with contact microphones. A year later, in the summer of 1968, I produced what I soon recog-nised as my first self-contained amplified instrument. With this clarification of my activity (paralleled by concert performances involving amplified objects and elec-tronic transformation of sounds played by live performers) I was able to progress as an instrument inventor, trying out a wider range of materials and microphones, and expanding my range of creations to include 'sound sculptures' for exhibitions and – unamplified – sound toys. An additional strong influence in this expansion, and in increasing my self-confidence in the visual aspects, has been my collaboration from time to time since 1969 with the artist John Furnival. Everything that follows is based on my own experience or on direct observation of the experiences of friends and colleagues. Although mine has been an exploratory, unplanned development, over the years most of the gaps have been filled in.

As an inventor of electroacoustic instruments I have been told on a number of occasions by electronic composers that they had worked for several hours in an electronic music studio to produce a particular sound that was very similar to one that I had just played on one of my instruments. (A simple example: slowly pulling one's finger over the bristles of an amplified toothbrush, or pulling a toothbrush in a similar way across an instrument amplified by a contact microphone, can resemble filtered white noise!) Such instruments need not only be used in concert perfor-mance, of course; several electronic composers have used a selection of 'my' sounds in tape compositions, and on a couple of occasions when I myself have worked with tape I have done the same.

This chapter will consist of a discussion of the various types of microphones that can be used, notes on some of the materials that are effective in instrument building and a more detailed description of four of the instruments that I have made.

Microphones

When I first set out to write this chapter, it only gradually dawned on me that no single microphone that I have ever used in any of my electroacoustic instruments is now commercially available in Britain. Models have been discontinued, manufacturers have gone out of business, and shops selling old-fashioned electrical bits and pieces have been replaced by shops specialising in microcomputers and pocket digital calculators or in disco equipment. In only ten years everything in the electronics world has changed.

In my original chapter, half finished, I took most of the space to describe the various microphones that had been so easy to obtain in London when I first began constructing instruments. This became far too complicated for a book of this nature. I have therefore considerably reduced the section devoted to microphones, in the expectation that anyone who wishes actually to build their own microphones will either already know more or less how to go about doing so, or realise the necessity of collaborating with someone who has the necessary technical background. I have given some hints on how to start, but few precise details. Each person experimenting with amplified sounds will have different aims and ideas, will try out different materials and would assemble a range of microphones different from my own even if all those that I have been able to choose from were still available. There are still a few relatively cheap microphones on the market under such names as 'lapel microphone' which, in the right hands, could probably produce excellent results, although the choice is considerably smaller than it was at the end of the 1960s. Anyone coming across any of the older types shouldn't hesitate to buy them on the off-chance that they might turn out to be ideal!

An electroacoustic instrument is one which relates, not necessarily in any immediately obvious manner, to one or more traditional instruments with the addition of a special microphone. In the context of this chapter it is further defined as an instrument that is virtually inaudible, at least in a concert, without the use of this microphone and an associated amplification system. The best known electroacoustic instrument is the electric guitar, invented in the middle 1930s, shortly after the less successful electroacoustic violins, cellos and pianos were built. Typically, the microphone is installed as a permanent part of the instrument in a position where the most faithful equivalent of the instrument's acoustic ancestor is achieved. The use of similar special microphones as alternatives to the normal 'air' microphones, merely to amplify a traditional instrument, concerns us here only insofar as such microphones serve for comparisons.

When inventing completely new electroacoustic instruments, fidelity to a known sound is less relevant. One must make one's own decision, relying on musical judgement, as to what the ideal sound of each instrument is to be. I usually either build the microphone permanently into the instrument, or provide a single position where the microphone is always fixed. Occasionally – mostly with magnetic microphones – I find that I wish to have a freer relationship between the microphone and the vibrating, sound-producing object. Sometimes an additional factor is the need to be able to pack the instrument away for transportation, which with fragile materials and certain kinds of contact microphones is best done by dismantling at least part of the instrument (ten of the instruments that I use most frequently in concerts pack away in a single cardboard box which measures only 27 x 27 x 14 cm). Since an electroacoustic instrument has no 'real' sound apart from what is heard over the loudspeaker (and this is likely to vary with different amplification systems and rooms even more than is the case with conventional instruments), the inventor may choose to exploit what would normally be considered as distortion or an uneven frequency response in order to focus on more unusual sound qualities.

Two main kinds of microphone are used: contact microphones and magnetic pick-ups. The former include a variety of commercial and home-made devices, such as 'normal' contact microphones, record cartridges, strain gauges, accelerometers, stethoscope microphones, throat microphones and microphone or hearing aid inserts; the latter are found on electric guitars, in certain old telephones, some military and industrial microphones and headphones and a few brands of cheaper hi-fi headphones.

Contact microphones

These function by being in direct physical contact with the object which is to be amplified, and are not sensitive to air vibrations unless these are so strong as to cause the microphone's container to vibrate, such as by speaking or blowing with one's mouth only a couple of centimetres away. Most types of contact microphone are rather fragile, and so particular care should be taken not to drop them or even to submit them to direct vibrations of too strong a nature, such as those of percussion instruments. The most useful contact microphones for our purposes are usually based on a piezoelectric ceramic crystal (these are the fragile types); a few use magnetic or other principles.

Until 1975 a cheap Japanese contact microphone, known variously as 'guitar' or 'harmonica' microphone, was widely available, but its importer at the time, Tandy Corporation (Radio Shack), withdrew it from their 1976 catalogue. It is possible that it will reappear again one day, since in the past it was unavailable for a long period on a couple of occasions, although never for such a long period as the current one. Another type of contact microphone that I have in the past found in Germany, Merula, may still be available, though it is several years since I have tried to buy one there; it costs about the same as the Japanese one but is of a higher quality, excellent for amplifying traditional stringed instruments, for which the Japanese microphones are inadequate. However, I have only used a Merula microphone for one of my invented instruments, which resembles an amplified fretted cello. Another potential source of contact microphones is in pop music stores, although their prices tend to be excessive.

The kinds of contact microphone that are comparatively easy to obtain are much more expensive – those made by firms such as FRAP and Barcus-Berry. These are specifically designed for individual instruments: guitars, other strings, woodwind, brass, piano and percussion. Perhaps the advent of these much higher-quality contact microphones was the cause of the demise of the cheap Japanese model, since they are ideal for a performer who is likely to buy just one such microphone during his or her working life.

Record cartridges were first used for electroacoustic sounds in *March (Imaginary Landscape No. 2)* by John Cage in 1942, and were later largely featured by him in *Cartridge Music* (1960), one of the earliest live-electronic compositions. In this latter work small items such as lengths of wire, matchsticks, hairpins and pipe-cleaners were inserted into the hole intended for the needle (so big in those days that one can hardly call it a stylus). Modern cartridges, designed for increasingly smaller styli, cannot be used in this way; the older the better, with the early 1960s being the time when cartridges ceased to be suitable for our purposes (mono only!). To use a cartridge as a permanent microphone in an electroacoustic instrument, one feature is of prime importance: a fixing screw set at 90°, or a slightly smaller angle, to the shaft of the needle and designed to hold it tightly in place. This is essential if a string is to be inserted into the cartridge, as on several of my instruments.

As can be expected, record cartridges have an excellent frequency response. I have used them mostly with metal strings (such as those on sale for electric guitars), one end of which is fixed into the cartridge with the fixing screw. Most other contact microphones must be fastened on to the vibrating object, or on to the surface to which this vibrating object is also fixed a short distance away. This is particularly important where the vibrations are very strong and sharp, which will tend to cause distortion of the sound when the microphone directly touches the object, and percussion instruments such as gongs, tam-tams and cymbals could even damage a crystal contact microphone unless some damping material is inserted between them, or the microphone is attached to part of the instrument's stand. If the microphone has some sort of clip, this can often be used; otherwise there is a wide choice of methods that include bolts, screws, wing-nuts, insulating or masking tape, rubber bands, springs and beeswax (this latter is often used for accelerometers and the single-instrument special contact microphones). It is always unwise to use glue: it may hinder the microphone from vibrating freely, and it makes any repair or adjustment of position difficult without damaging the microphone or the instrument.

The frequency responses of other contact microphones vary considerably. Excellent are accelerometers (obtainable from scientific instrument suppliers) and the single-instrument microphones as well as the more expensive general-purpose contact microphones such as the Merula; less good are the Japanese ones, microphones and hearing aid inserts and throat microphones, while stethoscope microphones have an especially strong low bass response. There is, however, a second factor that must be considered in conjunction with frequency response, and that is sensitivity. When dealing with smaller and more delicate vibrations than is the case when amplifying traditional instruments, many of the best quality contact microphones turn out to be ineffective, because the volume level is too low. Here the Japanese microphones have considerable advantages, in addition to their low cost. I have used well over one hundred of them in twelve years, which apart from anything else would have been impossibly expensive with better quality microphones. Their frequency response is adequate, particularly when there is no known original with which to compare the loudspeaker sound. I have always made my electroacoustic instruments in terms of the sound given by the microphones, using the microphones right from the start of the experimentation which is to result in an instrument rather than adding them at the last minute. When, out of interest, I have subsequently tried a Merula contact microphone on an instrument incorporating a Japanese one, the qualities for which I made the instrument have largely vanished – exactly the reverse of the procedure that would take place when comparing these two microphones' effect when used with, say, a violin.

In certain contexts one may want to amplify a large resonant object. Apart from the need, already discussed, to damp the vibrations when using a sensitive crystal contact microphone (which would not be the case, for example, with a Barcus-Berry or FRAP percussion microphone), excellent results can be achieved by using two or more different contact microphones of medium or poor frequency response. Each will give a very different version of the spectrum of the sound, and these can be selected individually or variously combined by employing a mixer channel for each microphone. Similarly, two identical microphones can be placed at different points on an instrument, or fixed or damped differently.

I have never used a throat microphone myself in any way apart from amplifying throat sounds, but I have heard them used effectively as contact microphones on a couple of occasions. It is usually necessary to replace the military or Post Office cable with screened audio cable. Of the other kinds of contact microphones mentioned above, a few comments can be added on each. Accelerometers are extremely expensive precision transducers used in laboratories for testing stresses in materials; I have seen one that had been made up much more cheaply in a university physics department, which worked well as a contact microphone. Strain gauges are used in a similar manner; they are inexpensive and make good general-purpose contact microphones.

The function of stethoscope microphones is self-explanatory; unfortunately the firm which manufactured the ones I have used no longer exists. Doubtless one could discover other brands through catalogues of medical equipment suppliers. Presumably the hearing aid inserts that I bought several years ago are now also unobtainable or obsolete; their size was 12 x 18 mm (some a bit smaller), mostly with very tiny bumps of solder to which a cable had to be wired. Around these inserts I wrapped foam rubber, like a sandwich, with the inside faces covered in glue (in this one instance, if repairs are needed, it is likely to be the foam rubber that gets damaged in dismantling the assembly, and this is easily and cheaply replaced). This reduced their functioning as air microphones and made them into fairly sensitive contact microphones with a frequency response largely restricted to a medium pitch range. I have found them useful in a few contexts. Conventional microphone inserts could also be tried out.

The next problem with contact microphones is their preamplification. Those based on piezoelectric crystals are extremely high in impedance (from about 1 meg-ohm upwards), but do not function satisfactorily with most high impedance micro-phone preamplifiers in mixers and tape recorders, as the output signal is too weak. The only easy solution is to use a low impedance microphone input (about the only instance where a high impedance source connected to a low impedance input will not cause any damage), which gives a normal signal strength, comparable to that of air and magnetic microphones; nevertheless this mismatch will cause considerable clipping of the resulting sound spectrum. In the case of invented instruments this is, once again, of less importance. But when I first tried out instruments of mine, whose sound had been chosen in terms of what the Japanese microphone connected to a low impedance preamplifier gave, with a specially designed high impedance micro-phone preamplifier (as has recently been built for me, in the form of a mixer), an unexpected range of sound was added; more so with some instruments than with others. Once again, the firms that make the high-quality single instrument contact microphones usually also manufacture, at a price, suitable preamplifiers. Accelero-meters are also likely to need special preamplifiers, and should *not* be mismatched into normal low or high impedance microphone preamplifiers.

The high-impedance microphone preamplifier was designed as part of a research project devoted to contact microphones that I undertook in Amsterdam at the end of 1977. I wished to be able to construct my own contact microphones, which would be less fragile than most commercial types, and whose qualities would lie between those of the Japanese ones (extremely sensitive but with poor frequency response) and the much more expensive ones for individual instruments (extremely good frequency response but not very sensitive). Clearly a gain in one aspect is likely to be at the expense of the other. The basis for these contact microphones is the piezoelectric ceramic crystal (PXE), which is quite cheap. Many different models of PXE are manufactured for a variety of purposes, including microphones, headphones and gramophone cartridges. Here are a few general points which may be helpful to anyone who intends to experiment with PXE. The microphone's container should be fairly sturdy, which is not as straightforward as it may sound because one does not have access to mass-production facilities or, usually, to metal casting or shaping equipment. The microscopically flexible nature of the crystal, and the direction or plane in which it bends, should be assisted by the way in which it is mounted, and it should be damped as little as possible by whatever is used to hold it in place. Deliberate distortion of the frequency response could be arrived at by changing the shape of the PXE crystals, which are circular, square or rectangular. Because excessive heat can destroy the nature of the crystal, the PXE should not be cut or sawn, but snapped or drilled ultrasonically. Similarly, if the output cable is to be soldered directly to the PXE, a low temperature soldering iron should be used.

Magnetic pick-ups

The variety of magnetic microphones is considerably less than that of contact microphones. A magnetic pick-up basically consists of a bar magnet around which enamelled (insulated) copper wire has been tightly coiled a considerable number of turns. This is much easier to construct and experiment with in a school science laboratory than a PXE-based contact microphone. Two points only need to be mentioned here: in order to solder an audio lead to the two ends of the copper wire, the enamelling must be scraped or filed off the last centimetre of each end; and there appears to be no simple formula for calculating the number of turns the wire should be coiled around the magnet – first wind a small number of turns, such as 50, and measure the impedance, and then calculate the number of turns required for a specific impedance in a similar ratio. More information can be found in any book which describes in detail the construction of an electric guitar.

Just as different kinds of contact microphones are suitable for different types of vibrating object, so magnetic pick-ups also have a specific area in which they are most effective. Only metallic objects with sufficient iron content will affect the magnetic field and produce a sound; as with the electric guitar, it is not necessary for the object actually to touch the magnet – in some of my instruments they touch and in others they don't.

The most expensive kind of magnetic microphone, but still comparable to medium-priced contact microphones, is the type used in electric guitars. They are the easiest to obtain and can be found in most shops catering for pop music instruments. I have not found them very suitable for my own needs, preferring ones with a single larger, stronger magnet. (But Mauricio Kagel has used an expensive model very effectively for a giant 'harp' in his composition *Unter Strom.*) One may find such magnetic units serving either as microphones *or* as loudspeakers (since each exactly reverses the functioning of the other, there is a point – in telephone systems and related apparatus – where the two are interchangeable). The first magnetic pick-ups that I used came from ex-RAF microphones, which much later I discovered had been used in Spitfires during the Second World War! Subsequently, once the supply of these dried up, I turned to telephone handset *ear*pieces (I have used nearly 100 microphones from each source, plus around 50 from other sources such as the earpieces of headphones used by the military or by telephone operators). It should be stressed that magnetic earpieces were only used in certain models of the older black Bakelite telephones in Britain, and in none of the present-day models. All magnetic microphones and earpieces (with the exception of those made for electric guitars) can be identified by the thin metal 'diaphragm' disc that is placed above the magnet, visible once the protective cover has been unscrewed or otherwise removed. This diaphragm operates when air from the speaker's mouth causes it to vibrate. In an electroacoustic instrument it is replaced by whatever ferrous metal object is to produce the sound (a diaphragm can also be used to alter the sound of an instrument by inserting it between the magnet and this object, and displacing it with regard to the magnet). When the diaphragm is in place it is sufficiently sensitive for the microphone to function not only as an air microphone but also as a contact microphone – such as in throat microphones, which are basically magnetic pick-ups with diaphragms.

An interesting effect that can be obtained by displacing the diaphragm will be described later one.

Some of the magnetic microphones that I use are telephone earpieces that have been removed by undoing two or four bolts and then screwed on to a small piece of wood through the bolt-holes; others are completely dismantled until just the magnet and coils are isolated, and can then be screwed on to the wooden base of an instrument from underneath, facing upwards, set into a small hole that has been specially cut. Nearly all of these magnets are U-shaped, and it is economical and effective to use *each* of the ends of the U to pick the vibration of a single string, spring or similar item (seen in cross-section: Ü).

Even with the range of similar-seeming telephone earpieces there can be considerable differences in impedance: I regularly use ones that have the extremes of 8.2 ohms and 2 kilohms. For most purposes one should try to use magnetic pick-ups which have an impedance of around 100-600 ohms. Some preamplifier inputs designed for low-impedance microphones will not even 'see' an input that is less than about 5 ohms, and treat it like a short circuit. Above 600 ohms, because magnetic microphones produce a stronger voltage than most crystal microphones, they should be connected to a high-impedance microphone input. When more than two parallel strings or springs are used, more than a single pick-up will be necessary, which does not happen with a contact microphone (apart from special filtering effects). It is usually preferable to connect them in series rather than in parallel, which increases rather than reduces the impedance, unless a large number of pick-ups are involved.

When the magnet and coil are left in the original Bakelite holder, some units will be solid, with two small slits in the plastic where the tops of the magnet ends come through, while others will contain an empty space between the magnet and the rim of the holder. Both kinds are useful, although I usually dismantle the former. Many unusual effects can be obtained with the latter, as, for example, with a spring stretched across the holder, which will only be damped by the two opposite edges of the rim and by the magnet itself; in a fraction of a second it is possible to alternate between any of these three plus a combination of the magnet with either edge of the rim.

The different characteristics of fairly similar pick-ups (impedance and voltage) mean that a particular object may sound much better with one pick-up than with another (see p.154), so that a selection of these can be valuable for trying out the object one wishes to amplify. As with my earlier comment on combining different contact microphones for a single large instrument, so it is possible to combine several different magnetic microphones. One of my instruments uses five different models, covering a wide range of impedance; these are combined by means of a mixer and not simply wired in series or parallel.

Although I have been careful to try out different microphones before deciding on the most suitable one for each instrument, it is often possible to obtain interesting sound variants by using totally different microphones. In a recent collective improvisation I decided after one minute that I would only use a 'wrong' microphone with each instrument from then until the end of the concert, and I was very surprised and pleased by the result.

Building electroacoustic instruments

Unlike other musical cultures, the tendency in Western music has been for instruments to become more neutral in sound. For example, the harpsichord was replaced by the piano, and the viol family by the violin family. These later instruments have to be able to cover a much wider range of musical styles and expression; a pianist can get away with playing music written for the harpsichord, but one cannot play genuine piano music from after the end of the eighteenth century on the harpsichord. Conversely because classical composers were, naturally, unable to compose for the new instruments that have come and continue to come into existence during the twentieth century, one can question the need to be able to play on them the kind of music written before they were invented. Should a new instrument be tuned to the tempered scale, or indeed to any predetermined scale? Few electronic tape compositions adhere rigidly to any scale, even if this is so far removed from the tempered system as to include no octave relationships. Today's new electroacoustic instruments should be used primarily for contemporary music, whether specially composed for those instruments, composed for unspecified instruments, or improvised. Because one is thus freed from the need to cater for a large chunk of musical history, it is possible once again in our music to obtain more unusual, rich and resonant sounds and to let future musicians make their own decisions as to whether or not they will use our new instruments; complex overtones can be stressed in a way that is much harder with traditional instruments, forms of impure note production (such as 'wolf notes') can be explored for their own inherent interest; sounds demanded by today's composers which previously were only available by treating traditional instruments in a way often contrary to their nature and possibly harmful (such as playing inside the piano or using the 'wrong' mouthpiece in the case of a wind instrument) turn out to be quite natural to electroacoustic instruments.

The advantage of using amplification with electroacoustic instruments is that one largely avoids the need for special resonators. The difference between the electric guitar and its acoustic predecessor clearly illustrates this: a solid block of wood, whose shape can vary quite substantially and is thus not crucial, replaces the carefully made hollow framework with which even slight changes can affect the sound detrimentally. A number of my own instruments are mounted on blockboard, a composite wood (somewhat similar to plywood) that is easily available and not too expensive. Little research needs to be done in trying out different woods, shapes or sizes or thicknesses for the resonator, taking into account its own resonant frequency and so on, because these are comparatively unimportant. Instead one needs to know a certain amount about the properties of this composite wood (which is made like a sandwich, with the grain of the two outer covers at right angles to the grain of the interior), about the vibrating objects which will make the sounds and about the

most suitable kinds of microphones. Another great advantage is the comparatively
little extra work that is needed in order to obtain really low notes, compared with
the substantial expense and sheer hard work that, for example, Harry Partch put
into his bass instruments. With long springs it is quite easy to stretch them or tune
them down so far that the fundamental disappears and one only hears the overtones,
as also happens with the lowest pedal notes of a large organ or the additional major
third added below the lowest A in the bass of a Bösendorfer grand piano; these,
however, only go down to about 16 and 22 Hz respectively, whereas my lowest
spring goes down to about 5 Hz.

On several occasions, without initially realising it, I have built into an electroacoustic instrument the equivalent of a piece of electronic music transformation
equipment such as a filter, reverberation unit or certain kinds of modulation.
Filtering by using different microphones on the same object or instrument (or identical ones at differently resonating positions) has already been described; a similar
effect can also be produced by using various damping materials, such as foam
rubber, to isolate the vibrating object from one of two or more microphones. In
addition, when a magnetic pick-up is mounted in the basic board, a diaphragm can
be inserted between the sound source and the pick-up.

It must be assumed that a certain amount of equipment will be available at any
school which wishes to build electroacoustic instruments. Apart from amplifiers
and loudspeakers (the more the merrier, since it can be confusing to share a loudspeaker), the most essential item is some device which has a microphone input. This
is unlikely to be the amplifier, unless pop group equipment is used. Ideal would be
a mixer with microphone inputs; a tape recorder with microphone inputs can also
be used (though not every tape recorder permits you to hear a sound on external
loudspeakers before it has been recorded). Without a mixer, it will only be possible
to hear as many instruments simultaneously as there are loudspeakers. If the
microphone inputs give a choice of 'low' or 'high' (impedance), it is wise to try
'high' first, and if the sound is very quiet with the volume control(s) turned up
quite high, then try 'low'.

In building electroacoustic instruments simple carpentry and soldering will be
needed. It is wise to get a group of children to use two or three different instruments
as models, not only because of the lack of contrast when they are played together,
but also so that queues do not form for a crucial tool that just happens to be in
short supply that week. Find out the correct name for the plugs required for the
microphone inputs: on many occasions I have been told 'I think it's a jack' because
it is the only term for a plug that many people have heard of, or because jacks are
used for almost every connection with pop music equipment.

Electrical safety precautions must be taken, primarily with magnetic microphones.
Though the microphones are not in themselves at all dangerous, an inadequately
maintained amplification system or lack of proper mains earthing in the building
can, as has happened with electric guitarists, prove fatal. For acoustic reasons, to
avoid hum, it sometimes turns out to be necessary to earth the actual magnet of

the pick-up in addition to the end of the coil that you choose to be earthed. Then, as already stated, the ferrous-metal object may touch the actual magnet and not hover above it. One of my instruments requires this, and I have added two complementary devices which I gather should be safe. The ideal one, however, is a small transformer, but a famous shop which specialises in transformers was unable to supply what a friend told me to get. There exists a device for electric guitarists, which probably includes a transformer, and it would be wise to invest in one of these per instrument if there are any doubts about the safety of any part of the electrical system.

Before describing four of my instruments in detail, I will write a bit more fully about my activity in this area. My first few instruments all use contact microphones. The first self-contained instrument, Shozyg I, contains a selection of small items, including two fretsaw blades, a small spring and a ball-bearing-mounted furniture castor (played by fingers, finger nails, a screwdriver, needle file, toothbrush, small electric motor etc.) which are amplified by two contact microphones for stereo and built inside the covers of an encyclopaedia volume, SHO-ZYG. Hence the title, which I have subsequently adopted to describe all the (mostly amplified) instruments I have built inside everyday containers: a matching second encyclopaedia volume, a larger book, two television sets, a radio set, breadbin, electric toaster, electric heater, accordion file, imitation mixing console (operated by zips instead of faders) and so on. One day I will probably have an exhibition of a shozyg kitchen and living room!

Towards the end of 1969 I began to use magnetic pick-ups for the first time. Initially I used one to amplify a spring that was 14 cm long and 3 mm in diameter, held above a complete pick-up in its original holder mounted on a small square of chipboard, with a key-ring fitted to each end of the spring, enabling it to be stretched to at least 40 cm. A word of warning here: there is a point beyond which all except the least flexible extension springs will no longer return to their original length. I use two versions of this particular spring, one of which is now nearly twice its original length. From this spring I developed the first in my family of Springboards (see Project 1), of which the first five all use identical springs, stretched up to 45 cm in length. With the same magnetic pick-up I also use an egg slicer (see Project 3).

Since magnetic pick-ups are used in about one third of my electroacoustic instruments, quite a large proportion of my sound materials are metal. With cartridges I also use metal strings or wire, and only with contact microphones do I sometimes use other materials: plastic (as in a plastic breadbin containing a 'keyboard' of six plastic spoons and stirrers mounted on inverted plastic cups and mugs, a plastic knife with serrated edge and 'to finish off with' a toothbrush), wood (usually for mounting other objects on, thus more a means of modifying the transmission of vibrations to the microphone) and nylon strings (fishing nylon; also useful for acoustic instruments, as for example with my *Lady Bracknell,* in which a length of fishing nylon attached to an empty coffee tin - like half a child's telephone - is

Plate 10   Hugh Davies and John Furnival − The Jack and Jill Box (Feelie Box)

rubbed with wetted fingers). In the several amplified Feelie Boxes that I have made with John Furnival there is a variety of small, primarily tactile surfaces which mostly produce very little sound even when amplified, such as: sandpaper, fur, carpeting, corduroy, metal foil, polystyrene, unusual shapes of plastic to be guessed at, gloves made of rubber, wool and string (stuffed with foam rubber, fir cones, plaster of Paris, soya beans, crinkly cellophane wrapping paper, electric light fittings and a bedspring), steel wool juxtaposed with cotton wool (one of our many built-in jokes), a nylon dish scourer, metal mesh, a Perspex triangle and corrugated cardboard (Plate 10).

The item I have used most of all is the spirally coiled spring. This comes in a great variety of shapes and sizes. There are basically three types of spring: (Ex)-tension, Torsion (rather similar to Extension) and Compression. I mainly use the first type: compression springs are less flexible by their very nature, and I normally perform on them in their original state and not built into an instrument, although the most flexible ones of this type can be manually compressed and even slightly expanded. Some compression springs are cone-shaped helices. Extension springs can be stretched manually as described above, either with both hands or, by fixing the other end to part of the instrument, with only one hand; or they can be fixed in place at both ends, as is the case with my Springboards. Not all springs are suitable: those made for the heating elements of electric fires do not have sufficient tension and never return to their original length, even if only stretched a small amount. A few others, mainly compression springs, are not made of primarily steel wire, but of a largely non-ferrous alloy, and thus have too little effect on the magnetic field of the microphone. Compression springs, especially those of thicker gauges, tend to have their ends filed flat so that they will stand upright on a magnetic pick-up rather than leaning at an angle like the tower of Pisa, with a continual risk of falling off the microphone. Extension springs often have their ends twisted into loops, which makes it easy to attach them to key-rings or screwhooks fixed to an instrument, or for screws to be inserted through the loops. A type of extension spring that is well known to children is the Slinky. This is somewhat limited in its range of sound, due to its very large diameter and because it is actually a very long length of wire and thus produces so low a fundamental that one primarily hears its overtones. If one were to mount a Slinky on a piece of wood it would need to be at least five yards long, and even then the Slinky would sag too much in the middle. It is probably at its best with one end resting on a table, amplified by a contact microphone. At the other extreme of extension springs are the easily obtainable 'typewriter springs', which are also somewhat limited, this time because they are rather too short to produce much variety of pitches.

When building a new instrument, it is often helpful to make a series of careful scale drawings in order to decide on the ideal layout, size and relative proportions. Occasionally this is insufficient, and a prototype must be made first. After constructing a few instruments one begins to see signs of a logical development and of one's own particular preferences, and elements of previous instruments are incorporated into new ones; sometimes one object that is only a small part of an instrument becomes the prototype for the whole of a completely new one. In many of my instruments the microphones are built into the constructions so that they remain fixed in the place that I have decided produces the best sound. With magnetic pick-ups this is not always so clearly defined, and in some cases the microphone is moved by hand into different positions around the instrument, or the instrument is similarly moved across the microphone. In the latter case the instrument is frequently a found object. A single spring held at each end by a key-ring virtually qualifies as such; but I am thinking more of the collection of found objects used in my composition *Salad*, in which four different egg slicers (different brands have the 'strings' tuned to different pitch ranges, though unfortunately 'they don't make them like they used to', and brands currently available use what I can only assume to be less ferrous alloys for their strings, resulting in a considerably weaker amplified sound), two 'identical' tomato slicers (with small saw-blades) and a cheese slicer (with a wire cutting edge) are amplified by five magnetic pick-ups, four of which are mounted together on a piece of chipboard (at the top of an old microphone stand) as a tightly fitting square.

When I have completed a new instrument I try to discover the most suitable context in which to use it, rather than imposing preconceived ideas onto it. Thus it might be played sitting down, sitting at a table, standing up, walking around (not so good with amplified instruments), crouching, kneeling or sitting on the floor. It might be suitable for a solo performance in a concert, for a more auxiliary role as part of a collection of instruments used by one player in a group improvisation, for an exhibition or as a toy – or a combination of these. I find improvisation helps me to learn more about my instruments' potentialities. In a classroom there is obviously a need to suggest some more coherent musical relationships. I find that a good way to start is with a small group, with instructions to hold a conversation or discussion using sounds instead of words. There will be occasional solos and duos, sometimes everyone plays at once causing a confused chaos, some statements consist of only a single sound or short phrase, others are very elaborate; some statements echo what another player has just played and expand it, others are contradictory. Just as happens with words. Another possibility is rhythmic pieces handled in the same way as with a group of percussion instruments. I should add that I have tried out such things, but only on a couple of occasions with children playing instruments made by me. The reason for this is simply that when coming from outside to work with a class of children for three hours or two days or a whole week I want the children to be able to play their instruments after I have gone home, which is unlikely to be possible when these are electroacoustic. Therefore when working with children I avoid amplification, and usually use bamboo as the main material since it is easy to work and sounds good. But I greatly welcome the present opportunity to pass on ideas about making electroacoustic instruments, even if it is at one remove.

With electroacoustic instruments it is difficult to hear your own sound in the loudspeaker clearly without being too loud in relation to other people who are playing traditional instruments, even if these are also amplified. The problem is considerably reduced when all the instruments are electoacoustic. Because there is little or no acoustic sound and the physical vibrations transmitted through the player's body are much smaller, monitoring one's sound in the loudspeaker becomes very important. It will be helpful for the players to have the opportunity of getting to know their instruments individually, to practise them alone just as with any conventional instrument, before starting to play together. One awkward thing that can happen with electroacoustic or amplified acoustic instruments when the microphone is fixed directly on the instrument, is that sometimes one is faced with the problem of taking one's hand or finger off the instrument or moving to a different finger position during a silence, since the microphones are often so sensitive that this movement will be audible over the loudspeaker. One solution is for each player to have a foot-operated volume pedal like an electric guitarist (I once made some boxes that could be attached to one's belt, for a similar purpose); however, familiarity with such quirks through practice can help to avoid such things or at least to cover them up. Similarly, when using contact microphones with an instrument that is to be played while sitting at a table, the table effectively becomes part of the instrument. Any unintentional bang or object dropped on to the table will be audible over the loudspeaker, unless the table is so heavy and solid that it has little resonance. A solution is to place a layer of foam rubber underneath the instrument, which would be particularly relevant when more than one instrument using any kind of microphone is played at the same table.

Project 1: Springboards

The background to this family has already been described. The first five Springboards all use the spring referred to, 14 cm long and 3 mm in diameter. Three models use four springs, one uses two, and one the grand total of fourteen. Each spring is amplified by means of half of a U-shaped magnetic pick-up. The layout of the springs in most models is parallel, making its kinship with the electric guitar clearer. Proportions: all Springboards are mounted on blockboard ½ in thick, and the three Springboards with four springs each measure, on average, 50 x 16 cm; the two-spring model is only 6 cm wide. The springs vary in length from 20 to 45 cm, arranged symmetrically like the cross-section of a pyramid: parallel lines whose centre points would makes a straight line at a right angle to them. The microphone is usually placed only slightly off-centre and not close to one end (typically it is about 4 cm from the centre point), so that the instrument does not have a right way round, but can be reversed. This produces slightly different timbres for those pitches that are available from both directions. The springs are fixed down by looping their ends over screwhooks (the smallest size that can be found at a well-stocked ironmongery) which are screwed into the top surface of the blockboard.

On the underside are mounted the pick-ups, screwed into place facing upwards, in holes approximately 1½ x 2 cm. These holes require care in cutting if the result is not to look messy: I normally drill several small-diameter holes around the perimeter (for which I have made a template on transparent paper, which is slightly smaller than the final hole size) and cut through the barriers between them with a Stanley knife, leaving a rough hole that is still somewhat smaller than needed. This is then expanded to the right shape and size with a small flat or half-round file. It is possible to mount the pick-up in such a way that the top ends of the magnet would be nearer to the springs by cutting away the outer sandwich layer on the underside of the blockboard around the microphone hole. While on the subject of the composition of the blockboard, I usually cut it so that – primarily for the visual appearance – the grain of the outer layer goes lengthwise; exceptions are the very narrow Springboards (3½ cm and 6 cm) with which I was afraid that the wood would be more prone to snapping due to the fact that the interior rectangular blocks would be cut into many short pieces placed side by side. As it is, these two instruments have one or two interior blocks that run lengthwise.

Apart from other comments made earlier in the section on magnetic pick-ups, there are two further items concerning microphones. The wires that come out at each end of the double coil (a coil around each arm of the U-shaped magnet) are very thin and fragile. I solder a short length of covered connecting wire to each pick-up wire, and fit their other ends into a two-way plastic terminal block that is screwed on to the underside of the blockboard; to the other side of the terminal block is connected the screened audio cable which has on its other end a plug appropriate to the microphone input. It does not matter which of the wires from the coil is treated as the earth and which as the signal. In some cases, as already mentioned, it may also be necessary to earth the actual magnet. If there are any audio problems – such as the microphone picking up radio or even television sound – a small ceramic disc capacitor of about 0.01 μF can be connected across the two wires from the pick-up by inserting it in one side of the terminal block (a higher value would start to clip the sound, acting as a filter). Concerning the choice of wiring more than one pick-up in series or parallel, see p.161.

I usually fit four medium-sized rubber feet on the corners of the underside of a Springboard, so that it will lie flat on a table rather than rocking around on the pick-up(s) and terminal block that protrude underneath. The final stage in the construction concerns the decoration of the top surface, with the springs temporarily removed. I prefer to use clear varnish (three layers) which brings out the grain of the wood; some kind of varnish is advisable to protect the wood from stains and grubby fingermarks. Children would probably enjoy painting, burning or carving a design, which could later be covered with clear varnish.

All springs, even the very shortest, produce medium to low pitches when played as 'open springs'. This is due to the lengths that would result if they were pulled out into straight wires. It is possible to tune a spring to a lower pitch, but not to a higher one; and indeed stretching a spring hardly changes its pitch, since the same amount of wire is still vibrating loosely, which is not the case with strings. Tuning is changed by selectively stretching alternate short lengths of a spring, each about 1 cm long, fairly vigorously so that these alternatively wider coils do not return to their original density. Performance technique is like that of the guitar, with the exception that the pick-up is the only point from which the vibrations will reach the listener: stopping a spring and then plucking it on the side away from the pick-up will give virtually no sound at all. To produce very high sounds, two fingers of one hand stop the spring, one on each side of the pick-up; so short a length of spring gives little resonance to the sound and in such a situation I tend to flick the spring with my fingernail rather than pluck it. Tremolos are effective at any pitch for producing sustained sounds. Needle files, screwdrivers and so on can be used in addition to fingers for playing and stopping the springs. Fingernails scraped rapidly along a spring will bring out the overtones of its fundamental, the faster the action, the higher the overtone. A separate, loose pick-up can also be used above the springs,

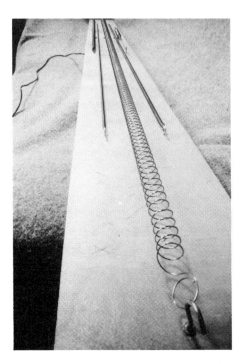

Plate 11 Hugh Davies – Springboard Mk VI (133 cm long)

partly to give a different version of the sound when operating with a stereophonic set-up and partly to play or stop the springs. An ensemble of different Springboards can also be very effective.

The later Springboards, whose family consists of a dozen at the time of writing, develop the same basic principles but uses a considerable variety of other extension springs (see Plate 11). Three of them develop a new principle first tried out in the early Springboard with fourteen springs. Pursuing the idea of springs radiating out from a key-ring with seven pick-ups mounted in a semicircle close to the key-ring (see Plate 12), I then made several springs of different qualities meet above a single pick-up at a small split-ring (like a key-ring) about 1 cm in diameter. These springs are sufficiently flexible for the ring to be shifted off-centre in different directions by one finger. A further development of this consists of a spider's web arrangement of about five short springs radiating out from this central ring to a larger concentric ring (which can itself consist of about ten short springs), from which in turn about five longer springs radiate outwards. Vibrations from these outer springs must pass through the inner web to reach the microphone, and it is possible to damp some of the inner springs selectively with one's fingers in order to change the route and the distance the vibration has to travel, affecting the timbre and pitch often quite substantially. The inner springs can, of course, also be played. When several springs

Plate 12 Hugh Davies playing his Springboard Mk III

converge at a single point such as a split-ring one often needs to damp some of the springs because they all tend to resonate from the vibrations produced by just one of them. When used deliberately, the player can control the reverberation imparted to the sound in a way that is similar to operating an electronic reverberation unit. Examples of four Springboards can be heard on the accompanying cassette. (*Cassette examples 8.1–8.4*).

Project 2: Bowed Diaphragms

I explained earlier (p.160) how the diaphragm of a magnetic pick-up functions. Two possible uses of the diaphragm are combined in my composition *Music for Bowed Diaphragms* (*Cassette example 8.5*). If the pick-up is retained in its original state as found in a telephone handset or other device, when the cover has been removed the diaphragm can be shifted off-centre, so that the pick-up's rim will damp the diaphragm disc in a variety of ways. This alters its frequency response, and has the effect of filtering the sound. The most interesting applications I have found for this are with the human voice (as I devised for *Group Composition VI* by the group *Gentle Fire*, of which I was a member; in this piece four old-style telephone earpieces were transferred to the mouthpiece of the handset so that the voices could be modified by the displacement of the diaphragms, and these sounds were then passed through two of the terminals of the telephone dials, enabling the filtered and distorted voices to be chopped up with interspersed silences) and with a 'bow'. The bow is actually a single strand of horsehair from a violin bow; this can also be used on a Springboard, where the hairs of a complete bow are inclined to get caught in the coils of the springs.

Music for Bowed Diaphragms is for five magnetic pick-ups with their original diaphragms. Each pick-up is different, and between them a wide range of impedance is covered. They are connected to the five channels of the stereo mixer that I always use in performances. Two of the pick-ups have solid top surfaces in which the magnet is embedded, the other three have gaps between the rim and the magnet. I use five bow-hairs, which can be pulled across the diaphragms (in various off-centre positions) either above the discs or between them and the pick-ups. A single bow-hair can be pulled across the edge of the disc, along its diameter, or moved around the protruding part of its circumference. All five bow-hairs can be pulled towards the player if they are between the diaphragms and the microphones. Since the bow-hairs are held fairly tightly between one's two hands they can also be plucked by a spare finger while held against a diaphragm edge, which leads to an unusual paradox. While the bow-hair travels across the edge of the diaphragm, it is a bow moving across an 'instrument' that is 'built into' the microphone; but if one then plucks the hair while it is still moving, it also becomes a string that is amplified by a microphone. The diaphragms are all mounted fairly closely together on a piece of block-board so that any two can be played, e.g. in stereo, by a single bow-hair.

I have experimented with two further possibilities using diaphragms. The first involves slightly filing down the Bakelite rim of a pick-up so that it provides a convex surface for the diaphragm (or a vibrating egg slicer) to rest on. The second consists of using the diaphragm as an instrument in its own right that can be moved across the microphone to create different sounds, and can be tapped, rubbed and scraped. To do this I sawed off one side of the disc to reduce its size somewhat, bolted a small handle on to the opposite side and inserted the handle through a slit that I had made in the side of the microphone's original screw-on Bakelite cover. As will no doubt be clear by now, in such a miniature and microscopic world as mine, tiny changes in construction and performance can produce great changes in the resulting sounds.

Project 3: From Egg Slicer to Aeolian Harp
When I first began to make instruments a couple of friends used to play egg slicers

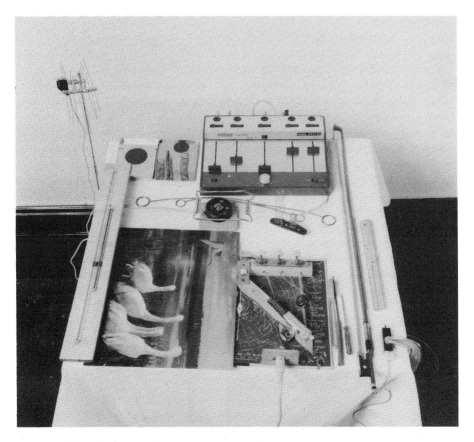

Plate 13 Hugh Davies — solo performance table
    Centre left: *Springboard with two springs*
    Rear left: *Aeolian harp, two diaphragms and springs in tin*
    Rear centre: *stereo mixer*
    Centre: *egg slicer on magnetic pick-up, behind it two springs with*
                    key-rings, to the right two springs vertical on a guitar pick-up
    Front centre: *Shozyg II*
    Front right: *guitar string in cartridge clamped to the table*

amplified by contact microphones. The strings of any egg slicer have quite a range of pitches, even though they are identical in gauge and length. By gently squeezing the longer sides together it is possible to alter the tension of the strings and therefore their pitch. I discovered that with the amplification level turned up higher it was possible to blow on the strings in addition to being able to pluck them. Furthermore, placing an egg slicer on or above a magnetic pick-up produces different timbres for these two qualities, and the pick-up's rim can also be used to stop the strings for higher pitches (see Plate 13). I use tomato and cheese slicers in a similar way.

I then wanted to construct a more varied egg slicer, either circular or shaped something like a harp. Several attempts at making a fairly small device that could be held in one hand failed because of the need to use tuning pegs of some kind which would take up more space than I wished, lacking as I did the factory machinery for tensioning and fixing the single long length of wire that is used for the strings of an egg slicer. I finally found a quite different solution, which does not really resemble an egg slicer but produces the kind of sound I was aiming at. Nine very fine fretsaw blades are mounted in a holder consisting of a sandwich of aluminium bars in three sections held together by bolts on either side of each blade. The blades protrude above and below in roughly equal proportions, giving eighteen different lengths and pitches. The holder fastens on to an old collapsible aerial fitted to a heavy base that stands on the floor, and there is a wingnut which enables the contact microphone to be attached to it. This instrument can also be both plucked and blown. Because of the ethereal qualities of the latter I have called the instrument, slightly inaccurately, Aeolian harp (plate 13), and indeed a strong wind will cause it to sound. This instrument seems to be the favourite out of all my instruments with the majority of people with whom I have talked at performances of mine, because of the delicate, floating sounds produced when one blows on it (*Cassette example 8.6*).

Project 4: Metal Rod 'Xylophone'

This instrument requires mainly soldering skills, and at the time of writing I have not developed it beyond a small prototype. I deliberately collected other people's rubbish for it, consisting of the ends of wires (between 1 and 4 cm long) that had been cut off electrical resistors and capacitors by friends who were fitting components on to electrical circuit boards. One could also purchase a similar type of tinned copper or steel wire, gauges between 18 and 24 swg. These wires are arranged by length and soldered to a piece of circuit board with holes so that the solder connections are underneath and the wires stick up vertically through the board. The underside ends of the wires should be wrapped together or around additional wires for strength, and longer lengths of wire could serve as two rods by bending them into a long thin U-shape. A contact microphone is fitted by placing a bolt with a wingnut on top through the circuit board to one side of the rods. Gently plucking the tips of the rods produces high clear sounds, which when recorded and played back at half-speed on a tape recorder sound like a xylophone or marimba; hence the contradiction in my title (*Cassette example 8.7*).

Appendix 1   Glossary

amplifier A device which increases the amplitude or strength of an electrical signal.

amplitude of an oscillating wave-form; strength of the signal measured about its mean point or average value, corresponding to the loudness of the sound.

analogue A representation of the variables of one medium in terms of another. The rise and fall of a voltage can be analogous to the rise and fall in the dynamics of a sound, for example. The term is often used in contradistinction to *digital*, where the difference to be stressed is that analogue signals are continuously variable, whereas digital signals are transmitted in previously defined units, however small.

attack The initial portion of a sound's or signal's envelope as it rises to its maximum amplitude.

balanced lines Twin-conductor screened cables used in professional audio applications, as opposed to the single-core screened cable where the screen is used as the return wire of the circuit and known as an 'unbalanced line'.

bulk eraser A powerful electromagnet designed to erase a full reel of tape in only a few seconds.

capstan Drive spindle of tape recorder.

cut-off point The setting on a filter which divides the passed from the rejected frequencies.

decay The final portion of a sound's or a signal's envelope as it declines to silence or, in some envelope shapers, to a predetermined *sustain* level.

decibel (Abbreviated dB). The ratio of two signal levels, which can refer to electrical signals or to sound intensities. Since the same ratio can apply to two signal levels of low intensity or to two signals of high intensity, it is often necessary to specify a fixed reference. Electrically the reference usually adopted is 1 milliwatt power in a 600 ohm line as the standard for 0 dB, expressed, as a fixed reference point, as dBm. The zero dBm rating also represents a level of 0.7746 volts. The table below gives the rating in watts and volts for different dBm levels.

dBm	wattage	voltage
+60	1000 W	774.6
+50	100 W	244.9.
+40	10 W	77.46
+30	1 W	24.49
+20	100 mW	7.746
+10	10 mW	2.449
0	1 mW	0.7746
-10	0.1 mW	0.2449
-20	0.01 mW	0.07746
-30	0.001 mW	0.02449

With sound intensities, since the ear is tremendously sensitive to pressure changes (on a scale of 1,000,000,000,000 to 1) a logarithmic scale to the base 10 is adopted, giving a range of approximately 14 to 1, each unit representing a bel. This scale is subdivided into units of 10, giving a range of 0 to 140 decibels. On this scale of sound intensities, a sound level of 1 dB is almost inaudible and a difference of 1 dB is hardly noticeable. A table giving a variety of acoustic conditions with their ratings in decibels is given below.

+120 dB	Pain threshold
+100 dB	Noisy factory
+ 90 dB	Pneumatic drill at 8 metres
+ 80 dB	Heavy lorry at 8 metres
+ 70 dB	Car at 8 metres
+ 60 dB	Orchestral strings and woodwind playing *ff*
+ 50 dB	Conversation
+ 40 dB	A quiet street in a residential area
+ 30 dB	A quiet day in the country
+ 20 dB	A whisper at one metre
+ 10 dB	Leaves rustling a few metres away

demagnetising   The process of removing residual magnetism, usually from tape recorder heads.

digital   A term used to indicate information conveyed in digits; it is often used in the context of the digital computer, where information is conveyed by the binary digit, or bit, corresponding to the smallest unit of information that can be conveyed. See also *analogue.*

edit   In tape composition, to trim or reorder lengths of recorded tape in order to obtain a desired sound sequence.

envelope   The contour or dynamic shape of a sound or signal characterised by its changes in amplitude.

equalisation   The process of modifying the amplitude and frequency response in a recording and reproducing system in order to optimise desired characteristics.

feedback   The return of a portion of the output of a circuit to the input. *Positive feedback* will tend to increase the output, *negative feedback* to decrease it. Positive feedback between a loudspeaker (output) and a microphone (input) can cause the phenomenon known as *howlround*, where the air between the microphone and loudspeaker is caused to vibrate at frequencies determined by acoustic resonances in the vicinity.

filter   A device that selectively transmits desired portions of the frequency spectrum of a given signal while suppressing others.

frequency   The number of cycles per second (c.p.s.) of a sound wave or signal. The unit is the hertz (abbreviated Hz).

fundamental	The lowest, or first, component (or *partial*) in a sound's frequency structure.
gain	Degree of amplification.
harmonic	A component of a sound having a frequency which is an integral multiple of its fundamental frequency. A harmonic having double the fundamental frequency is called the second harmonic. Harmonics are also known as *partials* or *overtones*.
hertz	The unit of frequency, abbreviated Hz. 1 Hz = 1 cycle per second.
howlround	See *feedback*.
impedance	That property of a circuit or component which restricts the flow of alternating current; expressed in ohms.
impedance matching	The choosing of devices or circuits of compatible impedance in order to achieve the maximum transfer of a signal from one to another.
input	A signal fed into a circuit, or the point of connection for the incoming signal.
jack	A device often used to terminate the permanent wiring of a circuit, electrical access to which is gained by inserting a plug.
line	The signal path throughout a circuit.
modulation	Variation of the frequency or amplitude of a signal's wave-form by means of another wave.
monitor	To listen to a signal being recorded.
oscillator	An electronic device that produces one or more periodic wave-forms of a definite frequency within a specific frequency range.
output	A signal coming out of a circuit, or the point of connection for the outcoming signal.
overtone	See *harmonic*.
parameter	A measurable, variable element. Parameters of sound include frequency, amplitude and duration.
peak	The greatest amplitude of a sound wave or signal in a given context.
phase	The fraction of period which has elapsed measured from some fixed origin. With respect to an oscillating wave-form, measurement is usually given in terms of degrees of a circle. Thus 360° would represent a wave-form advanced or retarded by a full period, 180° a wave-form advanced or retarded by a half-period, etc.
phasing	An effect obtained by splitting a given signal two ways and introducing a time-delay in one of them before they are recombined.
pinch wheel	In a tape recorder, the wheel that presses the tape to the moving capstan while in operation, withdrawing when not in use.

potentiometer	A *gain* control on audio equipment.
preamplifier	An *amplifier* used before the main amplifier, to bring very low level signals up to a level acceptable by the main amplifier's input stage. Microphone signals, for example, usually require preamplification.
real time	A term used to indicate a process that matches, unit for unit, clock time. A 'real-time composition' that lasts eight minutes has taken eight minutes to create; this usually indicates, therefore, an electroacoustic work.
signal	An electrical current whose fluctuations correspond to sound vibrations.
signal-to-noise ratio	A comparative measurement of the signal level in relation to the noise level of the circuit. Given in *decibels*.
transducer	A device which converts waves from one vibrating system to another. Microphones and loudspeakers are electroacoustic transducers. The vibrator–transducer mentioned in Chapters 1 and 2 of this book is a type of electromechanical transducer.
vocoder	A device for extracting the frequency-spectral variations of an input signal and imposing these upon another sound.
wave-form	The contour of a wave shown graphically in amplitude and time.

Appendix II Course outline

There are, no doubt, many ways of using a book of this nature. This section suggests one way in which the material might be graded as a series of activities corresponding to the first five years of secondary education. This plan may be adapted in various ways to outline other graded courses. For example, the series may be telescoped into a shorter, more intensive course. Each 'Year Grade' of the course gives a planned sequence of activities to be followed in the order given. Generally speaking, preliminary exercises and information precede classwork projects and creative assignments. In part, at least, each grade relies upon knowledge gained from an earlier grade. Chapter references are given in bold type, page references in normal type.

Year I

Listening via a microphone **2**, 26
Recording **1**, 5; **2**, 27; **3**, 46; **3**, 58; **6**, 108
Changing tape speed **1**, 6
Assignment 1 **2**, 43
Voice and Body Music **3**, 54
Bicycle Music **3**, 65
Machines **4**, 86

Year II

Tape recorder maintenance **1**, 5; **5**, 103
Trying out different microphones **1**, 7
Recording tones from oscillators **1**, 9; **2**, 40; **3**, 47
Voltage control principle **1**, 11
Envelope shaper **1**, 12; **2**, 40
Musical Numbers **6**, 111
Recording musical instruments **1**, 7; **3**, 60
Recording environmental sounds with portable tape recorders **2**, 27; **3**, 50; **3**, 62
Special recording projects **4**, 74
Acoustic processing **2**, 29
Mouth Tube **6**, 115
Drone Music **5**, 103
Assignment 3 **2**, 43
Multiple cassette recording **2**, 44

Year III

Recording with contact microphones **1**, 8; **2**, 29; and special purpose microphones **1**, 8
Editing **1**, 8; **2**, 34; **5**, 99
Playing sounds backwards **2**, 35
Tape loops **2**, 33
Use of leader tape **2**, 31
Rhythmic templates **2**, 32
Sampling **6**, 112
Vibrato **6**, 113
Variable speed **1**, 7; **6**, 112

Shortwave radio **6**, 111
Feedback **3**, 65; **6**, 110
Elementary mixing **2**, 39
Noise generator and filters **1**, 12
Copying tapes **2**, 36
Electromagnetic pick-ups **2**, 29; **8**, 159
Making audio leads **6**, 116
Circuit construction **6**, 123
Constructing a *Springboard* **8**, 168
Assignment 4 **2**, 43 and *Assignment 5* **2**, 43
'Opening the Cage' **4**, 87

Year IV

Mixing **1**, 18
Multiplying a single sound **2**, 37
Creating textures and masses **6**, 113
Dynamic shapes **6**, 120
Reverberation **1**, 17; **4**, 77; **5**, 94
Ring modulator **1**, 14
Synthesiser concept **1**, 15; Keyboards **1**, 16
The vibrator–transducer **1**, 24; **2**, 42
Circuit construction **6**, 123
Bowed Diaphragms **8**, 171
Assignment 2 **2**, 43
Tape with slide presentation **2**, 44

Year V

Envelope follower **1**, 21
Pitch-to-voltage converter **1**, 21
Sample and hold **1**, 22
Sequencer **1**, 17
'Painting' the tape **6**, 121
Reich's phasing technique **2**, 38
Circuit construction **6**, 129
'Aeolian Harp' **8**, 172
Metal Rod 'Xylophone' **8**, 174
Mapophone **6**, 122
Environmental Music **4**, 89
Musicmontage **7**, 133

Appendix III Select bibliography

The full bibliography of electronic music is now vast. In order to keep this select bibliography as useful and practicable as possible, the works listed are those recommended for further study or to provide information not available in the present book. Those works shown with an asterisk(*) contain extensive bibliographies; those shown with a dagger (†) contain valuable discographies.

Acoustics and technical books

Backus, J., *The Acoustic Foundations of Music* (Norton, 1969)
Borwick, J. (ed.), *Sound Recording Practice* (Oxford University Press, 1976)
Taylor, C., *The Physics of Musical Sounds* (English Universities Press, 1965)
Winckel, F., *Music, Sound and Sensation – A Modern Exposition** (Dover, 1967)

General works on electronic music – mainly for the listener

Ernst, D., *The Evolution of Electronic Music*† (Schirmer/Macmillan, 1977)
Griffiths, P., *A Guide to Electronic Music* (Thames and Hudson, 1979)
Schwartz, E., *Electronic Music – A Listener's Guide** (Secker and Warburg, 1973)

Electronic music in education

Drake, R., Hender, R. and Modugno, A.D., *How to Make Electronic Music*
  (Harmony/Educational Audio Visual, 1975)
Dwyer, T., *Making Electronic Music* (Oxford University Press, 1975)
Miliaret, G. (ed.), *The Psychology of the Use of Audio Visual Aids in Primary
  Education* (Harrap/Unesco, 1966)

Works giving information for the advanced practice of electronic music

Appleton, J.H. and Perera, R.C. (eds.), *The Development and Practice of Electronic
  Music* (Prentice-Hall, 1975)
Howe, H.S., Jr, *Electronic Music Synthesis* (Dent, 1975)
Keane, D., *Tape Music Composition** (Oxford University Press, 1980)
Strange, A., *Electronic Music – Systems, Techniques, Controls** (Wm C. Brown/
  Kalmus, 1972)

Instrument making, acoustic and electronic

Brosnoe, D., *Guitar Electronics: A Workbook* (dB Music Co., 1980)
Sawyer, D., *Vibrations – Making Unorthodox Musical Instruments* (Cambridge
  University Press, 1977)
Toop, D. (ed.), *New/Rediscovered Musical Instruments* (Quartz/Mirliton, 1974)

Reference works

Cross, L.M., *A Bibliography of Electronic Music* (University of Toronto Press/Oxford
  University Press, 1967)
Davies H., *International Electronic Music Catalog*† (Massachusetts Institute of
  Technology Press, 1968)

Miscellaneous related reading

Brandel, M., *The MAD Book of Word Power* (Warner Books, 1973)
Erickson, R., *Sound Structure in Music* (University of California Press, 1975)
Grayson, J. (ed.), *Sound Sculpture* (ARC Publications, 1975, available from PO Box 3044, Vancouver, British Columbia, Canada, V6B 3X5)
Halprin, L., *The RSVP Cycles – Creative Processes in the Human Environment* (Braziller, 1969)
Nyman, M., *Experimental Music – Cage and Beyond* (Studio Vista, 1974)
Partch, H., *Genesis of a Music* (Da Capo, 1977)
Reynolds, R., *Mind Models – New Forms of Musical Experience* (Praeger, 1975)
Schafer, R. Murray, *The Tuning of the World* (McClelland and Stewart, 1977)
Self, G., *Aural Adventures* (Novello, 1969)
Self, G., *New Sounds in Class* (Universal Edition, 1967)
Schwarz, T., *The Responsive Chord* (Anchor/Doubleday, 1973)
Williams, E. (ed.), *Anthology of Concrete Poetry* (Something Else Press, 1967)

Magazines and periodicals

Computer Music Journal Available in the UK from Vincent Coen, LP Enterprises, 313 Kingston Road, Ilford, Essex.
Electronotes Periodical devoted to synthesiser design and construction. Available from 1 Pheasant Lane, Ithaca, NY 14850, USA.
Interface Many articles devoted to electronic music. Published by Swets and Zeitlinger, NV Amsterdam.

The following now defunct magazines have many valuable articles and are worth seeking in libraries, photocopies or reprints:
Die Reihe English edition published by Theodore Presser Co., Pennsylvania, and Universal Edition, London. Vol. 1 (1958) was devoted to electronic music.
Electronic Music Review, Vols. 1–7. Trumansburg, New York. Ceased publication in 1969.
Source Magazine – Music of the Avant-Garde, Nos. 1-11. Sacramento, California. Has not appeared since 1972.
Synthesis Two issues appeared (1970, 1971) Published by Scully-Cutter Publishing, 1315 Fourth Street, SE, Minneapolis, Minnesota 55414, USA.

There have been occasional articles on electronic music in the following periodicals:
Contact – Today's Music Available from Philip Martin Music Books, 22 Huntington Road, York YO3 7RL, England. *Contact* Nos. 12 – 19 each contained an article on a British electronic music studio. No. 17 (Summer 1977) was a special Electronic Music Issue, and included an article on the work of Hugh Davies.
The Journal of Music Theory (Yale School of Music, New Haven, Connecticut 06520 USA)
Perspectives of New Music (PO Box 271, Yardley, Pennsylvania 19067, USA)
Sound International
Studio Sound

There have been many constructional articles of interest in the electronics press. These range from individual modules to complete synthesisers. For full information see the index to the relevant magazine. Dates given after the following titles indicate series articles of importance:

Electronics Today International July – August 1978
Elektor May – October 1977
Everyday Electronics February – April 1975 and April – June 1977 (microphone construction)
Hi-Fi for Pleasure
Popular Electronics June 1976
Practical Electronics February 1973 – February 1974
Sound Design (published by *Practical Electronics*)
Wireless World August – October 1973

Appendix IV Select discography

This selection has been made on grounds of both inherent interest and variety, and is arranged according to country of origin of the composition (not always the composer's home country). At the end is a selection of records of popular music with an important electronic component. Most records mentioned here are known to be available at the time of compilation (November 1980); others included are likely to be available in private collections or in record libraries.

Australia

Australian Digital Music (Works by Burt, Cary, Clynes, Conyngham), MOVE MS 3027 (MOVE Records, Box 266, Carlton South, Victoria 3053, Australia)

Belgium

Pousseur, Henri,   *Electre*, Universal Edition UE 13500
                Trois visages de Liège, Columbia MS 7051

Canada

Le Caine, Hugh,   *Dripsody*, Folkways FMS 33436
The Glass Orchestra, Music Gallery Editions (Toronto) MGE 10
Sonde, Music Gallery Editions (Toronto) MGE 14

Denmark

Pederson,   *STONED (and electronic symphony)*, obtainable from
   Gunner Møller,   Octopus Studio, giro 4272277, Dunhammervej 7,
                2400 København NV, Denmark

Finland

Finnish Electroacoustic Music (Works by Heininen, Honkanen, Lindeman, Rechberger, Romanowski, Ruohomäki, Sermilä), Fennica Nova LP FENO 5

France

Bayle, François,   *Grand polyphonie*, Harmonia Mundi AM 727.04
Ferrari, Luc,   *Presque rien no. 1*, DGG 2543004
                Visage V, Philips 835 485/86 AY; Philips 6526 003
Henry, Pierre,   *Orphée*, Philips 835484 LY
                Variations on a Door and a Sigh, Philips 836898 DSY
Parmegiani,   *De natura sonorum*, Harmonia Mundi AM 714.01
   Bernard,
Schaeffer, Pierre,   *Etude aux objects*, Philips 835 487 AY; Philips 6521 021
Schaeffer, Pierre   *Symphonie pour un homme seul*, Ducretet – Thomson
   and   DUC – 9; Philips 6510 012
   Henry, Pierre,
Xenakis, Iannis,   *Bohor; Orient-Occident; Diamorphoses;*
                Concret P-H; Nonesuch H-71246

Germany, West

Kagel, Mauricio,	*Acustica*, DGG 2707 059 (2 records)
	Transicion I, Philips 835 485/86 AY; Philips 836 897 DSY
	Unter Strom, DGG 2530 460
Ligeti, György,	*Artikulation*, Philips 835 485/86 AY
Stockhausen,	*Gesang de Jünglinge*, DGG 138811
Karlheinz,	*Hymnen*, 2-DGG 2707039
	Kontakte, DGG 138811
	Kurzwellen, 2-DGG 2707045
	Mikrophonie I; *Mikrophonie II*, Columbia MS 7355;
	DGG 2530 583
	Sirius, DGG 2707 122

Holland

Anthology of Dutch Electronic Tape Music (Includes works by Cats, Oyens, Kunst, Bergeijk, Doorn, Arras, Holt, Wentink, Andriessen, Smith and Campen), CV 7903 Composers' Voice, obtainable from Donemus, Paulus Potterstraat 14, 1071 CZ, Amsterdam, Holland (UK agents: Universal Edition)

Varèse, Edgard,	*Poème Electronique*, Columbia MS 6146; Columbia MG-31078

Italy

Berio, Luciano,	*Momenti; Omaggio a Joyce*, Philips 835 485/86 AY;
	Philips 836 897 DSY
	Visage, Turnabout TV 34046S
Cage, John,	*Fontana Mix*, Turnabout TV 34046S
Maderna, Bruno,	*Continuo*, Philips 835 485/86 AY
Musica Electronica Viva,	*Live Electronic Music Improvised*, Mainstream MS 5002
Pousseur, Henri,	*Scambi*, Philips 835 485/86 AY

Japan

Ichiyanagi, Toshi,	*Extended Voices*, Odyssey 3216 0156
Takemitsu, Toru,	*Vocalism Ai*; *Water Music*, Victor VICS 1334
Stockhausen, Karlheinz,	*Telemusik*, DGG 137012

Norway

(All on Philips – Norway, marketed by Polygram)

Berge, Sigurd,	*Five Electronic Sketches*, 6507.03
Fongaard, Bjørn,	*Galaxy* 839.241; Philips (France) 836 896 DSY
	The Space Concerto, 6507.034
Nordheim, Arne,	*Epitaffio*; *Respons 1*, 839.250 AY
	Colorazione; *Solitaire*; *Signals*, 854.005 AY
	Five Osaka Fragments, 6507.034
	Warszawa; *Pace*; *Lux et tenebrae*, 6507.042

Sweden

(CAP = Caprice)

Bodin, L.G.,	*Place of Plays*, CAP 1035
Hambraeus, Bengt,	*Rota 2; Tetragon*, CAP 1007
Hanson, Sten,	*Viarp I*, CAP 1035
Johnson, B.E.,	*Through the Mirror of Thirst*, CAP 1035
Lundsten, R. and	*Suite for electronic accordion; Feel; It*, HMV 4E0061–
Nilsson, L.,	34051
Mellnäs, Arne,	*Eufonie* CAP 1035
Morthensen, J.W.,	*Ultra*, CAP 1035
Persson, B.A.,	*Protein-imperialism*, Wergo WER 60047
Rabe, F.,	*VA??* Wergo,WER 60047

Many works of interest are available from Fylkingen Records, Fack, S – 102 60 Stockholm, Sweden, or from Sveriges Radio, S – 105 10 Stockholm, Sweden. Information also from: Swedish Information Centre, Tegnerlunden 3, Box 1539, 111 85 Stockholm.

United Kingdom

Bentley, Andrew	*Moan*, YORK YES 2
Birtwistle, Harrison	*Chronometer*, Argo ZRG 790
(Davies, Hugh)	*Music Improvisation Company*, Incus 17
	Music Improvisation Company, ECM 1005
Eastley, Max and Toop, David	*New and Rediscovered Musical Instruments*, Obscure No. 4
Eno, Brian	*Discreet Music*, Obscure No. 3
Lockwood, Anna	*Glass World*, Tangent TGS 104
Orton, Richard	*Kiss; For the Time Being; Clock Farm*, YORK YES 3
Souster, Tim	*Afghan Amplitudes; Arcane Artefact; Music from Afar; Spectral; Surfit*, Transatlantic TRAG 343 obtainable from OdB Editions, 37 Camden Park Road, London NW1 9AX
Wishart, Trevor	*Machine*, YORK YES 2 – 4
	Red Bird, YORK YES 7

The YORK discs are obtainable only from the Electronic Music Studio, University of York. The 3-record set YES 2 – 4 also contains works by Cardale, Gellhorn, Pickett and Wesley-Smith.

United States of America

Babbitt, Milton	*Ensembles for Synthesizer*, Columbia MS-7051
Bryant, Allan	*Space Guitars*, CRI SD 366
Cage, John	*Cartridge Music*, Mainstream 5015
Davidovsky, Mario	*Synchronisms 1 – 3*, CRI S-204

Gaburo, Kenneth	*Antiphony III (Pearl-white moments)*; *Antiphony IV (Poised)*; *Exit Music I*; *The Wasting of Lucrecetzia*; *Exit Music II: Fat Millie's Lament*, Nonesuch H-71199
Gravity Adjusters Expansion Band, Nocturne NRS 332	
Luening, Otto, and Ussachevsky, Vladimir	*A Poem in Cycles and Bells*; *Suite from King Lear*, CRI 112
Mimaroglu, Ilhan	*Tombeau d'Edgar Poe*; *Intermezzo*; *Bowery Bum*, Turnabout TV 34004
Reich, Steve	*Come Out*, Odyssey 3216 0160
Reynolds, Roger	*Ping*; *Traces*, CRI SD 285
Subotnick, Morton	*The Wild Bull*, Nonesuch H-71208 *Until Spring*, Odyssey Y34158
Wuorinen, Charles	*Time's Encomium*, Nonesuch H-71225

Many of the smaller labels can be obtained from New York Distribution Service, 500 Broadway, New York NY 10012.

Popular music

Pink Floyd,	*Dark Side of the Moon*, SHUL 804 *Ummagumma*, SHDW 1/2
Tangerine Dream	*Rubycon*, V 2025
Tomita,	*Snowflakes are Dancing*, RCA ARL-1-0488
Tonto's Expanding Headband	*Zero Time*, Atlantic K 40251

Radio ballads

| Charles Parker, | *Ballad of John Axon*, Argo DA 139 *Singing the Fishing*, Argo DA 142 |

Appendix V Manufacturers and suppliers

Synthesisers

ARP Instruments Inc., 45 Hartwell Ave., Lexington, Mass. 02173, USA

Buchla & Associates, Box 5051, Berkeley, Cal. 94705, USA

Dataton AB, Box 257, S-581 02 Linköping, SWEDEN (*System 3000*)

ElectroComp, Electronic Music Laboratories Inc., PO Box H, Vernon, Conn. 06066, USA

Electronic Dream Plant, Red Gables, Stonesfield Rd., Combe, Oxford OX7 2ER (*Wasp Synthesiser*)

Electronic Music Laboratory, I.W. Turner Inc., 31 Slocum Ave., Port Washington, NY 11050, USA

EMS Synthesisers, 277 Putney Bridge Road, London SW15

Moog Music Inc., Academy Street, Williamsville, NY 14221, USA

Rod Argent's Keyboards, 20 Denmark Street, London WC2H 8NA

Synthesiser kits and modules

Chadacre Electronics Ltd, 43 Chadacre Avenue, Clayhall, Ilford, Essex

DEW Ltd, 254 Ringwood Road, Ferndon, Dorset BH22 9AR

Eμ Systems, 417 Broadway, Santa Cruz, Cal. 95060, USA

Phonosonics, 22 High Street, Sidcup, Kent DA14 6EH

Powertran Electronics, Portway Industrial Estate, Andover, Hants SP10 3NM

Selidor Electronics, 6 Shirley Road, Southampton SO1 3EU

Serge Modular Music Systems, 572 Haight St., San Francisco, Cal. 94117, USA

Taylor Electronic Music Devices, PO Box 42, Greyfriars House, Chester CH1 2PW

Contact microphones

FRAP. UK distributor: Stateside Electronics, Unit 8, New Road, Ridgewood, Uckfield, Sussex TN22 5SX

Barcus-Berry. UK distributor: Guild Guitars (UK), 151 Portland Road, Hove, East Sussex

Merula. No model number or manufacturer's details available (West Germany)

C-ducer (a range of microphones for stringed instruments, including piano, and drums): C-Tape Developments, 7 Riverdale Road, East Twickenham, LONDON TW1 2BT

Strain gauges

Techni Measure, Eastern Dene, Hazlemere, High Wycombe, Bucks HP15 7BT (Many types, incl. PL-3)

RS Components, 13–17 Epworth Street, London EC2P 2HA (Single type, 2 versions, stock numbers 308-102 and 308-118) Also branches in Birmingham and Stockport.

PXE piezoelectric ceramic crystals

Edmundson Electronic Components Ltd., 30/50 Ossory Road, London SE1 5AN (distributors of Mullard = Philips)

Gulton Europe, The Hyde, Brighton, Sussex BN2 4JU (Glennite piezoceramics, incl. strain gauges)

Component suppliers

Maplin Electronic Supplies, PO Box 3, Rayleigh, Essex SS6 8LR (Components, tape heads and small microphone mixers)

Marshall Electronics, 40 – 42 Cricklewood Broadway, London NW2 3ET (Components)

Bi-Pak, PO Box 6, Ware, Herts. (Bargain packs of potentiometers, plugs, sockets, and audio leads)

Other addresses may be found in the popular electronics magazines.

Vibrator-transducer

Ling Dynamic Systems Ltd, Baldock Road, Royston, Herts. (100 Series Vibrators)

Appendix VI Electronic music studios in the United Kingdom

Those studios marked with an asterisk (*) offer part-time courses in electronic music open to the general public (see Appendix VII).

Department of Music, The University, Aberdeen

BBC Radiophonic Workshop, Delaware Rd, Maida Vale, London W9

Birmingham Arts Laboratory,* Holt Street, Birmingham

Department of Physics, University College, PO Box 78, Cardiff CF1 1XL

The Cockpit,* Gateforth St, London NW8 8EH

Centre for the Arts,* The City University, London EC1

Dartington College of the Arts, Totnes, Devon

The Music School, Palace Green, Durham DH1 3RL

Department of Music, University of East Anglia, Norwich, Norfolk

Department of Music, University of Glasgow, Glasgow GR 8QQ

Department of Music,* University of London Goldsmiths' College, New Cross, London SE14 6NW

Department of Music, The Polytechnic, Huddersfield, Yorkshire

Department of Music, University of Keele, Keele, Staffs. ST5 5BG

Leeds College of Music, Cookridge St, Leeds LS2 8BH

Royal Academy of Music, Marylebone Rd, London NW1 5HT

Royal College of Music, Prince Consort Rd, London SW7 2BS

Royal Northern College of Music, 124 Oxford Rd, Manchester M13 9RD

Spectro Arts Workshop, Bells Court, Pilgrim St, Newcastle-upon-Tyne NE1 6RH

Department of Music, University of Surrey, Guildford, Surrey.

West Square Electronic Music Studio,* Morley College, St George's Road, London SE1

Department of Music, University of York, Heslington, York YO1 5DD

Appendix VII Societies and courses

Electroacoustic Music Association (EMAS), Hon. Sec., 72 Hillside Rd, London
    N15 6NB
(This society publishes a newsletter four times a year and offers numerous services
to its members.)

Society for the Promotion of New Music (SPNM), 10 Stratford Place, London
    W1N 9AE
(This society promotes new music by British composers, including electroacoustic
music, and holds valuable composers' weekends which often feature electroacoustic
music.)

The studios which offer part-time courses in electronic music open to the general
public are indicated by an asterisk (*) in Appendix VI. Courses are also held at:
The City Literary Institute, Keeley House, Keeley St, London WC2B 4BA
Middlesex Polytechnic, Trent Park, Cockfosters, Barnet, Herts. EN4 0PT
Occasional courses featuring electronic music are organised by:
New Music in Action, Universal Edition, 2/3 Fareham St, London W1V 4DU
Dartington Summer School of Music, Registrar, 48 Ridgeway, London SW19 4QP

Appendix VIII Items on the accompanying cassette

A stereo cassette is available containing items illustrating five of the chapters in this book as follows:

Side A

Peter Warham: Electronic music in the primary school (Chapter 3)
(Pupils from Barlby Bridge Primary School, Selby, Yorks.)

3.1	The *Flying Scotsman*	0′ 46″
3.2	Selby Shipyard Launch	0′ 44″
3.3	'Thunder'	0′ 38″
3.4	'Bonfire Night'	0′ 36″
3.5	'Creepy Dance Music'	0′ 56″
3.6	Donna's tune	1′ 07″
3.7	'The Story of Jesus'	4′ 25″

Phil Ellis: Electronic music in the secondary school (Chapter 4)
(Pupils from Notley High School, Braintree, Essex)

Lower year-groups:

4.1	'Castle of Horror' (excerpt)	0′ 24″
4.2	Chord organ with echo chamber	0′ 35″
4.3	'Supernatural' wailing and decay	0′ 19″
4.4	Mini Korg Synthesiser melody	0′ 26″

Upper school individual work:

4.5	'Bells' (excerpt)	0′ 18″
4.6	Guitar and synthesiser	0′ 46″
4.7	'Long-Shanked Wading Bird' (excerpt)	0′ 50″
4.8	'Precipitation with Insight' (excerpt)	2′ 02″
4.9	'Albireo' (two excerpts)	2′ 28″

Tom Wanless: Electronic music in the secondary school (Chapter 5)
(Pupils from Sheldon Comprehensive School, Chippenham, Wilts.)

5.1	Drone with percussion	1′ 45″
5.2	As 5.1, but with added echo	0′ 30″
5.3	Harmonic series with percussion	1′ 45″
5.4	As 5.3, but with added echo	0′ 30″

Side B

5.5	A first electronic composition (4th-year boys)	1′ 24″
5.6	'Daydreams' (excerpt)	1′ 55″
5.7	'Vocal' piece	2′ 49″

Trevor Wishart: Musicmontage (Chapter 7)

7.1	*Red Bird* (sequence of excerpts)	6′ 30″

    a) Book swatting fly becoming doors slamming
    b) Word 'reasonable' becoming water
    c) Word 'listen' becoming birdsong
    d) Orchestration of birds and animals
    e) Garden sequence shattered by emerging voices
    f) Alarm clock becoming birdsong

Red Bird is an extended electroacoustic composition. The complete work is available on disc (see Discography under United Kingdom).

Hugh Davies: Electroacoustic instruments (Chapter 8)
(All instruments constructed, performed and recorded by Hugh Davies)
Project 1: Springboards

8.1	Springboard Mk IV (4 springs, parallel)	1′ 50″
	after one minute of left channel alone, an additional	
	hand-held magnetic pick-up converts the instrument to stereo.	
8.2	Bass Springboard Mk VI (5 springs, parallel)	1′ 15″
8.3	Springboard Mk III (14 springs, fan-shaped)	1′ 10″
	featuring variable reverberation by damping some of the springs	
8.4	Springboard Mk X (2 concentric rings of springs, like a spider's web)	0′ 50″
	one hand plays the rhythm unchangingly, the other selectively	
	damps the springs through which the vibrations reach the magnetic	
	pick-up	

Project 2: Bowed Diaphragms

8.5	*Music for Bowed Diaphragms* (excerpt)	1′ 20″

Project 3: From Egg Slicer to Aeolian Harp

8.6	a) Aeolian harp, played by a strong east wind (2 ex.)	0′ 45″
	b) Aeolian harp, blown by human breath	0′ 25″
	c) Egg slicer and Aeolian harp: both instruments	1′ 20″
	performed simultaneously; the egg slicer is plucked before the	
	Aeolian harp.	

Project 4: Metal Rod 'Xylophone'

8.7	a) Metal rod 'xylophone'	0′ 30″
	b) Ditto, a different passage played back at half speed	0′ 50″

Index

acoustic processing, 29, 113-16
'Aeolian harp', 172-4
amplifier, 3, 175, *see also* voltage-
    controlled amplifier
amplitude (of wave-forms), 10-11, 175
Anderson, Laurie, 122
attenuator, 126
aural cues, 135-7
Axon, John, GC, 46

balanced lines, 175
Berio, Luciano, 55, 106, 133
bias signal, 5
bulk eraser, 175

Cage, John, 34-5, 152
calculator, use of, 111
Carlos, Walter (later Wendy), 50
cassette recorders, 21, 44, 107
circuit construction, 123-30
clock-rate, 17
colour coding
    leader tape, 32
    resistors, 124-8
comb-filter, 14
Compute-a-Tune, 110
connections between equipment, 118
control voltage, 13, 17, 21
copying, 36-7
CSE Mode III examinations, 80, 92-3,
    105
curriculum, 44, 70-3

decibel, 5, 175-6
demagnetiser, 121
demagnetising, 176, *see also* tape
    recorder heads
distortion, 5, 109, 119

echo, 39, 94-5, 104
echo chamber, 77
editing, 9, 34, 61, 98-100, 176
editing kit, 8
electroacoustic instruments, 162-74
envelope, 12, 35-6, 176
envelope follower, 21, 127
envelope shaper, 3, 12-13, 16, 40, 101
environmental sounds, 29, 50-4, 62-4,
    89-91, 110
equalisation, 19, 176
erase head, 4, 5

feedback, 65, 110, 176, *see also*
    howlround
filters, 3, 13-14, 42, 101, 125, 176
    band-pass, 14
    band-reject, 14
    high-pass, 13
    low-pass, 13
    see also voltage-controlled filter
fixed filter bank, 14
frequency, of wave-forms, 10-11, 176
frequency follower, 21
frequency shifter, 3, 23
Furnival, John, 154
fuzz, 77, 119, 125, 128

gain, 12, 177
games, microphone, 27
generators, 3
    attack-decay, 126
    noise, 3, 101, 120
    white-noise, 11, 16, 42
'ghost tapes', 21
graphic equaliser, 14
group outputs (mixer), 19
guitar, electric, 3, 29, 50

hand winding, 7, 112
hardware, 3-25
harmonics, 10-11, 177
Hassell, Jon, 122
head reverberation, 18
hertz, 10, 23, 177
howlround, 65, 177, *see also* feedback

jack-field, 19
jew's harp, 29
joystick control, 23, 40

Kagel, Mauricio, 160
keyboards, 16-17, 40, 100
  touch-sensitive, 16, 79
kits, 130

landscape, musical, 134
leader tape, 31-2
leads, 95-6, 116-19
linear controller, 22, 40
line reference level, 5
location devices, 22-3
loops (tape), 32-3, 37, 38, 121
loudspeakers, 44
Lucier, Alvin, 114

MacColl, Ewan, 46
magnetic pick-ups, 160, 164
Mapophone, 122
matched pair (microphones), 7
Metal rod 'xylophone', 174
meter
  PPM, 5
  VU, 5, 95, 98, 104
microphones, 3, 7-8, 27, 58-9, 64-5,
    102, 109, 154-6
  capacitance, 7
  cardioid response, 7, 102
  contact, 8, 29, 115, 156-9
  omnidirectional, 7
Miliaret, G., 45
mixer, 3, 18-20, 128
mixing, 39, 98-100
monitor, 19, 177
montage (sound), 52, 133, 143
mouth tube, 115
multiplying a sound, 37
multitracking, 93, 96-8, 105

noise levels, 54
noise
  blue, 12
  pink, 12
  white, 12

octave divider, 129
organ, electric, 3, 20, 76
oscillator, 3, 9, 11, 40, 47, 100-1, 124,
    177, *see also* voltage-controlled
    oscillator

panpot (panoramic potentiometer), 19,
    23
Parker, Charles, 46
Partch, Harry, 163
performance, 43, 85
phase-shifting, 14, 77
phasing technique, 38, 129, 177
piano, electric, 3, 20
piezoelectric ceramic crystal (PXE), 159
pitch-to-voltage converter, 21
playback head, 4
potentiometer, 41, 124, 128,
    178, *see also* panpot
PPM (meter), *see* meter
processors, 3

quadraphonic systems, 23

radio ballads, 46
random voltage source, 22
real time, 21, 178
record head, 4
recording, 5, 27-31, 47, 51-4, 58-64,
    101-2, 108
Reich, Steve, 38
reverberation, 3, 17-18, 28, 42, 77,
    94-5, 101-2, 114
rhythmic templates, 32
ring modulator, 3, 14, 16, 101

sample-and-hold, 22
sampling, 112
sawtooth wave, 10-11
Schaeffer, Pierre, 9, 133
Schafer, R. Murray, 70
Self, George, 92
sequencer, 17
short-wave radio, 21, 111
Shozyg, 164

signal levels, 18-19
signal processing, 42
signal-to-noise ratio, 5, 178
sine tone, 15
sine wave, 10-11
sound library, 31
sound-on-sound, 4, 80
sound tray, 29
splicing, *see* editing
spring reverberation, 16-17
square wave, 10-11, 16
Stockhausen, Karlheinz, 38, 133, 153
studio design, 19-20
Stylophone, 21, 110
Subotnick, Morton, 21
synthesiser, 15-16, 72, 78, 79, 100, 107

tape, electromagnetic, 3, 5
    storage of, 31
    threading of, 35, 38, 112-13
tape loops, *see* loops
tape recorder, 3, 18-19, 27, 29, 38-9,
    45, 74, 93, 107-8, 111-14
    heads, 4, 95; cleaning of, 5-6, 103;
        demagnetising of, 5-6, 103
    inputs and outputs, 117
    maintenance, 5, 103
    speeds, 4, 6, 32, 48, 74, 94-5, 112
tape/slide presentation, 44, 85

telephone earpiece, use of, 29, 160-1
timbre, 10
toy instruments, 21
transducer, 176, *see also* vibrator-
        transducer
    electromagnetic, 29, *see* magnetic
        pick-ups
transformation, 145-7
triangle wave, 10-11, 101
trigger, electronic, 13, 22
tube filter, 29, 114

variable speed, 4, 6-7
Veroboard, 123
vibrato, 113
vibrator-transducer, 24-5, 42
vocoder, 116, 178
voltage control, 11
voltage-controlled amplifier (VCA), 12,
    16
voltage-controlled filter (VCF), 14, 16,
    125
voltage-controlled oscillator (VCO), 11,
    16, 22
volume unit (VU) meter, *see* meter

wah-wah pedal, 129
wave-forms, 9-11, 178
windshield, 8